60 Days For Jesus,
Volume 2

60 Days For Jesus, Volume 2

Understanding Christ Better, Two Months at a Time

Matt McMillen

A Production of Matt McMillen Ministries
(www.MattMcMillenMinistries.com)

*For Mark, Luke, John, and Faith. Our childhood wasn't easy,
but we had each other, and God used all of that stuff TOGETHER for good.
I love you all, and I'm glad God decided to make us siblings.*

CONTENTS

Month 2

"Let us, therefore, make every effort to enter that rest..."

HEBREWS 4:11

Make every *effort* to *rest*? How is this possible? Jesus
would soon show me...by *grace*. Only by accepting
the undiluted grace of what He has completely
finished *for* me, would I finally be able to enter that rest.

INTRODUCTION

60 Days For Jesus

"You'll never amount to anything and your parents will never get you back," my foster parent said to me with a cold, hard glare.

"You're a liar! That's not true!" I bursted out loud, after hearing such a devastating statement as a ten-year-old boy. Angry tears began to fill up and pour out of my eyes as I ran off through the hallway into my room, slamming my face into the pillow on my bed, screaming, then weeping uncontrollably.

The very thought of my family staying split up for good was the paramount of all my fears. The daily anxiety I faced as a young boy, needed no more added to it. So why was this person who was supposed to be fostering me temporarily, so cruel?

I don't know. But I do know who was behind their method of taking care of children—the enemy—whether they knew that or not. Why would I make such a claim? Because Jesus said the devil only has three main goals:

1. Steal.
2. Kill.
3. Destroy.

You can apply one, two, or all three, to any area of your life and if there is suffering, the devil is hard at work in the spiritual realm, effecting the *physical* realm—where we live in these bodies. The spiritual realm is eternal, like God, it's not bound by time and space. *We* are eternal too, in our spirits, just like God, who *is* spirit. *Our* spirits are made in His image, and are meant to live on into eternity. The spiritual part of us is what makes us humans beings so different than all of God's other creations. Our *spirits* are what Jesus came to save.

Sure, Christ came to give us an abundant life in these bodies, that's exactly what He said in John 10:10, right *after* He warned us about the three main objectives of the enemy. But this short trip here to planet earth is but a trial-run, a prequel to your *real* life in heaven, with God!

So if that's the case, then shouldn't heaven be what we focus on the most? ABSOLUTELY! Investing our time, talents, and resources into eternity should be supreme to all other aspects of our lives. I'm not saying that we should act weird, sitting around staring at the sky, begging God to hurry up and take us home—heck no! I'm saying we should begin to realize heaven is in us *right now*, this very moment, *as* believers.

Jesus Christ in spirit form—the Holy Spirit—*lives* in you, in full! He doesn't "come and go" based on your behavior, and His presence doesn't increase or decrease on certain levels which are contingent on your religious performances. He's there, in you, *once*, completely! As Christians, we are not waking up each day imploring His Spirit to "please be with us"—no way! He is already infused *with* our spirits!

I'll give you a near-perfect example of how He makes His home in us: This might sound strange, but if you could imagine a sperm becoming infused with an egg, *that's* what has happened with you and Jesus the very moment you believed He's forgiven you of your sins! Brand new, spiritually created, *eternal* DNA! A new life! You are infused together with Jesus forever, and nothing can change that! This is why He said you must be "born again."

You've been merged with Christ, compounded together, interwoven, placed *into*, combined with, married to, conjoined, baptized *in*, coupled, linked, unified, united, and born again *with* Him! You are a new creation *in* Jesus Christ! HE IS YOUR NEW IDENTITY! Understanding this fact as a Christian, with no fear about it, will change *everything* about your life!

For myself, I didn't understand this for so many years because of the misrepresentation of the gospel by others. For most of my life as a Christian, I thought Jesus was separate from me. I thought it was my job to just copycat Him and "follow" Him. Which sure, imitating Christ in action and attitude *will* happen as a Christian, but only in the proper way: *Organically. Without effort or forcing it.* Once you find yourself in a state of rest, you'll have it.

In the natural, this seems counterproductive because there is lots for us to do as Christ's ambassadors. However, our best production for Him only happens when we know He is in us and won't go away.

This supernatural epiphany allows you to stop striving to achieve more *of* Jesus, and instead, we simply rest *in* Jesus. This graceful rest happens once you realize that you and Him *are one*. After that, a newfound confidence unlike you've ever experienced before begins to sprout up and out of you! It is a confidence of knowing who you really are, a Child of God! A spirit who is actually *born of God*, like Jesus!

That's my goal with my writings, to help *you*, dear reader, understand the amazing power of Jesus Christ on the inside of your body! You have an eternal reservoir of heaven at your daily disposal! *Inside* you is a bold hope for each and every moment of your life! By allowing the Creator of the universe to live *through* your body, you will change the world! Your body is a tool! All you gotta do is let Him use it!

As you do this, you will produce a modern-day miracle...*unconditional love.* Love for God, love for others, and love for yourself. This deep love will overpower the enemy's feeble attempts of stealing, killing, and destroying your life! So let's go! I feel absolutely honored to have you spend the next 60 days with me! If you've not read *60 Days For Jesus, Volume 1*, please be sure to pick it up online!

Also, if you'd like to share any of these daily devotionals which you are about to read, they are always available for free on my website, www.mattmcmillen.com. Simply type in the title of the devotional in the search bar to find it. Other than that, there isn't much more to introduce to you, so let's begin! Thank you for allowing me to share my relationship with Jesus, with you! I hope I can help you know Him better through my personal stories and teachings. He's pretty great, you'll see!

Month 1

"Your love for one another will prove to the world that you are my disciples." ~Jesus

John 13:35

DAY 1

GET TO KNOW JESUS, GET TO KNOW GOD

"If you knew me, you would know my Father also." ~Jesus

SEE JOHN 8:19

Why is it so important to get to know Jesus? Because Jesus personifies the Creator of the universe! Jesus wasn't just some man strolling around being nice to people and granting wishes—no, He was, and still is, God in the flesh!

It's important to get to know Jesus and have an intimate spiritual relationship with Him because if God were to become a man, Jesus of Nazareth would *be* that man. When you see the face of Jesus, you see the face of God in actual "person form." The Father is spirit—not flesh. He's never been flesh. So when Jesus was born, He looked exactly like what the Father would look like as a man. This is why Jesus said, "Anyone who has seen me has seen the Father" (see John 14:9). The Father and the Son are not playing "good-cop bad-cop." Jesus came to earth to show you what God is like as a person—in *human* structure—His temperament, love, forgiveness, and personality. The One who is responsible for setting up stars, billions of light-years away, became a man and lived on one of His *own* planets for 33 years. For this very reason, getting to know

Jesus is extremely important because He reveals to us the actual character of God! That, and the fact that He is our Judge *and* Savior, both at the same time.

I read a story one time which really hit this point home for me—just *how close* God came to us through Jesus Christ. Here it is:

There was once a farmer who was a religious skeptic. He was sold on "the fact" that there was *not* a God, let alone a God who came to earth in human form to express His love to us.

One cold and nasty winter night, the man heard an irregular thumping at the kitchen door. He watched through the window as several tiny, shivering sparrows, obviously attracted by the warmth inside, were beating against the pane-glass window with no avail.

Touched, the farmer got all bundled up and headed out to the barn, trudging through deep, fresh snow. He opened the doors and expected the sparrows to go flying in out of the winter storm, but they refused. He even turned on the lights and tossed some hay into a corner, looked back up into the trees, waiting, but still the birds would not go into the barn.

He hollered at them, "Come on! It's nice in there! Go!" But they just scattered in all directions, and hid. The farmer kept trying to help these struggling birds because he knew they would surly die out in this storm, so he tried even more tactics to get them to go into safety.

He laid down a trail of cracker crumbs that led into the barn…nothing. He tried circling behind the birds to drive them toward the barn, still, they would not go through the doorway. Nothing worked. He, a huge alien creature, had terrified them. The birds simply could not comprehend in their little bird minds, that he actually had a deep desire to help them—not harm them.

So the farmer withdrew back into his house and watched the doomed sparrows from his kitchen window. As he stared out into the dreadful weather watching these little birds, a thought hit him: "If only I could become a bird for just a moment, one of them, then I wouldn't frighten them. I could personally show them the way into the warmth and safety I've prepared for them."

At that exact moment, another thought hit him. He had finally grasped why Jesus was born.

A prayer for you: *God, thank you for becoming a man. Thank you, Jesus. Thank you for showing me how to live and love, thank you for giving me hope and confidence. Thank you for showing me how valuable I am to you, at the Cross. Thank you for making your home in me! I am forever grateful! Right now, I lift up all who are reading this, directly to you. For those who want to know you deeper, reveal yourself even more. I know you are constantly guiding us, loving us, and protecting us, but today I'm asking that you help us to know you on the deepest level possible! Take us even FURTHER into this amazing relationship with you! LIVE THROUGH US! Use our hands, feet, mouths, and minds for great and mighty things! ETERNAL THINGS! Help us to not only change the world for the better during our short trip here, but also, help us to change the landscape of heaven with more and more souls who know you, and love you, personally. In your name Jesus, I pray, amen.*

Day 2

How Can I Know God Better?

"Faith comes from hearing the message, and the message is heard through the word about Christ."

Romans 10:17

Growing up, Grandma used to always quote Scripture to me during our conversations. Most of the time, I didn't even realize she was doing this, it was just part of her normal talking style. Sometimes, it would be years later, (and even now), that I would read or hear a Scripture, pause, look up, and say to myself, *"Grandma used to say that to me"*—and there it was, in the Bible. But she wouldn't always stop and say it was in the Bible.She gushed the Word of God, organically.

I was privy to the benefit of having this woman raise me, so as a young boy, teenager, and then young adult, my heart was constantly flooded with seeds of Jesus' teaching. Most of the time, I didn't want to hear it. Although sometimes I thought Grandma was strange, as did many other people, there was an underlying confidence she had, absolutely everyone respected her…but not out of fear.

And not only did she naturally display a spiritual poise unlike no other, she was a source of protection in a very odd way. Just being in her presence, any fear or anxiety that I had, would almost instantly go away.

Unbeknownst to me at the time, this was the Holy Spirit protruding from this fat little lady with the big smile and boisterous personality. I know that *now*, because sometimes I'll be around people and they'll say, "I don't know what it is about you, but there is something different"— only, they'll say this with a mannerism of confidence in me. When this happens, I'll usually respond with, "That's the Holy Spirit in me," and smile.

Jesus naturally shines OUT of us, when we are walking close with Him. Of course, it wasn't always like this, I fought God for most of my life, trying to replace Him with things, money, reputation, and people. And I believe deep in my heart, that if it weren't for Grandma's prayers, I'd be dead.

What we don't understand is that when we are living by the flesh, and we feel far from God (although we are not if we are saved, because Jesus is still infused with our spirit, which is a one-time event {1 Corinthians 6:17, Galatians 2:20}), it is the prayers of *others* keeping us safe. It is the prayers of others which unlocks God's power and favor over us. (For proof of this, look to Jesus healing the Officials' son, long distance, in John 4:43-54).

Grandma's prayers for me, and her prayers for many, *many* other people, did just that. And it wasn't just her prayers that have helped me become who I am today, it was also her style of teaching the gospel— which was never force-fed, but always on a platter, offered up with love. She never used guilt or condemnation on me, instead, she made Jesus look appealing—even when she was correcting me.

From the time I was a small boy in the 80's, to a teenager in the 90's, when Grandma would quote Scripture to me, or talk about God in our conversations, she always did so with gentleness and respect. She never pushed me to believe, but showed me grace. She never tried to instill fear in my heart, or barked at me for my blatant sinning, she just made Jesus look good, through *her* life.

She exuded a rock-solid confidence that the neighborhood wanted to be around, yet, she still had the softness of a spring flower...it was a strange paradox...like a lion and a lamb, both, at the same time. And everyone went to her, I MEAN EVERYONE, in their time of need for prayer, advice, and support.

"Go see Granny Mac."

She knew God, and we all knew it.

But how? How was this lady who cooked too much fried chicken so close to Jesus? What made her SO DIFFERENT in the fact that somehow, some*way*, God was *specially* with Grandma, at all times?…Simple: She flooded her heart with the words about Jesus with the consistency of an IV drip.

The Bible says, "Faith comes from hearing the message, and the message is heard through the word about Christ" (Romans 10:17). This is what made her different. This is what set her apart. She had a relationship with God, because she constantly sought it out.

I can remember getting up in the middle of the night to go to the bathroom, and she'd be sitting at the kitchen table reading her Bible. Or I'd come home from high-school for lunch, and she'd have me a Totino's personal pizza made, with extra cheese, and while I ate it, she'd be watching TBN and telling me how handsome I was.

Sometimes I'd walk in the back door at dusk, drenched in sweat from playing basketball at the sports complex, and she'd be on the phone praying with someone, again. "Grandma, I need to use the phone." "Oh hush your mouth, you can wait."

And she always wrote stuff down, and also, wrote many people letters of encouragement. Bible scriptures and notes about something she read about God, or heard on TV, were all over the place. She would even scribble all over the bills that had to be paid. "Matthew, hand me that envelope. I want to write something down."

She'd always be singing as well. This was one of my favorite things about her. She'd be running us kids around town, and the radio was broke, because so were we, so she'd be humming an old hymn. Sometimes, she'd just get louder and louder, until we'd start singing with her. Dishes would be piled up after dinner, and she wouldn't yell at us kids to clean up, instead, she'd just start hand-washing everything (because we didn't have a dish-washing machine) and all the while doing so, she'd be softly singing songs to Jesus.

She had a relationship with God, because she wanted it. She had a relationship with God, because she constantly flooded her heart with His words. Even now, at almost 90, I just talked to her yesterday, she won't be quiet about Jesus. "Matthew, please be praying for so and so," or "Matthew, how's Jennifer and the kids? Are you all doing good? I'm so proud of you, son."

She's lived her life by the Spirit of God *in* her. Not by rules, not by religious Christian laws, and not by using scare tactics to get people to stop doing dumb stuff…but by love. She loves Jesus. And because of that love for Jesus, she's loved everyone else the same. There are no words to type that will properly express how grateful I am to Grandma for showing me the real love of Jesus—for showing me how to get to know Him better. All I can say is "Thank you, Grandma. I was a life that was changed," and then do my best to help others do the same.

A prayer for you: *Heavenly Father, today I want to thank you for giving me my grandma. When I think about how blessed I am to have her blood running through my veins, I get a lump in my throat. You decided to bless me with her before you even formed this planet, and I'm SO thankful! Right now, I lift up all who are reading this, directly to you. For those who didn't get the benefit of having such a wonderful person in their lives, I ask that you reveal yourself to them. I ask that you help them come to know you on the deepest level possible, through the life of Christ! GIVE THEM A BRAND NEW FIRE ON THE INSIDE! Light a spark in their hearts, for your Word, and for all things Jesus! Instill in them a new confidence in your love, hope, and principles, which will last their lifetime, and then go on to later generations which will do great things for your Kingdom. In Jesus' name I pray, amen!*

DAY 3

JESUS DESTROYS BAD RELATIONSHIPS

*I tell you the truth, Jesus said to them, "No one
who has left home or wife or brothers or parents
or children for the sake of the kingdom of God
will fail to receive many times as much in this
age and, in the age to come, eternal life."*

LUKE 18:29-30

When you first read the above verse, it doesn't make sense. Leave my wife? Leave my parents? Leave my children?

That seems counterproductive to the gospel. I've read these verses before, and I always assumed that Jesus was talking about missionary work, which, you *could* use these three verses to teach about how important missionary work is. Fulfilling the Great Commission ("Go into all the world and preach the gospel" Mark 16:15), is very important! When this is complete, Jesus is returning!

But what's neat about the Bible is that as you grow in your relationship *with* and maturity *in* Christ, He will speak to you differently each time you read His Word. That happened to me this morning.

Sipping my coffee as I read, "leave everything and everyone for Christ to be rewarded on the deepest level possible," that doesn't *just* mean missionary work…it also means: Make Jesus first, above *every* relationship—EVERY relationship. One last time, EVERY RELATIONSHIP. Yeah, every relationship.

This is the hard part. It's hard because we want to have Jesus as "part" of *each* relationship we have (or at least we should, as Christians), but so often we refuse to make Him the main ingredient. Jesus does not approve of this.

As we live out life each day, it's so very easy to begin to find our identity in a certain person, or relationship; a slow fade occurs which results in us making not living for God how we should, because of a bad relationship. And oh, how we *love* bad relationships (insert sarcastic emoji here). What is a bad relationship? It's a link with another person which *could* be friendly, or non-friendly, but, IT IS NOT BASED ON THE APPROVAL OF GOD'S SPIRIT.

As indwellers of Christ, are we willing to have relationships how *He* approves? For example, are we willing to be loving, guiding leaders for our children like *God* wants us to be? Or are we just trying to be friends with them while ignoring our God-given responsibility of pointing them to Jesus as to how to handle our problems? Are we not holding them accountable for irresponsible behavior just so they don't reject us? That's a bad relationship.

Christ wants to make it better, but we must put Him above *even* our children. Friend, if we have Christ as the center of our lives, and our parenting as a planet which rotates around *Him*, only then we will be the best parents we possibly can be!

Same in your marriage, the closer you get to Jesus, the more you will learn just how valuable you *truly* are. In turn, you stop accepting unacceptable behavior as "normal."

God teaches you that it is *not* okay for your spouse to dishonor you socially or privately. He teaches you that it is 100% unacceptable for your spouse to refuse to contribute to your family, refuse to appreciate you, or to threaten you daily with divorce when you stand up to them.

He teaches you that it is NOT okay for your spouse to be physically or emotionally intimate with anyone other than you (male *or* female). You do NOT have to accept this bad behavior in this bad relationship! Why? Because you are worth more than that treatment! Your value is immeasurable! Christ at the Cross *proves* this!

If you will realize that you are *so* important to God, that He just *had* to send Jesus here to make sure you are taken care of, then you'll *finally* have the strength to confront your spouse about changes that MUST be made!

Frankly, He gives you armor. He gives you weapons (see Ephesians 6). This armor and these weapons allow you to fight a battle in a Christ-like way. When you stand up to unacceptable behavior in a bad marriage, respectfully, and lovingly; when bombs are bursting all around you, the enemy is screaming at you night and day…it may *feel* like you are being defeated, BUT YOU'RE NOT! God is keeping you safe. God is using this for good things.

When you have Jesus as your identity, He teaches you that your spouse can no longer disrespect you or behave in ways that God does not approve of. This lesson of "standing up to those who use you," or, "how to overcome codependency," whether it's your spouse, boyfriend, girlfriend, child, or ANY bad relationship, it requires *courage*. Courage is what will change your life. And courage is not the absence of fear, but instead, moving forward *despite* fear.

So if you have a relationship which was built on completely unacceptable behavior, by either you, or the other person, then expect a nuclear blast to go off when you decide to allow Jesus to live through you. Jesus requires *acceptable* behavior in relationships for those whom He loves. That's you.

If they aren't on board with you and Jesus, then, as Jesus said above, they'll be left behind. Sure, it will hurt to get rid of bad relationships, but you know what? Jesus has something better for you.

If they reject you and Jesus, please, understand this: That relationship was *not* wasted! Jesus will actually *use* the pain that was caused *from* that bad relationship for your purpose! That is, if you'll give it to Him! He will also give wisdom, character, endurance, and strength! And eventually He'll bless you with happy, healthy, whole relationships. Loving and *respectful* relationships…just like the one you have with Him

A prayer for you: *Good morning to you Heavenly Father! Thanks for waking me up today! Right now, I lift up all who are reading this, directly to you. I can attest to loved ones beginning to not like this new version of me because they could no longer control my actions by creating fear in me through their unacceptable behavior. You have made me brave! And you did this by teaching me my value! Please do the same for all who are reading this! Thank you for letting me see that my true strength is found in responding like Christ does, and praying for those who want to cause me harm because I won't let them do what they've always done. For these people here, whether it's their spouse, boyfriend, girlfriend, child, parent, relative, neighbor, pastor, church member, someone at work, or school—I DON'T KNOW, BUT YOU DO—give them courage to STAND UP! Give them the courage to make the changes in their lives that YOU want them to make! Give them courage to put Jesus first and to STOP accepting unacceptable behavior, or even, conducting the unacceptable behavior themselves. We can do all things through Christ in us! He gives us the strength! Amen, amen, and aaaaaamen. Thank you Jesus.*

Day 4

Can I Lose My Salvation?

*"if we are faithless, he remains faithful,
for he cannot disown himself."*

2 Timothy 2:13

Fear. This one word controlled my life for many years. So much so, that even when things were peaceful in my life, I still had this constant feeling of dread...as if *something* bad has *got* to happen to me soon. And if I didn't feel fear, I didn't feel right—even if I didn't know what to be fearful *of*.

There are a lot of contributing factors to this fear-filled mindset I had—even now, with the spiritual skill-set I've developed over time, the devil still tries to sneak angst and anxiety through the back door of my soul. However, the Holy Spirit *in me* points him out. I now recognize his tactics and I overcome his attempts to get me to shrink back in panic.

How have I come to this point? By realizing *Who* lives in me—God Himself! Once we establish this fact in our souls as Christians, we can then produce a relationship with Him through prayer, meditate on His love for us in Christ, as well as stand boldly on the promises of His Word! But growing up, when my mind was being developed, utter chaos would be the best way to describe my life. I had no defense against the fear in which Satan tormented me with.

My parents fought on a level that no kid should have to deal with. Mom cheated on Dad and was in and out of rehab. And my dad had no real relationship skills except for blowing up on people or ignoring them altogether. Along with the severe stress of having five kids, Mom and Dad couldn't seem to iron out their problems and eventually both of them lost custody of us after the divorce.

From a very young age, fear was being beat into my mind with a 20-pound sledgehammer. It's all I knew. *"What's going to happen to us?"* was a regular thought. There was no security or stability in my childhood whatsoever, so I naturally thought something bad was always about to happen—because it usually did.

Eventually, my brothers, sister and I were all split up into foster homes and children shelters. The fear that you develop as a small child in those places is heart-wrenching. Sleepless nights was a regular thing because of the steady flow of new kids constantly crying in their bunks, begging to go home. The fights in the halls and the bullying from the bigger kids with severe behavior problems also contributed to the stacking of fear in my young heart. I was scared to even go to the bathroom at night.

But those homes weren't the only thing which festered fear, you also had the school situation. School is supposed to be an enjoyable and social place to learn and develop lifelong friendships. That doesn't happen when you are yanked out of a school 3 or 4 times a year, just to be forced into another one.

As a ward of the State, all of the different schools you have to keep going to, while being labeled as "the new foster kid," or "the children's shelter kid," these situations fertilized the fear in my heart on a grand scale. Uncontrollable shaking, sweating, and stuttering became something that I hated about myself. *"Why am I like this?!"* Back then, I didn't know. Now I do…*Fear*.

Eventually, I too developed very bad behavior in class, along with an hard-nosed aggressiveness, just to have a defense mechanism. I also became jealous of the kids who had a normal family, those who didn't have to move all the time. The bottom line was, not many more things created fear in me as a child, than school. The devil tried to destroy my life, starting at a very young age.

So let's fast forward to my late twenties, I'm ready to finally give my life to Christ—*completely*. I didn't want to pussy-foot around any longer, I had enough of trying to fix my life, my way. And sure, I was saved as a kid, had I died I would have gone to heaven, but I sure didn't realize it because of the *religious* fear shoved into my soul by others over time. Religious fear ruins more lives than we Christians can possibly imagine. *No* relationship should be based on fear, especially one with your Creator.

The Bible says that "the fear of the Lord is the *beginning* of all wisdom" (see Proverbs 9:10), not the middle, and not the end. My blood pressure rises a little when I think about the Christians who use the "method of fear" to get others to want to get to know God. It's disgusting.

The fact was, I was almost 30 and my life looked like the landscape of a forest after a major fire; black, burnt, smoldering, and lonely. In order to prove that I *was* worth something, I became extremely successful in business. Come to find out, that didn't make me NOT afraid anymore. It was weird. The "American Dream" didn't fix me. So I decided to just numb these feelings of fear with alcohol, porn, sex, video game binges, and anything else to get my mind off of this deep and constant panic in my heart— nothing worked.

I then thought going to church would fix me! Nope! What I got at church was a country club of perfect people who didn't understand someone such as me. I was way too "overly-motivated" according to them. I needed to cool my jets because "God isn't here to entertain me or to help me achieve my dreams." Sure, I knew I was an extremely determined individual, but still, I was a person longing for something *more*. They didn't accept me for who I was or where I was at in my life; they just yelled out things like, "You ain't livin' right!" "Be holy!" And even, "You are supposed to make disciples out of disciples!"…I was like, "How? By being like you? I don't get it." So I was rejected, and rejection creates fear if you allow it to, and then *that* type of fear creates *anger*.

I wanted to find peace and confidence in a group of Christians. Instead, what I got at that particular church was conditional "church love": harsh judgment, cold shoulders, and a steady disturbance in my soul each time I walked out of the door on Sunday after service.

The pastors spoke out of both sides of their mouths, saying such things as, "Believe and be completely forgiven!" And then the next week, "You gotta have EVIDENCE that you're saved!" Such double-talk. They wouldn't make up their minds and the Holy Spirit wouldn't allow my heart to believe their two-time teaching. It was very frustrating. And frustration creates *more* fear!

"Which is it? Am I completely forgiven? Or do I need to do stuff to make sure I stay forgiven? BE CLEAR!"…They weren't. They just swept these very simple questions under the rug with confusing Christianese and more "do stuff." So I pipped up because that's just who I am. I might not have done it with much grace, but I was still learning how to handle my problems how Christ wanted me to. Eventually I was shunned and asked to "get plugged in at another church." So I did. Hindsight is 20/20, and I honestly wish I didn't wait so darned long to move on because the church I'm currently at has been just what I needed—grace. Real, unconditional, unapologetic, grace.

But at my previous church, instead of *freedom* from fear being—which I desperately longed for—I got a set of rules to follow and a "do better" sheet to fill out. I got *religion*. Religion ruins lives, *creates* debilitating fear, as well as anger and self-righteousness. *Relationship* on the other hand, does not. A relationship with Christ based on your love for Him, and finally understanding your value *to* Him, will break you free from any and all religious bondages. I had to learn this the hard way.

I got sermons which taught me, "You have no business trying to get God to help you reach your goals in life! That ain't the gospel! God doesn't give you seven steps to change your life for the better!" They nit-picked everything *good* about every other preacher and teacher. They stirred up dissension and judged everyone on a very high level—a level which even they weren't abiding by. According to them, there had to be *proof* of my saving through a lifestyle change. And me, being an over-achiever, the cogs began turning in my mind.

"Hmmmmm…okay…What level of good do I need to have? Where is the tipping point of my lifestyle change that will get God to finally approve of me?…I'll just become the very BEST at this 'being good' stuff."

Legalism ensued, and I began to come off as super-aggressive about "making people" be "good" like me. You know, a so-called "good Christian man," a "godly man"? Not only did I start pushing God on others tremendously, but I also began to shun and cut off those who weren't like me because the church said I shouldn't have anything to do with non-believers or the Christians who didn't have proof of *being* a Christian through a lifestyle change. I had become someone I previously hated, a religious Christian—a "church person"—and my life was more miserable than ever. To top it off, my level of fear was deeper than it had ever been before.

I was also subliminally being trained that Jesus' sacrifice wasn't *completely* good enough, and I had to add to it (do my part) in order to *keep* my salvation, by confessing every sin. The problem was this: what about the sins I *don't* confess, or the ones I forget about, or the ones I overlook and justify, never to be talked about again? Do those not count? I was being taught that God graded me on a curve, based on *my* performance, and He does not. Jesus has finished everything *for* me. The Father looks at Him *in* me. This is where my perfection comes from—Christ actually *inside* me, not anything my mind or body does.

Thankfully, as I sought out Jesus on my own, I learned that this "confessing of every sin" was Scripture being taken out of context. With this method, why not just sin away and then ask for forgiveness once a day, or once a week, or once a month, or whenever? Sounds pretty dumb. Sounds like a *non*-relationship, and that's what I was being taught.

I was told outright that if I didn't *do* certain things, or *stop* doing certain things, or have a higher level of repentance, that I didn't belong. FEAR. FEAR. FEAR. FEAR. FEAR. FEAR…

I was looking for *freedom* from fear, and what I got in that church *contributed* to my fears on a much grander scale! A lie was planted in my soul by Satan himself, "I *must* live up to the approval of these Christian people, or else I'm not really a Christian."

So, what happened?...I *kept* seeking Jesus! I didn't give up on knowing Him *deeply*! I knew that He already lived in me, but I wanted to get to know Him more each day! I *needed* peace, I needed it! I needed released from fear! And something in me kept saying this would be found in understanding who Jesus Christ really is. So I began my own daily personal study of His life, I asked Him to *change* my life and remove my fear—He has done just that—in spades!

The number one thing Jesus has done is teach me how to replace my fear with His unconditional love for me. This is a by-product of finally understanding my infinite value *to* Him. Once we understand our value to Him, everything in our lives changes for the better!

Here are some tips that I believe will help you if you struggle with a crippling fear of God—*especially* if you are afraid of losing your ticket to heaven. Why did I build up to this nearly taboo subject in the manner in which I did? Because the horror of losing your salvation is the number one fear of every Christian who doesn't fully understand God's love for them in Christ:

1. **God's love for you is perfect, so you have nothing to fear.** In 1 John 4, the Bible says that "perfect love casts out all fear, because fear has to do with punishment." Once you place your faith in Christ as your Savior, you don't have to be afraid of hell any longer because you are *not* going to be eternally punished. You ain't going there! SO STOP BEING AFRAID! Jesus paid for your release, in full, at the Cross (see John 3:16-18). When you feel like your "saving" is at stake because of mistakes you are making, or lack of religious works, don't believe it. The devil is "the accuser" (see Revelation 12:10), so no matter what you do, good *or* bad, he will attempt to pester you in spirit. Simply

begin to speak God's promises over your life when you feel this fear coming on you. Feelings don't count when it comes to the truth of your salvation—only the facts do. You *are* saved, once you believe in Jesus' forgiveness. I repeat, ONCE.

2. **You only get saved once, not multiple times.** Hebrews 10:10, 1 Peter 3:18, and Romans 6:10 are very clear about this. Salvation is a one-time event. Further, the New Covenant is not an agreement between us and God, but a contract between the Father and Son—*we* are simply the beneficiaries to this contract. We don't create it, add to it, or sustain it. Instead, we open up our hearts and receive it by grace through faith (see Hebrews 8:13, Ephesians 2:8,9). The good news is, based on this New Covenant of the shedding of perfect blood one *final* time—which is what God requires for forgiveness, *blood*, not our asking (see Hebrews 9:22)—God's wrath over the sin of the world has been completely satisfied at the Cross! The blood of Jesus actually *worked*! Of course, you still have to accept it by faith—actually believe that Jesus did this for *you*, and then invite Him into your heart to live—but after that, it's over. You are saved, no matter your sin—past, present, or future. Keep in mind, *all* of your sins were in the future when Jesus died. To add on top of this good news, Hebrews 7:25 states that Jesus is able to save us completely as long as He lives—and He isn't dying again and again in heaven, each time we sin! HE WILL LIVE FOREVER! SO WE WILL *STAY* SAVED! Lastly, it's important to know that God doesn't grade on a curve. James 2:10 makes this perfectly clear: It's all or nothing if you are trying to obey God's laws in order to be accepted by Him. To counteract such legalism, the Bible actually says we are adopted into the family of God and marked with a seal until the day of redemption (see Ephesians 1)—we've had a DNA swap with Christ! (See Romans 6, Galatians 2:20). So please know you are not *kinda* adopted into His family, "until you straighten up

enough," and you are not *kinda* marked with a seal until Christ returns, "if you don't get enough brownie-points with your pastor"—IT'S FINISHED (see John 19:30).

3. **Religious Christians will take Scripture out of context to create fear, even after you are saved.** First of all, let me define "religious Christians." I mean no disrespect. I'm simply referring to Christians who find their identity in how much they "do" for God, how "little" they sin, as well as their "level" of repentance. They do not believe Jesus finished everything *for* us. They think there is more to it than *just* believing He's forgiven us of our sins. Religious Christians have created new "laws" by taking Scripture out of context, which have nothing to do with the undiluted grace-filled gospel. These post-Cross laws keep people on a hamster-wheel of religious works of trying to *stay* in God's good graces. It's demonic. They want us to *add on* to what Jesus *has done*. They tell us this is the only way to *complete* our salvation. These actions included churchy laws such as: *our* works, *our* behavior/attitude repentance, speaking in tongues, physical baptism, church attendance, church volunteering, mission trips/evangelism, pastoral approval, confession, fasting, tithing, Scripture memorization—I could continue—but the brass tax *to* these laws are the key words, *I do*. "Look at what *I do* to earn my spot with God." "Look at what *I do* to *keep* my spot with God." Any statement which begins with *I do* is wrong, and is non-gospel. THE GOSPEL IS ABOUT WHAT JESUS *HAS* DONE! Everything we *now do* is because Jesus *has done* everything for us! So our motivation is a LOVING RELATIONSHIP! We *want* to show Him that we love Him! That's it! Nothing more, nothing less! What's worse is the religious Christians look down on those who aren't *just* like them, or striving to *be* like them. They want you to think that you owe *them*—you don't! They may even smile, but deep down, they are bitter, harsh, uber-judgmental, fair-weather friends, who will block you from their lives if you

don't do exactly as they say and fall in line. Fear, guilt, condemnation, and using the Bible as a weapon is their M.O. So *recognize* them by their fruit, begin to *think* good thoughts about them—FIND SOMETHING—and pray they will finally come to understand the deep love of Christ. But do NOT be afraid of them. Your salvation is set—once. So look them in the eye with confidence and show them Christ in you.

4. **There is no part of the New Testament that says a Christian can lose their salvation.** This is the wonderful news that sets people free, but the religious Christians hate it because they think everyone will go buck-wild in sin. Which, truth be told, the opposite actually happens when we finally realize we are 100% like Christ in spirit, no matter the behavior of our flesh or lack of mind renewal (my life is proof of this). The Spirit will never lead us to sin. *When* we sin, which we will a lot, that is *not* Christ in us but our flesh along with our un-renewed minds. Sinning is *not* Him—and *He* is who we are *after* salvation (see Romans 6, Galatians 2:20). However, these types of Christians will cherry-pick certain Scriptures to try to prove we *can* lose our salvation. Honestly, they are cutting off their own noses to spite their face because the same grace they are against, they too, will desperately need. But let's break down a couple of those taken-out-of-context verses. Jesus said, in Matthew 7, "Depart from me, I never knew you," to the people who were bragging on all they've done for Him. But the key word here is *never*. He never knew them! Instead, all *they* knew were their religious works, and the "tagging on" of the name of Jesus, after. Here is another: Hebrews 10:26 says, "If we deliberately keep on sinning after we have received the knowledge of the truth, no sacrifice for sins is left," and this is true, but only for *non*-believers. The author of Hebrews was saying, "If you hear or read about the sacrifice that Jesus made for your sins, and you reject it, you have *knowledge* of the truth. *That* is what is unforgivable." Why? Because you *will* keep on sinning,

after becoming a Christian, because you are a human being—and God does not grade you on a curve. What shocked me the most about this verse—what had created SO MUCH FEAR in my life—was to finally realize the fact that the entire book of Hebrews was written to...HEBREWS! Jews! Those who kept bringing the blood of bulls and goats back into the temple to *be* forgiven—even *after* they heard the gospel! Therefore, this verse *is* correct, when KEPT IN CONTEXT: "no sacrifice for sins is left." "Sacrifice," as in, the blood of animals, NOT JESUS! Hebrews 10:26 is written to those who had taste-tested the gospel (heard about Jesus' final blood sacrifice as the Messiah), yet these Jews still wanted to hedge their bets on the old way of being forgiven by sacrificing animals when it no longer worked! So please remember that any part of the Bible which makes you think you can lose your salvation, read it in context. Always keep in mind *who* the audience is, why *what's* being written is being written, AND READ ALL AROUND IT. Are believers or non-believers being written to, or about? What you'll soon realize is God's love and grace through Christ's blood supersedes *all* laws, commands, and fear-filled Scripture! So don't be afraid of losing your salvation any longer! IT'S YOURS FOREVER!

A prayer for you: *Good morning Heavenly Father! It's very early here as I write, Jennifer and Grace are still nestled in bed; I'm so grateful for them—for my family. Thank you. I'm also grateful for my home, my job, and my good health. Thank you, Lord. Right now, I lift up all who are reading this, directly to you. For those who are extremely fearful of you, begin to wash them with your peace and security, found in Christ, today. Reveal to them your unconditional love. I'm asking for a new protection over their minds against the enemy's lies which attempt to produce doubts of your real love. And for those who have given up on you because of the false-adverting of a fear-filled gospel taught by others, reveal THE TRUTH to them! Christ in us AS our perfection! Help* *them to refocus on WHO lives in them the VERY MOMENT they believe He's forgiven them—Jesus! Help them to realize it's HIS sacrifice at the Cross which has brought us near to you forever! Establish your grace as the foundation in their hearts—thank you for such grace. Thank you for Jesus. In His name I pray, amen.*

DAY 5

JESUS IS A GOOD GARDENER

"But the fruit of the Spirit is love, joy, peace, patience,
kindness, goodness, faithfulness, gentleness and
self-control. Against such things there is no law."

GALATIANS 5:22,23

God wants us to produce "good fruit" with our lives. How do we do this? By allowing Jesus to live through us! How do we allow Jesus to live through us? We *begin* making choices He approves of and we *stop* making choices He doesn't approve of, based on His character. And you might ask, "But Matt, why can't I just believe and do what I want, since I'm already saved?"

I gotta be honest with you, I did that for most of my Christian life, and God soon taught me the main reason why we start to do anything for Him, or stop doing certain things He doesn't *want* us to do is this: BECAUSE WE LOVE HIM.

Everything else we do as a Christian should be in the drop-down menu of *our love for Him.* And if you think about it, every strong relationship is built on both parties starting (or stopping) an action because of their deep love for the other individual. Same with us and God. Jesus

25

showed *His* love for us at the Cross, and now *we* must have action in our love for Him as well.

Real love for others is backed up by action. Without action, love is paper-thin and conditional, it is fair-weathered at best. In any relationship, without action *and* sacrifice, eventually one of the individuals will begin to take severe advantage of the other.

Jesus doesn't want this. He wants a *strong* union with you! That's why He sacrificed His own life and went through the pain and discomfort of crucifixion! He backed *up* His love for you with ACTION!

The good news is, as long as your heart is beating Jesus never gives up on you. It's *us* who gives up on Him, with our actions. I was the worst person I knew when it came to taking advantage of His love and kindness.

So when we *finally* begin to show Jesus that we love Him, *through* our actions, we start to "grow good fruit"—Paul calls this the "fruit of the Spirit" (see Galatians 5:22,23). And what does fruit do?…Nothing, it just grows, easily and organically, never forcing itself *to* grow. JESUS IS THE VINE THAT WE ARE CONNECTED TO. When we attempt to do things on our own, apart from Him, we can grow *no* good fruit.

When we try to *force* spiritual fruit growth, we fall into the trap of *religious* works, or "works of the flesh," resulting in us attempting to do God's job, in turn, creating severe frustration. You'll recognize this when you find yourself trying to make things happen in which you have no power to *make* happen. The devil then gets you atrociously upset from that point on. God wants you to have peace! He wants you grow *organic* spiritual fruit! Peace is a piece of this fruit! (For a full list of Spiritual fruit, see Galatians 5:22, 23).

Here is a parable Jesus told about how God is inspecting the fruit in our lives, checking to see if anything is growing, and, just how very important it is to spread the gospel for Him.

As you read this, keep in mind we don't *do* anything to *earn* God's approval, or to be saved (being saved is a free gift through your faith and acceptance of Jesus' forgiveness); so instead of worrying about that, we should have a daily goal of doing good things on earth and spreading the gospel while resting in God's grace, because we *love* our Creator, others, and ourselves.

In this parable, notice that Jesus is pleading *our* case, and that *He* is the one fertilizing our soil, therefore trying to *help us* grow spiritual fruit! He is pleading with the Father to give us more time to change our lives into being spiritually fruitful!

"A man had a fig tree growing in his vineyard, and he went to look for fruit on it but did not find any. So he said to the man who took care of the vineyard, 'For three years now I've been coming to look for fruit on this fig tree and haven't found any. Cut it down! Why should it use up the soil?' 'Sir,' the man replied, 'leave it alone for one more year, and I'll dig around it and fertilize it. If it bears fruit next year, fine! If not, then cut it down'" (Luke 13:6-9).

So today, my friends, please ask Jesus to teach you how to grow good fruit, and He will! He loves you and wants your life to be beautiful and *spiritually* fruitful—through Him!

A prayer for you: *God, I want to thank you for another day alive on planet earth. So many people didn't get this opportunity, so thank you! Right now, I lift up all who are reading this, directly to you. For the ones who really like the idea of having a close, loving, respectful relationship with you, touch their hearts on a deep level today. Give them a sincere desire to change their behavior for you, because they love you! Help them to ALLOW Jesus to cultivate their souls so that they can have so much good fruit growing in their lives, people are tripping over it! In Christ's name I pray, amen!*

DAY 6

When You Want To Quit Drinking, But Can't

*"Then you will know the truth, and
the truth will set you free." ~Jesus*

John 8:32

It always starts out innocently, doesn't it? We usually don't plan on taking it too far, we just want to have a few drinks. For me, it had become a habit, just *something* I did. Like brushing my teeth, going to gym, or going to work. Drinking was a normal, regular part of my life. *"But don't call me an alcoholic, because I'm not!"* That's how I thought.

Barbecues, dinners, sitting pool-side in the backyard, ball games, visits to family members' houses, after work, chillin' around the bonfire, doing yard work, watching TV...whatever. Having an ice-cold beer in my hand was part of my life. I was beer connoisseur, I could pick out the good from the bad. But honestly, I'd drink anything to get a buzz. Beer, wine, whisky, foo-foo drinks, whatever. Just give it to me! GOTTTA GET THAT BUZZ! OH, AND *KEEP* IT!

I've heard that 70% of regularly-drinking people are in denial *about* their drinking as being a problem—like I was—actually, still am, only I'm in recovery instead of denial, and I will be for life. The religious

Christians will want you to think you'll never have a desire for it once you get saved, but that's total horse crap. Recovery is a life-long process because you have flesh, and your mind needs renewed, so be easy on yourself.

Once you shed this shell, and enter into God's presence for eternity, *then* you'll be transformed into a being who no longer has desires that go against God's will (see 1 Corinthians 15:52). Until then, relax. You gotta live with yourself. You are not a problem for God, and, you are no *surprise* to God either.

But so many people who actually *do* have a drinking problem (and not everyone does, some can take it or leave it), think that if they aren't waking up in the middle of the night with the shakes, they don't *really* have an issue with it. Fair enough. I thought that too.

I was not just a functioning alcoholic, but a successful one. "I ain't like those weak people. Those drunks." I'd defend myself to the death if you wanted to try to say something about my overindulgence of this nectar from hell.

My wife and I were having a conversation the other day, about alcoholics, after a friend of ours' mom was hit and killed by a drunk driver on the interstate. Jennifer said, "I think they need tougher laws." As a former boozer I was quick to correct that, because drunk-driving laws are already pretty brutal—some of the toughest laws of the land. What we have here in America, and truth be told, worldwide, is not a drinking issue, or a lack-of-tough-laws issue, but a *soul* issue. We gotta get to the bottom of people's souls—their minds, free will, and emotions—to find out *why* they are drinking, and then address *that*.

Laws won't change lives, only a *soul change* will change lives—and Jesus said He came to give us rest for our souls (see Matthew 11:29). Our *feelings*—our emotions—are a part of our soul. So to make changes, we must ask ourselves *why* are we feeling *like* we're feeling?

In regard to laws, when you are arrested for a drunk driving incident—hopefully without killing anyone—you gotta take classes to be informed on just *how bad* alcohol abuse is, what it does to your body, and the tragedies it causes for so many families. So it's not from lack of information, but from a lack of *healing* for what's going on *inside* us.

I should know, I got my first DWI when I was 19, and my second when I was 21. I'm now 35 and I've been sober nearly two and a half years, but if I had been pulled over for each time I drank and drove, you would not be reading this. I would be locked away for life.

What we need to do is address the reasons why people are drinking, which is ultimately embedded in their souls. Problem-drinking is *not* a disease, it's a rotten fruit that grows in our lives from a poor soul condition. We are looking for a *feeling* to make us "all better," when what we need is our minds renewed by the Holy Spirit.

Addiction is a spiritual issue, so it must be addressed, supernaturally. This is the root. Pull up the root, and the fruit won't grow.

When we drink, we are trying to alter our feelings, period. I like lists, so here is a short list that will help you understand us better—that is, if you don't. And for those of you who have an issue with the drink, this will be completely relatable about how you *feel*, and why you take that first sip:

1. If we feel sad, we want to feel glad.
2. If we feel insecure, we want to feel confident.
3. If we are bored, we want to feel excited.
4. If we are already excited, we want to feel even *more* excited.
5. If we feel lonely, we want to make that feeling go away (this can be accomplished by drinking with others, or by yourself).
6. If we feel uncomfortable around others, we want to fit in and feel comfortable by drinking.
7. If we feel uncomfortable around others, we want to *not* fit in and feel comfortable by drinking.
8. If we have a bad day at work, we want to feel better *after* work.
9. If we have a great day at work, we want to celebrate *after* work.
10. If we feel like we are not appreciated by someone, we want to make that feeling go away.

11. If we feel like we *are* appreciated by someone, we want to drink because we're happy.
12. If we feel afraid, we want to feel brave.
13. If we feel brave, we want to *stay* feeling brave.

I know that 13 points is an off-number, but honestly I had to stop myself from going on to the next number! I could go on, and on, and on, probably coming up with nearly 100 reasons *why* we want to drink—which is *all* based on our feelings!

WE. WANT. TO. FEEL. DIFFERENT.

We want to be comfortable in our own skin.

SO WHAT ARE WE SUPPOSED TO DO?! WHO CAN POSSIBLY HELP US?!

...Jesus.

Jesus can help us with this major problem, this *soul* issue. How? By teaching you who you really are! Which is an infinitely loved child of the one and only *true* God, CREATOR OF THE UNIVERSE! The religious Christians have done such a bad job of teaching the world their true identity in Christ! All they've done is shame the world and bark out scare tactics! THIS KEEPS PEOPLE DRUNK, HIGH, ANGRY, LOST, FRUSTRATED, AND EVENTUALLY SUICIDAL!

They've made God out to be someone who He's not! And in the wake of that destruction, hordes of people have turned *away* from Him to address the very *real* soul issues they have, all because they think He's here to punish them! HE ISN'T!

Once you *simply* place your *faith* in Jesus, YOU AREN'T GOING TO BE PUNISHED! (See Romans 3:21,22). We've been taught to work to *stay* saved, or to *stop* doing certain things to *keep* our salvation, but all along IT'S BEEN FREE! You can't work to keep something that you didn't *work to get* in the first place! The religious Christians haven't earned ANYTHING! Neither can you! Neither can I! Their self-righteousness is nastier than any drunkard who begs God daily, "PLEASE TAKE THIS AWAY FROM ME!"

SO PLEASE, wrap your mind around THIS TRUTH: Even if you *never* stop drinking, God still loves you the same! THIS IS AMAZING NEWS! And it is this GOOD NEWS which gives you the POWER to—not just quit drinking—BUT *BEGIN* A BRAND NEW LIFE IN CHRIST!

My friend, Jesus wants to help you understand your *value*—which is priceless! PLEASE, BELIEVE THIS! You don't *stop* doing something, or *start* doing something, to *achieve* your value from God! It's already been established at the Cross! JUST STEP *INTO* IT, AND RECEIVE IT!

This will heal your soul. In turn, this will adjust your feelings. In turn, this will give you the power to never drink another drop. Once you finally do understand your value in His free gift at the Cross, then you'll soon realize you're allowed to bring all of your feelings to Him, no matter what, at all times. That is, your good, bad, or indifferent feelings. This is called a *relationship*! And God longs to have one with you through Christ! THIS RELATIONSHIP WILL OBLITERATE YOUR DRINKING PROBLEM.

What gives Jesus this ability? Simple. He is your Creator in the flesh; He wrote the instruction manual on humans. The Bible says that "all things were created through Him and for Him," and that, "in Him all things hold together" (see Colossians 1:16,17). That's not just referring to the sun, the moon, the stars, or this planet—but YOU!

You are Jesus' prized possession! He gave you your ability to *have* feelings for a reason! Ultimately, that reason is to enjoy an eternal relationship with Him in heaven, forever! This is why He wants you to begin bringing *every* feeling to Him, so that He can help you address it, and then *use* it for good, for others, and for your purpose!

He doesn't want you to change your feelings, oh no...that's what drinking does. Feelings are not good or bad, they are just that...*feelings*. It is you who decides what to do with them, and it is your soul which directs your hands, feet, and mouth—*about* your feelings.

When Jesus lives in your heart, He begins to give your soul, *rest*. Then, through His grace, He gives you the strength to make the right choices in regard to your feelings—rather than drink to change them. And I know that not everyone reading this has a drinking problem, but if you have to ponder for one second, "Do *I* have an issue with drinking?" simply ask God. He will guide your heart into the truth, through the Holy Spirit. And Jesus said that it's the truth that will set you free (see John 8:32).

We need truth. Truth is good for us. For me, I didn't want to hear the truth about who I was, or about my life *denying* the fact I had no business drinking alcohol. I was arrogant. I was in denial—part of the 70%. "I don't have a problem, you do! Look at yourself!" "I can control this!" "I'm not addicted!" "I'M FREE TO DRINK, SO BACK OFF!"

Sure, I was free to drink. But I wasn't free *not* to drink. I was a complete slave to my feelings. They led me, I didn't lead them. When all along Jesus simply wanted me to start bringing absolutely every part of my life to Him, *including* my feelings, so we could begin doing wonderful, eternal things, *together*. He wants the same for you! He created you, He loves you, He's not mad at you or disappointed in you...He just wants to begin a relationship with you, through your heart, which will change your soul and life. He wants to begin this today...right now. C'mon... let's go. Jesus is ready and you are too. YES, you really are!

A prayer for you: *Heavenly Father, today I'm so grateful! I'm grateful for your protection over me and others, when I did so many dumb things while drinking. When I heard about my friend's mom being killed by a drunk driver, my heart sank. Not just for him and his family, but also for the person who killed her. That could have easily been me who did that, and I know it! Thank you for your hand of protection* *over my life during that difficult stage of growth! Thank you for placing angels around my vehicle each time I started the ignition while buzzed! I don't deserve to be here, but you were good to me, and you kept me safe. I'm SO humbled today. Thank you. Right now, I lift up all who are reading this, directly to you. For those who feel like drinking is just a part of who they are, and that they CAN'T change, DELETE THIS FROM THEIR MINDS! I rebuke any spirit of addiction from their bodies, right now, in Jesus' name! Help them to begin to understand and recognize the lies from the hottest places of hell, which are meant to keep them in bondage! SET THEM FREE THIS VERY MOMENT! And for the family members and friends of problem drinkers, help them too. Begin to supernaturally teach them how to understand that the drinker in their lives is not trying to cause problems, but just wants to feel different. Begin to help them establish healthy boundaries, and strengthen them so they can enforce those boundaries with love, respect, and confidence! Help them to NOT enable the drinker any longer! I bind the spirit of codependency in the name of Jesus! LEAVE THEM ALONE! Teach them what healthy relationships REALLY look like, based on THEIR relationship with Christ! Teach them their VALUE! In His name I pray, amen.*

DAY 7

THE TRUTH ABOUT CONFESSING OUR SINS

"If we confess our sins, he is faithful and just and will
forgive us our sins and purify us from all unrighteousness."

1 JOHN 1:9

Have you ever been told that you must confess every single sin in order to be *completely* forgiven by God? And if you didn't, or if you forgot to confess any, you're not *really* forgiven? What does such a statement create in a person?…One word, *fear*.

So if this legalistic proclamation of *confession of every sin in order to be acceptable to God* creates fear for a Christian, then a red flag should immediately go up in our souls alerting us that *this* is a lie from hell. Here's why:

1. **The Bible says God hasn't given *any* Christian a spirit of fear, but of power, love, and a sound mind—as in a *peaceful* mind (see 2 Timothy 1:7).** I'm going repeat myself here for emphasis. God has *not* given us a spirit of fear (that Spirit is Himself, *in* spirit, the Holy Spirit), but of POWER, LOVE, AND A SOUND MIND. So, worrying about confessing every

single sin, right down to the fibs you tell your kids about the Easter Bunny, is a big fat lie from Satan which is meant to *create* fear. You don't even have the human ability to keep track of all the many sins you commit, plus, you don't always *notice* your sins. And if you say you do, then you're lying, therefore compounding your sins.

2. **The Bible says there is no fear in God's love because it's a *perfect* love—and His perfect love casts out *all* fear because fear has to do with PUNISHMENT (see 1 John 4:18).** The Apostle John knew very well that Jesus had taken on the brunt of all our punishment *from* the Father. How would he know this? Because he saw it happen with his very own eyes at the Cross (see John 19:26). Further, the Bible is clear about the Messiah's *punishment* sacrifice for the world. This was written about hundreds of years before Jesus was even born (see Isaiah 53:5). So because we will *not* be eternally punished for one single sin, after placing our faith in Jesus, we have *nothing* to fear. The biblical fact is *no Christian* will give an account for *any* sin, only unbelievers will. Sure, we will all stand before the throne, Christian or not, but Jesus has secured our verdict as "not guilty" (see John 3:17,18).

The religious Christians who try to instill fear in the souls of other believers, they simply don't understand what Jesus has truly done for us. Instead, they are too focused on what we are dead to, *sin* (see Romans 6:11). Why beat a dead horse for previously misbehaving? It's pointless, it's dead.

You'll hear them say disturbing things like, "If you've *truly* repented, only then will you not sin any longer. And if you *keep* sinning, after you *thought* you got saved, then you didn't really get saved! You're not a *true* Christian unless you prove it with your works and repentance! You gotta repent every single day, of every single sin, and confess it to God! If you don't, then *you* will be in a hotter place of hell than the unbelievers because you *knew* right from wrong, yet you didn't confess it!"

My reply to this is, "…Really?…So tell me, how do *you* keep track of all your sins? A legal pad, or on your phone? Do you write them down so you can confess them later, or immediately? And what about the sins you forget about? The ones you overlook, belittle, or incorrectly justify as if they are *not* sins, but they really are?"

"Matt, you're a fool! Those sins don't count! Those are the sins which are covered by God's grace! A real Christian would know this!"

"Hmmmmm…so now *those* sins don't count, but the sins you remember to confess *do* count? I thought God was going to rightfully punish me for *all* the sins I don't confess? So which is it? You gotta make up your mind here. With your incorrect method, some sins count, and some don't. So God grades us on a curve? A curve which is based on our memory combined with a quasi-forgiveness? And you just called me a fool, which Jesus said in Matthew 5, if you call someone a fool you're in danger of hell. So are you gonna write that sin down *now*, or just confess it later by memory?"

"I'm done with this! I'm not having a Bible discussion with you any longer! You'll get what you deserve from God Almighty! I'll be praying for you harder than anyone else I know! You'll *pay* for this false teaching of the true word of God!"

…I've had that conversation, nearly verbatim, many times. When you start telling people they are completely forgiven *one time* through their faith in what Jesus has done at the Cross, the angry religious spirits come out of the woodwork to attack. But I ain't scared—oh I used to be, but *now* I know the truth. Their loud words, nasty emails, or all-capped comments with seven exclamation points are comparable to a toothless dog barking on a short chain. Harmless. All bark. No bite.

I now know *who* lives in me, they will never get me to be of God, *ever* again.

These types find their identity in an *anti*-grace, "Oh we *can't* be completely forgiven one time. We gotta keep confessing!" And do you see what happens? Religious pride happens. Unnecessary aggression happens. Going crazy trying to prove that Christians are *not* really forgiven "all the way," happens. It's sad because the very same people who claim you must confess every sin to be forgiven of it, they have *nothing* to back it up except attempting to create more fear. A fear that deep down *they* feel the most, so they want us to feel it too. Don't fall for it. Jesus told us all the time not to be afraid, and He meant it.

We have nothing to fear as Christians. Nothing. God loves us and wants us to have peace. Of course, I'm speaking about the fear of eternal punishment on any level, or fear of a demotion in heaven because of sin. Those things will not happen to believers in Christ.

Now, will *earthly* punishments come from making poor choices? Sure they will. If I go out and kill a man, and then plead to the judge that I shouldn't be punished because I'm a Christian, he'll probably move me up to the front of the line at death row. So yes, earthly punishment does still happen for Christians, but eternal punishment does not. Thankfully, God is merciful so even when we *do* deserve to be punished here on earth, He is monitoring those situations as well, working all things out *together*, for good (see Romans 8:28).

But this notion of confessing every sin *after* we are saved, in order to *stay* saved, is ludicrous. So let's look at the *one* Scripture—in context—which has created such confusion, and then break it down, 1 John 1:9:

> *"If we confess our sins, he is faithful and just and will*
> *forgive us our sins and purify us from all unrighteousness."*

First of all, as with every book in the Bible, we must look at *who* 1 John is primarily being written to, then look *around* the verse in question. If we *don't* do this, we can conveniently cherry-pick single verses here and there, pile them up, and then form a brick wall of fear and condemnation. Through this approach, which is used by many who don't understand the gospel very well, we can easily make God out to be someone who He's not.

The devil even attempted this trick on Jesus; that is, taking Scripture out of context to confuse and cause harm (see Matthew 4, Luke 4, Mark 1). And isn't that just like the devil? He places a *hint* of truth in with his lies in order to accomplish his work of stealing, killing, and destroying. I'll not go there in this devotional, because I could write forever on the subject, but even the devil has memorized the Bible.

When 1 John 1:9 is kept in context, what we are reading in this particular verse is not even directed towards Christians. John is making a case *for* Christ. He's not telling those who believed in Jesus as their Savior what they need to do to *be* saved. Instead, he's saying what a Christian's *life* should look like organically as they walk by the Spirit of Christ in them—*after* being saved.

All throughout 1 John he is explaining the actions and attitudes which come *from* Christ *in* us. He's *not* saying that these actions or attitudes *achieve* Christ in us. That part, which is called *salvation*, only comes by grace through simple *faith*. He tells us so in one of his other books, "For God so loved the world that he gave his one and only Son, that whoever believes in him shall not perish but have eternal life" (John 3:16).

The book of 1 John was primarily written to the *Gnostics*. Gnostics were people who believed our physical bodies were nasty, dirty, and all-around, just plain bad. They thought that in order to be one with God all they had to do was give away all their stuff and seek out wisdom. Because they thought the bodies of human beings were so flawed, they stuck to the notion of, "God would *never* belittle Himself by becoming an actual person." Hence, the Gnostics refused to believe in Jesus as the Son of God, all because the Christians kept claiming Jesus was a man.

For this very reason, John opens up his epistle by saying he *touched* Jesus (see 1 John 1:1). John makes the claim that he was an eye-witness to Christ *as* a person, emphasizing the fact that he had a *physical* relationship with God's own Son.

Second, and here's where we get to the brass-tax of the confession verse in question: the Gnostics believed there was *no such thing as sin*. There mindset was, "I'm not sinful because sin does not exist." This is the primary reason why John wrote: "If we confess our sin, he is faithful and just and will forgive us our sin..." as in, THE VERY FIRST TIME WE CONFESS THAT WE ACTUALLY *HAVE* SIN!

John was trying to get them to say, "You know what? I actually *do* have sin in me which needs God's forgiveness. I *must* confess I'm sinful *without* Jesus' blood. I *need* to be forgiven." This is why John says in the verse *before* that, "If we claim to be without sin, we deceive ourselves and the truth is not in us" (1 John 1:8).

And then look at the verse right after 1 John 1:9, which ties this all together and proves that the Gnostics believed they had *never* sinned, "If we claim we have not sinned, we make him out to be a liar and his word is not in us" (1 John 1:10).

The truth about the endless confessing of our sins is that it is *not* confessing which saves us but *only* the blood of Jesus and our faith *in* His blood as the truth *for* the forgiveness of our sin. Hebrews 9:22 is very clear about God needing *blood* to remove sin—*not* our words.

Further, according to the Old Testament Law (which non-Jews, us gentiles, weren't even invited to *read*, let alone *obey*), it wasn't the Jews' *confessing* which covered up their sins, but only the blood of animals. To top that off, this huge animal bloodbath party was only required, get this, ONCE A YEAR, at the Day of Atonement!

And the Jews got forgiveness *for an entire year* through this big day of animal bloodshed! They didn't get forgiveness for just an hour, day, or week—BUT FOR ALL YEAR! They weren't required to sacrifice animals each time they sinned, but only *annually*! So what makes us think that on *this* side of the Cross, as gentiles—NON-JEWS—our *words* will take away our sin?! They won't! WORDS *NEVER* TOOK AWAY SIN! *No* amount of babbling, begging, and pleading about our screw-ups can cleanse our spirits, *only* what Jesus' blood did for us at the Cross can!

To add to this point, the once-a-year slaughtering of animals at the Day of Atonement only covered up, or "atoned for" the Jews' sins—that blood never *took away* the sins for good. That's why they had to do it once a year! But Jesus' blood actually took *away* our sins, forever! (See Hebrews 10:4, 1 John 3:5, John 1:29).

Friend, Jesus has completed all the confessing you'll ever need to do in order to *be* saved, as well as *keep* your saving. He did so when He said,

"IT IS FINISHED!" These three words were the ultimate confession of sin! (See John 19:30). After that, He sat down at the right hand of God and a *New* Covenant began—a *better* covenant. Not one based on the blood of bulls and goats, but on the perfect human blood of Jesus Christ, the Messiah.

This New Covenant is between the Father and Son, *we* are simply the beneficiaries (see Hebrews 8:13). We've done nothing to create this contract, neither can we sustain it by our efforts. All we do is just *receive it* by faith and say, "Thank you." The best news is that you will *stay* saved as long as Jesus lives! And He isn't dying again and again up in heaven each time you sin! (See Hebrews 7:25). IT'S OVER! DONE! FINISHED! HE IS RISEN!

By Jesus giving up His perfect, sinless blood, once for all time, He has brought *everyone* into fellowship with God, not just the Jews (see Galatians 3:28). And now, because of such kindness and grace shown to us by our Creator—that He would sacrifice His own Son for us— and because Jesus will never shed His blood again, it's our job to simply *believe* that His blood *has* forgiven us, as in *one time*. This faith then gives us access to *His* perfection as He makes His home in our hearts! It's not about anything *we* do or don't do, but about what Jesus has done! (See Romans 10:9, Hebrews 10:10, Romans 6:10, 1 Peter 3:18, Ephesians 2:8,9, 3:17).

So today, my friends, know this: Jesus Christ has finished everything required by God on your behalf, which is to complete all of the laws and commandments perfectly, with love. He is your representative, your advocate, your Savior, and your obligatory sinless bloody lamb. The Father now sees Jesus *inside* you, in spirit—the Holy Spirit—and He is more than satisfied with Him. To top that off, He will *stay* satisfied, even if you never confess another thing for the rest of your life.

A prayer for the day: *Heavenly Father, what an amazing plan you thought out! You loved us so much you just HAD to create us! But you knew ahead of time that we would fail because of the option of sin. Yet,* *it was ALSO you who gave us this option because without the ability to make our own choices, we wouldn't have the ability to CHOOSE to love you back! Instead, we'd all be unlovable robots. But through your pre-planning and grace, you've allowed us to make our own choices and I am grateful. You not only created us with free will, but you also wanted to make a way to remove our sin forever. That way, is Jesus. Thank you, Thank you, THANK YOU SO MUCH for Jesus' blood sacrifice at the Cross! Amen!*

DAY 8

PASTORS HAVE THE ABILITY TO BE INCORRECT

"So Christ himself gave the apostles, the prophets, the
evangelists, the pastors and teachers, to equip his people
for works of service, so that the body of Christ may be
built up until we all reach unity in the faith and in
the knowledge of the Son of God and become mature,
attaining to the whole measure of the fullness of Christ"

EPHESIANS 4:11-13

P astors have a tough job, they have my full respect. Sometimes I think to myself, *"Could I start my own church and be a pastor?"* The Holy Spirit immediately corrects me each time, "No, you're not ready for that. You don't have the temperament."

Understandable. And you know what? I'm fine with that. I get asked quite often, "What church do you preach at?" Or, "What times are your services?" I even get called "Pastor Matt," and it makes me feel honored, but at the same time, I chuckle a little. I'm not a pastor. I'm a regular person, just like 99% of the world's Christian population. I'm a regular person who has developed a close relationship with Jesus by seeking Him out each day through His Word, Christian books, prayer, music, preaching, teaching, videos, movies, articles, blogs, TV shows, ANYTHING "JESUS"—I study. I'm simply a Jesus junkie. I can *not* get enough of Him.

What I've done is, I've taken *that* relationship with Jesus, and combined it with my God-given gift of communication, which has *then* supernaturally resulted in me walking out my destiny. And I gotta tell ya, it feels good. Even when the world is crashing around me, I *still* have a peace in my heart that is unshakable, and it's Christ in me.

All I've really done is become loving and respectful to Jesus through my words and actions because of what He did for me, for free. I had no clue the amount of people who would actually pay attention to what I had to say each day.

This is proof that God does more than we can ever imagine when His power is at work within us (see Ephesians 3:20).

And my destiny is simple: Bring attention to Jesus by allowing Him to live *through* me. I'm just like you. No better, no worse. We're the same in the eyes of God. He does not have favorite kids. He does not love us *more* because of our good behavior, or *less* because of our bad behavior. This same love is applied to *pastors* as well, only, they are on a platform.

This is a *huge* responsibility. People are looking to them for life's answers, so they better be sure to find their complete identity in Christ—not in themselves. As I've sat back over the years and watched pastors *pastor*, I've noticed a few things:

1. **People place so much of their faith into *that* single person, as if he (or she) is unable to be wrong.** I've been guilty of this, and it took me being blindsided by a trusted pastor to realize that just because you preach, that doesn't mean you fully understand the love of Christ. Our identity must never be found in a pastor, but instead, it should be found in Christ alone.
2. **People want to be extremely close to pastors, sometimes even more than they do Jesus.** This is not fair to the pastor. Yes, they want to help you, they want to be involved in your

life, but please understand that they have a family life as well. Take it easy on them. For some people, they have placed the opinion of their pastor *so high*, that when they are rejected by the pastor (because the pastor is trying to establish some healthy boundaries) they get angry and act as if God Himself is rejecting them. Some, even give up on their faith altogether because of the rejection of a pastor. Don't do that. If you do, the devil has won. LOVE your pastor, but know that he is just a man (or woman).

3. **Pastors get attacked more than the average Christian.** Of course, the devil doesn't like anyone making the lives of people better by pointing them to Jesus, let alone through teaching or leading them in a Christ-like way. So that dingle-berry from hell will come rushing in with gale-force winds to knock the pastor off his feet through the *hate* of non-believers, *and* through the uber-critical religious people. If the pastor is firmly planted in Christ, he'll not budge. If he's not, he's toast.

4. **Some pastors teach too much fear, while others won't come near "fear" teaching.** Peter said that we are to be "well balanced" (see 1 Peter 5:8), this should apply to *all* aspects of our lives. For pastors, this should be applied to their teachings. If all you teach about is fulfilling your congregations' dreams, you are selling your people short. And if all you teach about is how "backsliding" (which is not even a word in the New Testament) will land you in the deepest part of hell, you're wrong too. Keep the scales balanced. Teach truth *and* love, 50/50.

Yes, God wants to help us fulfill our dreams, but He is much more interested in molding our souls into Christ's image through *trusting* Him, than He is is making sure we have a fancy car or a big house. But at the same time, God couldn't care less if you have a fancy car and a big home if you are firmly planted in Christ's love. Those things won't send you to hell, or make you lose your salvation. They are simply details.

Also, try to remember: More money means we can reach *more* people. It's a good thing! It's not money that is the root of evil, but the *love* of it, the replacing of *Christ* with it.

I gotta tell ya something else that I've noticed. Some pastors are extremely self-righteous. So much so, that they find their complete identity in that *position*, in that *title*, in how they *look*, rather than in Christ.

Sure, they might know Jesus, but does Jesus fully engulf their souls? Or does doctrine? Or does their suit? Or, their refusal to *wear* a suit? Have they made *themselves* more holy than they really are by what they are *doing*?…

I can't judge that. I can only ask the questions. I *used* to judge them in this way and God soon slapped that out of my mouth, gently, of course.

They should ask themselves this: "*Has my position as pastor replaced the love of Jesus in my heart? Have I become cold? Is my identity found in my title, or is it found in my love for Jesus?*" And lastly, "*Am I showing others who Jesus really is, or am I showing them ME?*"

Do they have an unconditional, grace-filled, Christ-like love? Or do they have a rewards system for their church members? They must choose wisely because one type *heals* lives, and the other, ruins them.

Some pastors even lie to their congregations, saying such things as, "If you're not having any problems in your life, then you should be questioning your salvation." This is terrible. This is called *fear-mongering*, and fear will not work. So if that's you, stop it.

John said that "there is no fear in love, because fear has to do with punishment." Once we place our faith in Jesus, we no longer have to *worry* about being eternally punished. He also said that "God *is* love," and that "perfect love casts out *all* fear" (see 1 John 4).

God's love for us in Christ is PERFECT. And we have access to this perfect love, by grace, through faith (simply believe that Jesus is the Savior of your sins {see Ephesians 2:8,9}). God doesn't *want* you to be afraid of Him. Yes, He wants you to be afraid of life and death without Him—those are healthy fears. But as far as flinching all day long? No way. STOP BEING AFRAID OF GOD. Love Him, and show Him the respect that He deserves, but know that He is your loving Father. He *loves* you.

A lot of people have been hurt by pastors tremendously, myself included. I've seen some put on one face in the pulpit, but in a one-on-one setting, they are a different person. I'll not go into that, but if you pick up my book, *True Purpose In Jesus Christ*, I devote nearly an entire chapter to it.

But on the other hand, if it weren't for the pastors who truly know the heart Christ, and them teaching me, leading me, and guiding me...I don't think I'd be where I'm at today. The pastors who've encouraged me, telling me that God loves me infinitely *despite* my sin, yet, they told me that my sin had to go if I wanted to get the most out of my life—*those* are the pastors who have molded me into the man I am today. So thank you.

The more I think about pastors, overall, the more they have my sincere respect. Just the amount of relationship juggling is mind-boggling. Everybody wants to be a part of their pastor's life, and that's impossible. Yes, I'm sure he or she cares deeply for you, but there is no way that they can have a normal life, and be scrambling around a web of needy people 24/7—even though I'm sure they want to. So give them a break. Don't resent your pastor like the devil wants you to do. *Think* of them with love, no matter what.

So today, my friends, know this: Yes, your pastor *does* have the ability to be incorrect. Just like you do, and just like I do. None of us are perfect in word, thought, or deed, no matter our positions. But the great news is, on the inside of us is a perfect Savior! So let's all do as Jesus said and make sure that everyone knows we are following His lead. How do we do that?...Simple. By our *love* (see John 13:35).

A prayer for you: *Heavenly Father, this morning I lift up all pastors to you, ALL OF THEM, all throughout the world. Nothing is too big for you, so I'm praying a world-wide prayer today. I ask that you bless each and every pastor with peace today. Help them to understand the love of Christ on the deepest level possible, and then help them teach it to* *their people. Lift them up if they are down, REJUVENATE THEM! And if they've placed themselves higher than Christ, knock them off their pedestal, but do it gently. Help every pastor today to be a blessing! They CAN change the world for the better! I ask that you instill in each and every pastor's heart, Jesus, deeply, and on a whole new level! Thank you, Lord. Amen.*

Day 9

What Are You Doing With What God Gave You?

*"Well done, good and faithful servant! You have been
faithful with a few things; I will put you in charge of
many things. Come and share your master's happiness!"*

Matthew 25:23

You are one of God's greatest investments! YES! YOU! When you meet Him after you die, or Christ returns, He will be expecting a return on His investment. He's not looking for you to do anything you *can't* do, but He *is* expecting you to do what you *can* do for Him. Here is a parable that Jesus told His disciples about why we should be getting to work for God—not to earn anything—but because we love Him.

Getting to work for God is very important! *Using* what He's given each of us in the form of gifts and talents is not contingent on receiving our salvation, but it *is* contingent on stocking the halls of heaven with souls and making lives better here on earth! That's what we live for!

And, just like a loving husband does certain things for his wife, in order to make her proud, so do we, as Christians, do certain things to make God proud. No, these actions don't earn us status with Him, but instead, simply shows Him that we care.

In the following parable, this version of the Bible calls what God has given you to invest, "bags of gold," but other versions call what God has given us, "talents." This is where we get the expression "use your talents for God." As you can see here, He has given all of us a different amount! Using the talents He's given us, is what's most important to Him. Check this out:

"Again, it will be like a man going on a journey, who called his servants and entrusted his wealth to them. To one he gave five bags of gold, to another two bags, and to another one bag, each according to his ability. Then he went on his journey.

The man who had received five bags of gold went at once and put his money to work and gained five bags more. So also, the one with two bags of gold gained two more. But the man who had received one bag went off, dug a hole in the ground and hid his master's money.

After a long time the master of those servants returned and set-tled accounts with them. The man who had received five bags of gold brought the other five. 'Master,' he said, 'you entrusted me with five bags of gold. See, I have gained five more.'

His master replied, 'Well done, good and faithful servant! You have been faithful with a few things; I will put you in charge of many things. Come and share your master's happiness!'

The man with two bags of gold also came. 'Master,' he said, 'you entrusted me with two bags of gold; see, I have gained two more.'

His master replied, 'Well done, good and faithful servant! You have been faithful with a few things; I will put you in charge of many things. Come and share your master's happiness!'

Then the man who had received one bag of gold came. 'Master,' he said, 'I knew that you are a hard man, harvesting where you have not sown and gathering where you have not scattered seed. So I was afraid and went out and hid your gold in the ground. See, here is what belongs to you.'

His master replied, 'You wicked, lazy servant! So you knew that I harvest where I have not sown and gather where I have not scattered seed? Well then, you should have put my money on deposit with the bankers, so that when I returned I would have received it back with interest. So take the bag of gold from him and give it to the one who has ten bags. For whoever has will be given more, and they will have an abundance. Whoever does not have, even what they have will be taken from them. And throw that worthless servant outside, into the darkness, where there will be weeping and gnashing of teeth.'" (Matthew 25:14-30)

Friend, I know the end of this parable sounds really harsh, and this does not apply to Christians losing their salvation because they've not done enough—but Jesus is trying to get the point across that God has placed you here for a reason: TO SPREAD THE GOSPEL! He's given you gifts, *talents*, resources, and time! He wants you to *use what you've got* to multiply the population of heaven, and to show people how to live an abundant life in Christ!

SO BEGIN TODAY! JUST SAY, "GOD, USE ME!" AND HE WILL! Don't hide your talents any longer! USE THEM FOR GOD! This is why you live!

A prayer for you: *Well good morning God! Thanks for a great night's sleep, and thanks for waking me up again today. You are a good God! I also want to thank you for pestering the heck out of me, and getting me to finally use my own talent of writing and communication, for you. For years, I used both AGAINST YOU, and I realize that. Thanks for not giving up on me! Right now, I lift up all who are reading this, directly to you. For those who are thinking, "What is my talent?" reveal it to them! Show them exactly what it is. They probably already know, but make it clear! Also, show them that they are allowed to try out anything they want, and if it's part of their purpose, you will make it successful! Help them to set goals, and to keep moving forward! Help them to hone their talent into something beautiful, and spiritually fruitful! And keep the* *devil away from them when he says, "There's nothing special about you." I rebuke that liar from their hearts! YOU'VE SAID that you've given ALL of us different levels of talents, so we know it's true! In Christ's name I pray, amen.*

DAY 10

WHEN GOD ASKS YOU TO DO THE UNTHINKABLE

"Then he reached out his hand and took the knife
to slay his son. But the angel of the Lord called
out to him from heaven, 'Abraham! Abraham!'"

GENESIS 22:11

Are you allowing Jesus to live *through* you? If not, and you think that by doing so, you won't have to make any tough decisions, you'd be very wrong. Sometimes God asks us to do some pretty scary things— stuff that you wouldn't ever think was directed by Him. He will ask us to move forward in certain situations to test us, strengthen us, and hone our *complete trust in Him*...alone.

And if you *are* allowing Him to live through you, He will ask you do to certain things which seem counterproductive to your faith. Let me tell you about that part of being a Christian—the scary part.

Maybe the greatest example of God asking someone who loves and respects Him (through their words and actions) to do something petrifying, is Abraham. In the book of Genesis, there's a story of a man and his wife, Abraham and Sarah, whom God promised they would have many descendants. Abraham was told, "I will make you the father of many nations. I will make you fruitful. I will make your descendants as numerous as the stars in the sky, and sand on the seashore." The problem was… Sarah was barren.

So year, after year, after *year* went by, and both Sarah and Abraham began to get very old—still, no biological children. They even tried to rush God's plan at one point, and instead, got a microwaved blessing: a child with their maidservant. Sarah talked Abraham into sleeping with Hagar, and he obliged, resulting in Ishmael being born.

But that forced blessing only caused more problems for them. Ishmael wasn't God's best idea, He planned on Issac being born at *just* the right time! Long story short, Sarah finally got pregnant as a really old lady. Abraham was exactly one hundred years old when Issac was born.

They thought it was so funny that an old lady would be nursing a newborn that they laughed as Sarah did just that (see Genesis 21:6,7). The name *Issac* means laughter!

This new baby boy was looked upon as *very* special! Issac was doted on like a prince! Just imagine if something happened to him! Imagine if God decided to test Abraham by *removing* Issac from his life…forever. That's exactly what happened.

God asked Abraham to do the unthinkable—to sacrifice his one and only son as an offering to Him. Keep in mind, this story is BC, Jesus wasn't yet born, so God still required innocent blood as a sacrifice for sins. Usually this was the blood of animals, but God asked Abraham to offer up his son.

Rightfully, Abraham didn't want to do such a thing. I can picture him pleading his case in agony, "God you said that I would be a father of many nations, and then you give me this huge blessing just in the nick of time! And now you want to take it away?! WHY!?"

Whether or not God gave Abraham a reason why, Genesis doesn't say, but this unthinkable act sets the tone in my own life. This seemingly unfair request from God to Abraham, reminds me that when I am doing my very best to trust God myself, to love Jesus and do His will, but yet,

He still asks me to do something that seems as if it's from the devil, I get taken back. I have to regroup—is this *really* from God?

Now, I gotta tell you, if I was still doing things my own way—making poor choices that go against God's Spirit—I wouldn't be able to decipher such difficult requests as being from heaven or hell, but now, I can. And even if I'm incorrect, God will still use my mistakes for good, because He sees my effort and my soul's desires.

Friend, sometimes God wants you to take that ONE THING, or that ONE PERSON—who or *what* you are finding your identity in, and then hand it over to Him. That person, place, or thing that you believe you just can't live without, God wants you to say, "Here, I trust you. I'm giving this to you. Do what you want with it. You can allow me to keep this in my life, or you can remove it. I know that you love me. I know that you are good. I know that you are sovereign, and you always provide a way. I'm laying this down at your feet and putting *you* first. *All* of my value is now in you. No one else. Nothing else.

So Abraham made his way up the mountain with his son, made an alter, bound Issac and placed him on it. SHAKING, DISTRAUGHT, PETRIFIED...he lifted up the knife, high above his head...and just as he was about to slay his one and only beloved son, an angel said, "ABRAHAM! ABRAHAM!"

"Here I am," he replied.

"Don't kill your son. Now I know you fear (respect) God because you didn't even withhold your only son from Him. There is a ram caught in a bush over there, use it as your sacrifice."

GOD PROVIDED A WAY! AT THE ELEVENTH HOUR, WHEN ALL SEEMED LOST, GOD PROVIDED A WAY! GOD SHOWED ABRAHAM WHAT REAL TRUST IN HIM IS!

Because of this event, Abraham named that mountain, *The Lord Will Provide.*

So today, my friends, know this: The Lord will provide. The Lord will provide. THE LORD WILL PROVIDE! Trust Him! Get to know Jesus! As this happens day by day, He will begin to mold you into someone very strong, someone very confident, and someone who is willing to shake up their entire lives…because God asks you to. DO IT! If you are letting Him live through you, what you think is the most painful thing you will ever do, *that* will be what makes you a spiritual legend! A person who changed the course of history, forever, like Abraham! DON'T BE AFRAID!

A prayer for you: *Heavenly Father, today I want to thank you for scary situations. A few years ago, there's no way I'd be thanking you for such a thing. I kept making dumb choices and handling all of my problems the exact opposite way that you wanted me to. But now, I'm doing my best to submit to gracefully your ways, so I know that when I have to make difficult decisions, it's because you are trying to take me to a new level of faith. GIVE ME STRENGTH. GIVE ME TRUST. I NEED IT VERY MUCH! Right now, I lift up all who are reading this, directly to you. For those who want the power to be able to change their lives, GIVE IT TO THEM! Give them wisdom and guidance as they step off the cliff and into your hands! YOU ARE ALWAYS WITH US! Thank you! We are ready for the new things, just ahead. We love you. In Jesus' name we pray, amen.*

DAY 11

How Do I Remove My Sin? Simple. You Can't.

"I will remember your sin no more." ~God

ISAIAH 43:25

One of the biggest misconceptions of non-believers, and even Christians who just don't know any better, is that none of us have the ability to *remove* sin from ourselves—no matter how hard we try.

Sure, we can act and think a little "less" sinful, and even strive to no end to *completely* stop sinning, but, you'll soon see that you can't. If you *think* you actually *have* achieved status with God through becoming less sinful in word and deed, or that you've actually stopped sinning completely—then you no longer need Jesus. You've achieved the goal of becoming a Pharisee, not a Child of God.

And yes, Jesus said to the woman caught in adultery, "Go and sin no more" (see John 8:11). But keep in mind, Jesus hadn't yet died, so He was still teaching Old Testament law. Why? Because He was setting people up. He wanted to show them that being 100% sin-free was impossible, and that there *needed* to be another way—*other* than ourselves. This is why He said that He is "*the* way," (see John 14:6).

My friend, Jesus doesn't like sin at all, so much so, He took the punishment for ALL SIN on *Himself* in order to make us right with the Father. In Hebrews it says, "But now he (Jesus) has appeared *once for all* at the end of the ages to *do away with sin* by the sacrifice of himself" (Hebrews 10:26).

He did it. Not us.

I repeat: *HE* did it, not us.

For the self-righteous Christians who have "completely straightened out their lives," those who claim to not be like us "dirty old sinners," these people can't fathom this truth. They think that what they *did* to get right with God, and what they currently do *for* God, makes them acceptable *to* God. This is highly incorrect. They can try all they like to keep their righteousness, but they didn't *earn* any righteousness in the first place.

No amount of their effort removed any sin.

No amount of *their* effort removed any sin.

For those who still can't get this: NO AMOUNT OF THEIR EFFORT REMOVED ANY SIN.

Past, present, or future.

Only Jesus' blood did—*if* they believe in Him as their Savior.

Of course, this will bruise the egos of the religious people who don't understand God's grace; those who find their identity in "how good" they are, the tally of their trips to church, or how often they volunteer. Their hearts are hard in the worst way—to the *deepest* form of God's love, which is for *everyone*—despite sin. "Hate the sin, love the sinner!" they'll say… NO. *Love* the sinner, hate your *own* sin. This is how it should truly be.

These Christians have removed grace from the good news, so it's not good for anyone else but them. What's most sad is that this is the very worst form of evangelism because they are misrepresenting the unconditional love of Christ. They've turned back the clock 2,000 years and become modern-day *Christian* Pharisees. Lost people don't want to be like these types of Christians and I don't blame them, because I don't want to be like them either.

And on the flip-side, for those of you who won't give Christianity a chance because you know that you'll never be able to stop sinning, you are correct by half. No, you can't. Everyone sins, a lot. Those who say they don't are self-righteous fools because God doesn't grade us on a curve—we MUST be perfect. There is no middle ground. And only Jesus can do this *for* us (see Matthew 5:48, James 2:10, Romans 6).

The great news is this: We can't wear out God's grace through the blood of Christ. There is no tipping point. Religious Christians will stand up and walk-out at this idea, but again, they *too* will be in desperate need of this grace. Grace *can't* be earned; if it can't be earned, then it can't be lost. If it *could* be, then it wouldn't be called grace, it would be called *earned rewards*.

So, because of this *good news* (that's what the word *gospel* means), we can come to this conclusion:

When you place your faith in Christ *once*—not multiple times—*He* removes your sin, completely and for good, because you become a *new* creation in your spirit (see Hebrews 10:10, 2 Corinthians 5:17).

Yes, you can always *begin* to allow Him to live through you on a deeper level, but know that the reason you *already have* an unsettling feeling each time you now sin is because your spirit is brand new—it's infused with Christ! Your spirit *can't* keep on "practicing" sin, as in "get better by doing repeatedly," it no longer has that ability (see 1 John 3:9). So now, *when* you sin, you'll feel like a horse is kicking you on the inside. Some Christians have gotten good at ignoring this feeling, but it's still there.

So if we can't wear out God's kindness, our goal should now be this: *Because* of the sacrifice of Christ we should now *want* to do the right things *for* Him. Why? Because we love Him! Jesus even said this Himself, "If anyone loves me they will obey my teaching" (John 14:23). He didn't say, "DO WHAT I SAY OR GO TO HELL!" "BE SALT!" "BE LIGHT!" "GO MAKE PEOPLE OBEY THIS GOOD NEWS, NOW, OR ELSE!"

No…Jesus gave us…*grace*. Sweet…grace…He also gave us the ability to *choose* to become who He wants us to become. And then He piled on top of GRACE and the power of CHOICE—unconditional love and mercy…What a wonderful God that He would give us these gifts through Christ!

After we finally realize just how amazing God's gift is to us through Jesus, everything changes. You will then have the *ability* to do your very best *not* to sin, *through* His grace. Why? Because you love Him, *and*, because you are no longer afraid of being punished (see 1 John 4:18).

So today, my friends, know this: Once we truly understand our identity in Christ, that we are BLEMISH-FREE (because of His work, not ours), we will then be able to walk out each day *with* Him and enjoy the rest, goodness, hope, and confidence that only *He* provides.

A prayer for you: *Good morning Lord! What a beautiful day you've given me! I want to thank you for the sound of singing, excited birds outside my window! How wonderful it is to hear their enthusiasm for this brand new day. I ask that you give me that same enthusiasm to spread your good news as I walk out the door today. Right now I lift up everyone reading this directly to you. For those who have been lied to about your kindness—how you remove our sin completely, through Jesus—I ask that you renew their minds with your grace. As believers, help them to realize that because of Christ, their sin is 100% gone. All of it. Forever. Thank you for teaching me this! In Jesus' name I pray, amen.*

DAY 12

HOW TO DEFEND YOURSELF AS A CHRISTIAN

"When you are brought before synagogues, rulers and authorities, do not worry about how you will defend yourselves or what you will say, for the Holy Spirit will teach you at that time what you should say." ~Jesus

LUKE 12:11,12

Let's face it, not everyone is excited about you being a Christian—that includes both non-believers *and* believers.

As a matter of fact, some of the people in your life who are used to getting their way with the old version of you, now, are just plain furious. Their tactics no longer work. When this ensues, prepare yourself—no, don't just prepare yourself, HAVE YOUR MIND MADE UP AHEAD OF TIME, to do a few things:

1. **Forgive.** You must remember that the entire premise of Christianity is based on forgiveness—not justice, not revenge, not tit-for-tat—but 100% *undeserved* forgiveness. So if you are wanting Christ to help you defend yourself in unfair situations, you must have in your heart forgiveness-mode *before* you are even wronged.

"BUT MATT IT'S NOT FAIR! IT HURTS! HOW CAN GOD LET THIS HAPPEN TO ME WHEN I'M JUST TRYING MY BEST TO LIVE THROUGH HIM?! I WANT TO GET THEM BACK! YOU JUST DON'T UNDERSTAND!"... Friend, I can relate. I know what it's like to feel disoriented while following Jesus because you just took a sucker-punch to the face. You're gonna be fine. This will strengthen you. Always remember that God is with you and *He's* not causing this, the devil is, *through* people. God is actually *using* this for a good future purpose. So prepare yourself ahead of time and *know* that attacks are coming your way, and decide *before* you get attacked, to forgive. To make it easier to forgive beforehand, stay focused on what *you* did to Jesus at the Cross because of your sin. He decided to forgive you ahead of time, and so should we, with others.

2. **Don't take the bait, don't retaliate.** This was a very difficult thing for me to learn because I'm a passionate person, and I'm well-versed. My vocabulary is dense, it's a gift that I can use *for* God, or against Him. I have a wonderful ability to debate with the best of them, and if I have to I can plead my case and get you back verbally, splendidly. But that's not what God wants me to do. Even now, I have to consciously allow the Holy Spirit to make me *pause, pray, proceed* when I get punched in the gut with an attack from others. Just the other day, I had a supposedly Christian man rip into me on social media. My initial response was to attack back, but I didn't, even though every fiber of my being (my flesh) was telling me to. But even worse than not commenting back, I white-washed my newfound resentment for this man by blocking him on Facebook while saying to myself, "I don't need this crap." It wasn't 45 seconds later that the Holy Spirit told me to *unblock* Him, and then send him a message telling him how much God loves him and that He has a great plan for his life. This was like eating a rotten lemon, but afterwards, I felt good. I had overcame evil with good (Romans 12:21). I think he was in shock

because he responded with, "Thanks, that's what's so good about faith." Weird.

3. **Don't force your defense.** I lived most of my life *forcing* how I felt, verbally. This is not good because we are both spirit *and* flesh. Our flesh's mouth has no scruples, so when we let it run wild even when pleading our case, bad things happen. Further, Jesus said we shouldn't even worry about what we should say when we have to defend ourselves, but instead, the Holy Spirit will give us the words (see Luke 12:11,12). So what I've realized is when I feel myself about to *force* words out of my mouth (or through the typing of my fingers) in my defense, I'll just be quiet. For too many years, I just spouted out whatever *whenever*, trying to defend myself. I can't live like that and enjoy the peace of God *in* me, even when I'm coming under attack by people who hate me, dislike me, or who are simply jealous of me. If I do, then I'll respond in sinful anger. The problem with responding in sinful anger is we always regret what we said, or did, and then we spend more time feeling guilty and cleaning things up than it was worth. It's just like my drinking. Sure, I "just" wanted to get a buzz to release my feelings and relax, but the hangovers and dumb choices I made while *getting* that buzz was never worth it. So instead of defending yourself with your words, defend yourself with prayer. Find your comfort in Christ. Ask God, "Tell me what to say." Most of the time, He'll tell you to just keep your mouth shut and let Him deal with those who are treating you poorly. And when you finally *do* have something to say, it solves problems, God's way.

So today, my friends, know this: You don't *need* to defend yourself! God will do that for you! He is your loving heavenly Father! He protects you at all times, even in the middle of the storm! He knows what you can handle! YOU ARE STRONG IN CHRIST! He sees what's going on and your time is coming! KEEP PASSING YOUR TESTS! He sees clearly, that some people—even Christians—will try to goad you into defending yourself sinfully, and *then* try to use that sin against you. Don't do it. Mind your own business, pray for those who hate you, and be FULL OF JOY in the meantime! You are attaining the full measure of your faith by doing so, and becoming more like Christ in your mind and body!

A prayer for you: *Good morning Lord! What a spectacular morning it is here in Missouri! I want to thank you for a good night's rest, for my good health, and for Jesus. Right now, I lift up all who are reading this, directly to you. Those who are in a severe battle, those who and are tempted to handle things their own way, strengthen them! Show them that it is in our WEAKNESS of not doing things OUR WAY, that we become strong as an oak tree–that we we become STRONG LIKE CHRIST! Establish your ways in them, and then give them the courage to walk them out! In Jesus' mighty name I pray, amen.*

DAY 13

WHAT MAKES YOU GOOD ENOUGH FOR GOD?

"...I consider them garbage, that I may gain Christ and be found in him, not having a righteousness of my own that comes from the law, but that which is through faith in Christ—the righteousness that comes from God on the basis of faith."

PHILIPPIANS 3:8,9

I almost titled this devotional, "What Makes You Righteous In God's Eyes?" but that sounded a little religious. So I swapped the word *righteous* for *good enough*, because really, that's all righteousness is—being settled-up with God, or, *in good standing*.

SO JUST *WHAT IS IT* THAT MAKES YOU RIGHTEOUS?! This is a question that can either ruin your life, make you become bitter, frustrated, *self*-righteous, angry, or scared—or—the *truth* about your righteousness with God can set you free!

Why has it become so difficult to get the truth of our 100% righteousness down pat? Simple: Because of the twisting of the truth by those who don't *know* the truth. The Christians who think they are *more* righteous because of their church works, Scripture memorization, and lack of sins of the flesh.

These types of Christians destroy lives, rather than heal them. They condemn others, rather than care for them. They antagonize, rather than evangelize. I was affected severely by this brand of "Christianity." When I was looking for the unconditional love of Jesus, I didn't get that. Instead, I got conditional love from those who didn't know Jesus on a personal level—all they knew was *religion*.

Why would I say that? Because if they *did* know Jesus intimately, they would treat others *differently*. They are sin-focused and works-based, rather than being full of grace as they should be. They might have a *dash* of grace, but when you only having a small amount of grace, you can't even taste it; a flavorless gospel ensues.

Jesus said we should be *salt* (see Matthew 5:13). And what does salt do? It gives flavor, and it preserves. That's not happening as much as it should be, in the Body of Christ.

So many Christians like to judge others harshly, no matter if they are a Christian or not; they are hyper-critical and call grace "cheap." When really, grace is not cheap at all. It is the most expensive thing ever—for Jesus, not us. For us, it's completely free. And this grace doesn't *just* save us, it also *empowers us* each day to allow Christ to live *through* us.

I used to have a lot of hate in my soul towards religious Christians, those who honestly believe that what they do, or don't do, *makes* them righteous. Even typing that, my blood pressure goes up just a tad. It's a sore spot for me in my soul that Jesus is still healing day by day. I'm not there completely, but I'm soooooooo much better than I used to be. Just like the urge to drink, the Holy Spirit has taught me to be conscious of this feeling of resentment, and to bring it to Him *immediately*.

And I guess I'm like this because I've been so hurt by "church people" who thought they *were* righteous. These people attempted to make me feel like I *wasn't* righteous—"like them"—when really, *they* were only *self*-righteous. My dad, for example, has allowed self-righteous people in the church to ruin his relationship with God when it comes to being involved with an *actual* church. It's just not important to him.

Sure, Dad's a Christian and he loves God, but his pride towards those in church has kept him from being involved *at* church. I mimicked this for a long time, and I finally had to come to the realization that just because Dad is like this, doesn't mean I have to be. I *want* to go to church. Yes, I *am* The Church, because of my faith in Christ (see 1 Corinthians 6:19)—but I still want to go and gather with others *weekly* to learn and praise God *corporately*. IT IS GOOD!

What Dad has allowed to fester, and keep him where he's at, I've battled with the help of Christ in me:

1. **Bless those who curse you** (Luke 6:28, Romans 12:14)
2. **Pray for those who hate you** (Matthew 5:44)
3. **Don't be overcome by evil, but overcome evil with good** (Romans 12:21)

We cannot allow the devil to make me hate people, no matter if they hate us or not. It's like the Will Smith song, *Just The Two of Us*, "...hate in your heart will consume you too."

So try your very best to remember that what others do or don't do doesn't *make* them righteous, *or* unrighteous. Our righteousness is free, and it has *been* free from day one of our belief! And it does not come in increments. So who is righteous? *Anyone* who has placed their faith in Jesus. Period.

Like Dad, I wanted to shut off the church world and just have my own little one-on-one relationship with Jesus, but the Holy Spirit quickly corrected that—although at first I fought it.

I am NOT allowed to have disdain in my heart for anyone! Believers, or not! Christ owns *all* the real estate in my heart, so the very moment I feel ill feelings or harsh judgment towards anyone for anything, I have to consciously allow Him to correct that. If I don't, I'll live a sorry, blameful, bitter, fruitless life.

Here are some tips that I believe will help you when it comes to dealing with self-righteous people. Learn from my mistakes and don't be like me—don't attack them. You'll regret it even if they *are* wrong. Instead, begin to *think* of them with love, just like Jesus does for you:

1. **TRY TO REMEMBER THEY'VE NOT EARNED A THING.** This was difficult for me in the beginning of wanting to *really* have some fruit in my life for Jesus. I'm very aggressive and overly-competitive. I want to win at everything—which has been a blessing for me at times, and other times, a cursing (when it's out of balance). So when I saw what other Christians were doing, I wanted to compete with their works. This is wrong. We don't compete, we are on the same team! TEAM JESUS! And, all we have is 100% free! It *can't* be competed for—or won, or lost! It doesn't matter if someone's been doing stuff for Jesus for 5 days, or 50 years, all we have is free. Free. Free. Free. WE'VE NOT EARNED ANYTHING. WE *CAN'T* EARN ANYTHING FROM GOD. Jesus already earned it all. Now, enjoy it, and grow fruit! Fruit that will last! (See John 15:16).

2. **FAITH IN JESUS IS OUR *ONLY* RIGHTEOUSNESS.** This statement will upset the religious Christians. If you have a religious spirit that normally pesters you, you'll probably judge me harshly for saying this—or you won't fully believe it. The self-righteous believers who look at what they do (or refuse to do) "for" Jesus, *as* their identity (rather than their *faith* in Him alone) will absolutely *hate* this. Why? Because they find their identity in THEMSELVES doing stuff FOR God. Here's a rule of thumb that will help you overcome this Pharisaical nastiness: When you feel yourself being pressured to do something, or *not* do something, in order to *stay* in good standing with God, let that be a red flag to take a step back and remember only your belief *in* Jesus is your good standing. This fact will empower you to do more for God, as well as remove any sinful actions of the flesh or soul. This amazing power comes from understanding your full value of your identity in Christ alone.

3. **STOP BEING AFRAID OF GOD.** The fear of God is a major weapon of control and manipulation that the religious Christians use. And sure, the Bible says that "the fear of the Lord is the beginning of all wisdom" (see Proverbs 9:10)—THE *BEGINNING*—not the end, and not the middle. We all start out by understanding that God is really big, that He has standards we should gracefully strive for each day, and sure, we *need* to get on His side. And it is our faith in *Jesus* which does this— not anything we do or don't do (see Ephesians 2:8,9). After *that* belief originates (once we accept Christ's forgiveness of our sin) we need to STOP being afraid of God! You can't enjoy a relationship with someone whom you fear because you won't really love them. This is why John said, "there is no fear in love, God *is* love, God's love for you is perfect, and perfect love casts out *all* fear" (see 1 John 4). *Fear* has to do with punishment, and because of Jesus we aren't going to be eternally punished. This is good news! GOD'S LOVE FOR YOU IS *PERFECT!* HE LOVED YOU EVEN BEFORE HE FORMED THIS PLANET! JESUS' LIFE, DEATH, AND RESURRECTION PROVES THIS! Simply ignore the scare tactics of others and enjoy Him!

So today, my friends, know this: You *are* good enough for God *if* you've accepted Christ's forgiveness by simply believing. "But Matt, what about—" NOPE! NOPE! NOPE! Stop paying so much attention to what you've been taught is *wrong*, and *start* paying attention to who is right—which is YOU, right now, today, this very moment…because of Christ *in* you! ENJOY!

A prayer for you: *Heavenly Father, I just gotta thank you for the seasons of blessings in my life, you are so good to me. The pain that I've gone through has produced wonderful, ripe fruit! THANK YOU! Right now, I lift up all who are reading this, directly to you. For those who have had their lives destroyed by cold, legalistic religion, help them.*

I'm asking that you supernaturally wipe the slate clean in their souls! If you could JUST get them to understand WHO they really are— their true identity in Christ's finished work—then they would begin to love themselves, love you, and love others properly! HELP THEM TO DO THIS TODAY! GIVE THEM PEACE, COMFORT, CONFIDENCE, AND A SOUND MIND! In Christ's holy name I pray, amen.

DAY 14

Do You Even *Want* To Change Your Life?

*When Jesus saw him lying there and learned
that he had been in this condition for a long
time, he asked him, "Do you want to get well?"*

JOHN 5:6

For years, I didn't want what Jesus had to offer, my body and soul was still too rebellious. I wanted to do things *my* way! The problem with "my way," is that Jesus did not approve of it. The blueprint that He had laid out for me (and everyone), by allowing Him to live *through* me—I did not want to build my life on that. I didn't yet *want* it. I didn't trust him enough to do things His way.

So what happened to me? Old Matt (the matt who hadn't yet allowed Jesus to renew his mind) kept banging his head against the same dumb wall, and then blaming the wall for his headache. Old Matt kept going around the same *stupid* mountain, and then blaming the mountain for my poor sense of direction. Then one day, I finally had a come-to moment, "I gotta change."

I gotta change.

Not people, not circumstances, but me.

I was ruining my entire life trying to change people and circumstances in which I had no power *to* change. So the Holy Spirit finally convinced me of this: "Stop getting upset about what you *can't* control, instead just do your best to control what you *can*, my way. Then you'll have peace."

EUREKA! I'VE GOT IT! CHANGE *ME*! Well alrighty then!

But I believe that in order to have these "come-to moments," we gotta try things out our own way long enough to realize *our* way don't work. Some people have this moment of repentance early in life, some in the middle, and some even decide to change—to *want* it—after they are old and gray, which is a very good thing! 9 years old or 90, as long as your heart is still beating, it's never too late to make healthy changes. God keeps us alive for a reason—that reason, is to become exactly like Jesus, gracefully.

The sad thing is, some people never decide to change. They simply do not want it. And they don't want it because they think they don't need it—and they think they don't need it because of a nasty little word that the devil plants in our souls: pride. Pride is the root of all sins as well as a terrible life! Out of pride grows:

1. **Unforgivness.** If a *Christian* is too full of pride in their souls to realize Christ forgave *them* unconditionally, that they refuse to give that *same* forgiveness away to others, then they can expect a frustrating life. This change they refuse to make, COMPLETE FORGIVENESS, is the same as them punching themselves in the mouth. It's dumb, and pointless. The devil licks his chops at unforgivness. We must remember that the entire premise of Christianity is based on forgiveness. So when someone continues to bring up old hurts caused by others, and the sins which have already been taken care of by God—those hurts and sins are now on *them, and them alone*. Unforgiveness is like a magnet that compels the faults of others to yourself. Drop it like a hot rock, and make a decision to forgive like Christ forgave you.

2. **Self-Pity.** In John 5, When Jesus approached an invalid sitting my the pool of Bethesda, a man who had been in self-pity for 38 years, Jesus said to Him, "Do you even want to get well?" The man replied with the same stale excuse that he'd been giving everyone for years, "Nobody will help me." Jesus didn't reply with, "Oh, you poor baby, let me do that for you." No, He said, "GET UP!" Jesus is *not* an enabler! Religious Christians want you to think He is! He's not! And YOU don't have to be either! Self-pity is not gonna work with Jesus—He *will* point out your excuses, *to* you—and then expect you to do something about it, *with Him.* So make a decision TODAY, to refuse to be in self-pity any longer!

3. **Sin-Soaked Choices.** I was the worst with this, as my pride gave me tons of excuses to sin. *"Get drunk! You deserve it! Relax! You work hard! Nobody appreciates you anyway!"* Or, *"Go ahead and watch that porn, nobody is watching. You've not had sex in a while, it's no big deal."* Or even, *"Get them back! They need to get what's coming to them so they can learn a lesson!"* SIN. SOAKED. CHOICES... They grow right out of the pride of our souls. It wasn't until I finally humbled myself to Christ's ways of handling my problems that I began to *change* my choices. I began to allow the Holy Spirit to convict me of the *wrong* ways of handling things—but I had to want it.

4. **Arrogance.** Please don't get arrogance confused with confidence. God wants you to be confident! It is in our confidence that we do the most work for Him! SO *EXUDE* CONFIDENCE AT ALL TIMES! EVEN WHEN YOU ARE WEAK! Try to remember that God's power is made perfect in our weakness (see 2 Corinthians 12:9). Arrogance, however, is a *branch* of pride. It says, "I don't need to change anything. I'm never wrong. People *make* me like this." Arrogance looks upon others—both, those who are far from God, and even well-meaning Christians— with a hyper-critical attitude. It's nasty. When God tries to gently

smack this out of your hands, let Him. Getting corrected by God never feels good but it's supposed to shock us into paying attention to Him.

My friend, God is simply looking for us to *want* to change! He's not trying to bribe us *to* change—we gotta want it! Jesus never helped anyone who didn't want to be helped! He gladly helped those who *came* to Him—those who wanted what He had to offer! Which is a brand new life!

What you will soon realize is that after you want to change (and you actually begin to) God teaches you that *you* can't change people, and that you can't make *them* want to change. No matter how badly you want it *for* them, they are the ones who have to decide to remove their pride enough, themselves, to ask Jesus to change their hearts, minds, and lives—YOU, CAN'T.

Oh but the devil sure wants you to ruin your life *trying* to change others, because he knows you can't. So when you feel yourself getting frustrated, just take a step back, and relax. Let God handle it. Begin to set healthy boundaries with love and respect, and then enforce those boundaries the same. You have to detach yourself from people who don't want to make healthy changes.

God has taught me in my journey of *wanting to change* that it's okay to separate myself from those who *don't* want to change. If someone is hitting the crack-pipe, and you're getting dressed for church, that won't work. Sure, that's an extreme example, but for even the most subtle differences, *both* people in a relationship have to want to change for God—or it will fail.

If it doesn't fail, it will become extremely one-sided and codependent. God does not approve of selfishness *or* codependency.

So after you've given your absolute all and have done all you possible *can* do, and still the other person wants nothing to do with making healthy changes for the benefit of your relationship, then it's *okay* to separate yourself from them. Let me repeat: IT'S OKAY. And if you don't, you will destroy your life, value, and self-worth *trying* to change them.

The religious Christians who are codependent enablers won't agree with separating yourself from the people who refuse to make healthy changes; but for your own mental, spiritual, and emotional health—yes, it's allowed. DETACH AND SEPARATE YOURSELF. Let them hit rock-bottom, then they'll have more of a chance to *want* to change. Just like Jesus can't help people who don't want to be helped, neither can you.

Move along, pray for them diligently, and let them know that if at any point in time they want to change, you'll be there for them—until then, you won't. THIS IS POSSIBLE TO DO. Stop loving people to death, and stop ruining your life "standing in the gap" for those who want nothing to do with change.

So today, my friends, know this: YOU CAN CHANGE! YES, *YOU*! Get your mind off of trying to change *people* and *circumstances*, and instead, focus on allowing God to change *you*! How? By wanting it! You gotta want it! You gotta say, "Lord, I'm ready now. I'm ready for you. Change me!" After that, brace yourself...because nothing will ever be the same!

A prayer for you: *Heavenly Father, you are such a patient, good God. Thank you for helping me change my entire life after I wanted to change. Right now, I lift up all these readers directly to you. I ask that you lovingly convict them of any mindset which might be holding them back from WANTING Jesus to be deeply involved in their lives. REVEAL IT! Help them to change their minds. Help them to WANT to change. You will always give us opportunities to change, but we still gotta decide on our own to "GET UP!" just like the man laying by the pool. Give us that extra nudge to WANT to get up today, so that you can change our entire lives for the better! In Christ's name, amen.*

DAY 15

WHAT IS YOUR STORY?

*"I have testimony weightier than that of John. For
the works that the Father has given me to finish—
the very works that I am doing—testify that the
Father has sent me. And the Father who sent me
has himself testified concerning me..." ~Jesus*

JOHN 5:36,37

We all have a story to tell, it's just, some of us never tell it. Either because we are ashamed of it, embarrassed by it, or because the plans for our story didn't pan out how we wanted them to, we hide it. But *all* of us have a story to tell—our story is our *testimony*.

The most important testimony of all time is Jesus'. His testimony changed eternity. But just imagine if Jesus stayed quiet and never told His story? What if He knew what His mission was, but yet, He didn't speak about it, didn't teach people, or what if He refused to tell the world about His true identity? What *if* He simply went to the Cross, with no explanation?...We would have no clue about *what* He expected from us after He left. We wouldn't even *have* the opportunity *to* believe.

So *half* of our salvation is found in the words Jesus spoke. Our *saving* is one-half Cross, one-half Word. We needed Jesus to speak! Without it, there would be no *truth*. Thats why Jesus said, "I *am* the truth" (see John 14:6, my emphasis added). And without Christ's truth through His words, we would have no blueprint for our lives.

This is why we need YOUR story! Yes, YOURS! YOU! DEAR READER! WE NEED YOU! We don't need more fake-happy pictures on social media, we need some grit! We need some dirt! We need knees bending and index fingers pointing up! STORIES! TESTIMONIES! We *need* them! We need to know what Jesus has done for *you*—and, what He is *currently* doing! We need your testimony!

Are you a Christian? THEN SPEAK UP! Why would you just keep everything to yourself? Is it because you are stuck in a sin pattern? SO WHAT! SPEAK! How do you think you will ever break free?! It is when we bring out darkness into the light, we can finally get set free!

Are you not sharing your testimony because your meticulously-laid plans fell through? Or is it because someone has attempted to ruin your life, and now you are heartbroken?! THAT'S OKAY! SPEAK UP! SPEAK OUT! HOW DO YOU THINK YOU WILL EVER HEAL?! Where do you think your newfound confidence will come from?! IT WON'T BE BY YOUR OWN MAKING!

SO SPEEEEEEEEEEAK!

We *need* you to speak! Christ *lives* in you, and YES, you are going to heaven because you believe He is your Savior, but now He wants you to USE YOUR VOICE FOR HIM—right here, right now! *Your life doesn't have to be perfect before you start to do this!*

My friend, don't waste your story. The Bible says that we overcome the power of the enemy through the blood of Christ *and* our testimony (see Revelation 12:11), it's both. So when you keep your story to yourself, you are giving the devil his way—you are allowing Him to keep you shut up.

WHY NOT SMACK HIM IN THE MOUTH?! WHY NOT *TALK ABOUT WHAT'S GOING ON?* Why not talk about what's going on, or what *has* been going on? Why not show other people that just because you are a Christian, everything isn't always perfect or easy, but instead, everything is *always* being paid close attention to by our loving Heavenly Father?

Why not? I mean, after all, He is working all things out together for our good, anyway? (See Romans 8:28).

What are you doing? What are you waiting for? Everything to line up before you start to use your testimony to help others? Sure, you may enjoy seasons of ease and blessings, but nothing will be perfect until you shed this shell—SO TELL YOUR STORY AS IT IS. Has an unloving Christian told you to keep your mouth shut until you straighten out your life? They can shove that junk in their pipe and smoke it because that is *not* how this works!

Everything in your life doesn't have to be perfect before you become vocal about your past, or even your current struggles. Instead, please begin to understand that *Jesus* is your perfection—*you* don't have to be, and neither do your circumstances! Remember, it is *in* your weakness that you become strong! (See 2 Corinthians 12:10). It is *in* your testimony that you can help other people see that it is Christ holding everything together—it's not what *you* do, but what He has already done!

Please. Speak. UP.

Tell your story. We need it. There is someone out there right now, who is waiting for it. Your testimony about what Jesus has done in your life is the key to unlocking the strength they are looking for. Your story is what will show them what confidence in Christ looks like. Be brave. Begin to tell your story, today.

A prayer for you: *Good morning, God. Thank you for another day alive! What an honor it is to have life! Today, I want to thank you for giving me the courage to share my life's testimony like I do. People ask me sometimes, "How do you say all that personal stuff?" And honestly, I don't know. My answer is usually, "Jesus wants me to be salt and light, so that's what I'm doing." It's gotta be Christ in me because I wouldn't* *dare say some of the stuff I do. So I know He's using it! Right now, I lift up all who are reading this, directly to you. For those who are on the fence about telling their story, please pull them off. Once they fall into Jesus, they'll begin to understand that they don't have to look perfect, but instead, they simply have to point to Christ as their perfection! Fill them up with your love, hope, peace, and CONFIDENCE as they begin to tell their story with absolutely bravery! In Christ's awesome name I pray. Amen.*

DAY 16

JESUS WILL NEVER REJECT YOU—EVER!

"…whoever comes to me I will never drive away." ~Jesus

JOHN 6:37

C an you repeat that opening verse with me? Only this time, I want you to picture Jesus looking directly at you as He says it:

"Whoever comes to me I will never drive away."

Whoever means *whoever*!

So let's do it again:

"If *you*, _____ (insert full name here), come to me, I will never drive you away."

YOU are a whoever! YEAH! You really are! "But Matt, what about *this* about me—" "NOPE!" Remove that thinking from your mind! You've been taught wrong! Jesus' love for you is *not* conditional! Once you accept His forgiveness by simply believing it as the truth for your sin, even *you* can't stop this! (See 2 Timothy 2:13).

No matter what it is about you—as long as you believe in Him as your Savior, ONE TIME—as in, the first time—Jesus will never reject you, never abandon you, and He will never *remove* His love from you—NO MATTER WHAT! Friend, He loved you before you were even forgiven, He even had a good plan for you then (see Romans 5:8). So how much more do you think He will take care of you now that you are a joint-heir to heaven with Him? (See Romans 8:17).

The fact is this: You *can't* wear out the blood of Jesus, the Cross actually worked! As long as Jesus lives, this promise of His (which is heaven, and His unconditional love for us, here on earth) stays in effect! (See Hebrews 7:25). Oh my goodness, when I first grasped this amazing truth, I thought I was going to explode!

I thought, "You mean...you still love me despite my alcoholism? You still care for me despite my difficulty to forgive? Despite my bursts of anger? Despite my greed? You mean to tell me that I don't have to be completely perfect in word or deed before you will accept me? REALLY?! How can that be?!"

Jesus spoke to my heart, "Because I finished everything *for* you." This love is what will change you, not more rules, not more religion, but understanding that what *we* do means nothing compared to what *Christ* has done. That's it. I finally found it—what we are all looking for—an actual relationship with God! That's what Jesus provides! And just *why* does He allow it to be so simple to have access to God? So *completely different* than what many Christians say?

Because so many Christians don't understand God's grace. Because once you realize you *can't* do anything to lose His love, you actually begin to care for Him. You actually begin to put His feelings first. He begins to matter. Soon enough, what matters to Him, matters to you. Only *then* will you start to change everything, and for the right reasons; it's all because you know He loves you 100% unconditionally and without limit—and why would you want to abuse that? Why would you want to take advantage of such love... You don't.

We change for Jesus because we know that He loves us even if we *never* change. In turn, this creates a new, deep love for Him which empowers us to do whatever it is He is asking us to do—despite the cost. We no longer care about sex, money, our reputation, making sure we "feel good" all the time, or appeasing others to gain their approval—whether in the religious or secular community, it does not matter. Instead, we care about what Jesus cares about, which is loving God with all of our heart, body, and soul—and loving people as *we* love ourselves. And we learn to love ourselves by coming to understand Jesus' unconditional love for us; a love so deep, we can't ever lose it.

This is why Jesus wants you to come to Him as you are! He will never, ever, EVER reject you! As I've personally done this, (kept coming to Him despite my failures, rather than be afraid of Him), and the years have gone by, what I've soon found out was that the *root* of my problem of drinking wasn't even drinking in itself! Drinking too much too often as a form of a stress-reliever was just a fruit grown in my life, from another deep issue I was having, which could only be fixed by Christ—*codependency*.

The major problem with codependency is you do *not* love yourself like Jesus does. You think you *have* to have the love of another person—despite the cost of what they are doing to you. In turn, you allow such people to get away with things that they shouldn't be getting away with just to make sure they don't reject you, cause you major problems, or leave you altogether.

I drank to cover that issue up. What I *should* have been doing is finding my identity in *Christ's* unconditional love for me, establishing healthy boundaries which needed to be respected, and then enforcing those boundaries with love, respect, and an even-temper.

It wasn't only my drinking which caused me so many problems—that action was just a fruit which grew in my life *from* codependency (among many other things in my soul that had to be purged out by the Holy Spirit).

WHAT I HAD TO DO WAS DIG UP THE ROOT AND PLANT NEW SEEDS!

I take full responsibility for the poor choices I made while drinking, however, the *root* of my drinking was deeply imbedded in my severe case of codependency. If you're not familiar with what codependency is, simply put, it's a disease of the soul. It's a part of our mindset which must be renewed by Christ! An example of codependency is:

> *Allowing unacceptable behavior from others, as if it's normal, just to keep them in your life. Codependent people hesitate to stand up to them, or rock the boat, because of what they will DO to them; that is, the aggression they will have to face by saying the other person's actions is causing them severe pain.*

THIS IS NOT OKAY! THIS IS NOT HEALTHY!

I'm very thankful to God that He has opened up my eyes to this demonic cycle. In certain relationships I allowed very poor treatment to happen to me, and I just swept it under a *Christian-rug* or ignored it altogether. That, or I put some legalistic whipped-cream on it and forced myself to eat it. I had become a frustrated, drunk door-mat, with a short fuse, all because I wouldn't stand up to those who refused to make healthy changes for the benefit of our relationship—or do so in the *proper* manner. Rather than deal with unacceptable treatment in a normal way, I turned it inward. To make matters worse, I kept numbing those feelings with booze. Once I got sober, I *kept* trying to continue to ignore unacceptable behavior from others, and God wouldn't let me!

He said "No, you need to confront this."

"BUT I DON'T KNOW HOW! Why don't *you* just change them?! You can do anything!"

He replied, "I don't change people. I give them the opportunity to change, but they still have to choose it."

"Well…alright, then you are gonna have to give me the strength and grace to pull this off because I don't have it in me."

He did, and He continues to.

As I've kept praying for wisdom about how to deal with codependent situations, God has lead me to books and teachers on codependency, and *how* to defeat it. He's taught me how to *recover* from this crippling soul disease, just like He did with my problem drinking. He's given me new skills, and I'm grateful.

But this epiphany came out of the original realization that Jesus loves me no matter what—that *He* will never drive me away! It was that fact, that undying love, which set me on this new path. It wasn't my "trying harder" not to sin, it was me *continuing* to go to Christ *knowing* that I was loved *despite* my sin. We find rest in learning that Jesus will never reject us…*a rest for your soul*. So even if people reject you, *He* never will.

So today, my friends, know this: Whatever it is you are struggling with, and I mean WHATEVER, go to Jesus. I didn't say stop struggling, then go to Jesus. I'm saying GO TO JESUS AS YOU ARE! The *stopping* of whatever you are struggling with is just the beginning! He *won't* reject you for it! SO GO! GO! GO! Go to Him! STOP WAITING TO STRAIGHTEN UP FIRST! Stop waiting to have "proof" for Him that you're a "good Christian"—HE WANTS YOU IN THE RAW! This is where your new life begins!

He takes that grit, grime, and dirt, shines it up, reshapes it, and molds it into something beautiful! You'll soon realize that even as He continues to form you into His image, AND IT HURTS SO BAD, it still feels *heavenly*. The reason *why* is because you are attaining the full measure of your faith: *Becoming like Christ through pain.*

A prayer for you: *God I want to thank you today for my transparency. Sometimes I look at the stuff you tell me to write about, and I'm like, "Who is that person? How does he say such private things about himself?" It's almost an out-of-body experience as you humble me enough to tell my story in order to help those who are struggling with the same things. Keep doing it. Keep making me into who you want me to be. Right now, I lift up all who are reading this, directly to you. For those who are struggling with guilt, shame, and condemnation, help them to feel your deep, unconditional love—a love which will never reject them no matter what. Give them that extra BOOST today! Give them a brand new PASSION and ENTHUSIASM for you! Help them to come to you as they are, and simply say, "Help me." I know you will, as you did it for me! Amen.*

DAY 17

JESUS IS ABOUT TO RUIN ALL YOUR PLANS

"The enemy comes in like a flood."

SEE ISAIAH 59:19

I know the title of this devotional may seem like a downer, but let me explain. If you've decided to follow Jesus, and you are excited, well good! PRAISE GOD! HALLELUJAH! Welcome to my Family! AWESOME THINGS ARE ABOUT TO HAPPEN IN YOUR LIFE!

...But let's just keep things real about this new life. When you first believed in Christ as your Savior, you were spiritually shoved to the frontline of a supernatural battle. You are now a soldier in the Kingdom of God who fights with grace, not because of anything you are doing, but because of *who* resides *in* you. Therefore, a flood is coming your way, from hell.

When you made the choice to give your heart and life to Jesus, I mean *really* put your all into this thing—none of that little "Sunday morning peek-in stuff"—the devil sent out reinforcements from the darkest parts of hell. IT'S COMING...but don't be afraid.

These wicked reinforcements are going to begin to wash over your life, attempting to get you to revert back to your pre-Jesus state of living. So be ready, a flood is coming, a MONSOON. The Bible says, "the enemy comes in like a flood" (Isaiah 59:19). And what does a flood do? It covers everything! It's impossible to stop! It comes RUSHING IN, and tries to knock you over, destroy your home, ruin your life, and then kill you by drowning!

But that's okay...you ain't moving this time. This flood is simply the devil and his demonic crew. JUST LET THEM TRY THEIR BEST TO KNOCK YOU OVER–THEY CAN'T. Inside you are BRAND NEW ROOTS! Yes, you may *bend* as the flood comes washing through your life! You will feel like you are about to snap and break!...But...you won't. Jesus Christ *in* you is holding you firm.

YOU ARE NOW *BUILT* ON THE ROCK OF JESUS CHRIST HIMSELF! You ain't going anywhere! That flood doesn't stand a chance! Instead, it will wash away all of the things and people that shouldn't *be* in your life! LET THAT STUFF GO! LET *THEM* GO! Stop being afraid to go on without *it*, or *them*! After all, the only people who will be washed away are those who aren't built on that rock with you! Stop ruining your life trying to keep people *in* your life who don't want anything to do with you or Jesus! Let that flood wash them away. It won't be easy, but you have to let...go...

Addictions, habits, mindsets, and people, all will be washed away... but you won't. And just *how* do you *not* get washed away by the flood of the enemy? HOW DO YOU STAY PUT WHILE EVERYTHING ELSE DRIFTS FAR OFF, INTO THE DISTANCE?! Jesus tells us:

> *"Therefore everyone who HEARS THESE WORDS OF*
> *MINE AND PUTS THEM INTO PRACTICE is like*
> *a wise man who built his house on the rock. The rain came*
> *down, the streams rose, and the winds blew and beat against*
> *that house; yet it did not fall, because it had its foundation*
> *on the rock" (Matthew 7:24,25 my emphasis added).*

WE HEAR HIS WORDS AND PUT THEM INTO PRACTICE! THIS IS HOW WE BUILD UP OUR CONFIDENCE IN WHAT

WE ARE NOW DOING! THIS IS HOW WE BUILD OUR HOUSE ON THE ROCK!

And we discern His words by looking *around* those words in Scripture, *in context.* If you don't look at Scripture in context, you will be *conned* by the text. When we read, we must always consider a few things. Is He speaking to *us*, as post-Cross Christians? Or is He speaking to the legalistic Pharisees who all they knew were religious rules and self-righteousness?

As we read each section of the Bible *in context*, is He teaching us grace? Or was He setting up those who needed to be shown the *one thing* they lacked for perfection, which was faith in Him, alone? The key is to insert the words "*I* do"—as in me, not Jesus, or me *plus* Jesus. It has to be *only* Jesus, and our faith in *that*. Jesus is not interested in us living by Old Testament laws, rules, and religious regulations, but instead by His Spirit in us, coming out of us, organically (see Galatians 5:22,23).

He wasn't speaking in hyperbole when He said you *must* be perfect—you *have* to be perfect in order to be in the presence of God forever! But the *only* way you can possibly accomplish perfection is through a *spiritual* death and resurrection, by grace through faith—not by anything you can possibly do on your own, or by anything you *think* you can add *to it* to keep it, or sustain it. It's free at your taking from the beginning—and it always will be (see Romans 6, Ephesians 2:8,9). Jesus then tells us how *can* get swept away by this flood:

> *"But everyone who hears these words of mine and DOES*
> *NOT PUT THEM INTO PRACTICE is like a*
> *foolish man who built his house on sand. The rain*
> *came down, the streams rose, and the winds blew*
> *and beat against that house, and it fell with a great*
> *crash" (Matthew 7:26,27 my emphasis added).*

We are not building our new lives on sand, but on a firm foundation—A ROCK—*the* Rock, Jesus! As we allow Him to live *out* of us, little by little, what the enemy tries to use for our harm, he is actually doing us a favor by washing away harmful things and people who aren't built on this rock with us!

I KNOW IT'S PAINFUL! IT'S OKAY TO FEEL THAT PAIN! FEEL IT! FEEL IT, AND BRING IT TO JESUS! HE WILL GIVE YOU YOUR COMFORT! BUT DON'T YOU DARE TRY MAKE THINGS STAY THAT ARE CURRENTLY BEING DRAGGED AWAY BY THE FLOOD! LET IT GO!

Jesus is making new things happen for you now. He makes *all things new*! (See Revelation 21:5). And when you really dig your heels in with Jesus—and develop a close relationship—it may look like things are falling apart, but they're not. Instead, everything is coming together. A cleansing is taking place. The loose articles are being washed away. Don't go back to how you were because that's *not* you anymore. Don't hold on to stuff, places, and people. Allow this flood to reshape the landscape of your life. This too shall pass! And you will look back and be amazed at what God was doing as He ripped up the roots of your life, planted new seeds, allowed a flood to happen, and then watched proudly as you grew big and strong in Christ!

A prayer for you: *Good morning Lord! Thank you for this day! This is gonna be a great day because I know you love me, and you are with me. Right now, I lift up all who are reading this, directly to you. So many of them are doing their best to allow you to live through them, but they are experiencing very difficult times. Please, help them. GIVE THEM STRENGTH! You say in Isaiah, "Behold, I am doing a new thing; now it springs forth, do you not perceive it? I will make a way in the wilderness and rivers in the desert." WE KNOW YOU ARE DOING NEW THINGS! We trust you! But please help them to STAND FIRM IN JESUS as they walk through your way in the wilderness, and as they drink from the rivers you provide in this new desert. We KNOW that you are good! We DO trust you! So bring on the rain and the flood, let it wash away everything that you don't want in their lives! WE WILL STAND STRONG AND FIRMLY ROOTED IN CHRIST! Thank you for everything. Amen.*

DAY 18

HELL IS REAL

*"I told you that you would die in your sins; if
you do not believe that I am the one I claim to
be, you will indeed die in your sins." ~Jesus*

JOHN 8:24

Nobody likes to talk about hell. It's not very popular to tell someone, "Hey, you know that sin you have in your life? If you don't
ask Christ into your heart to forgive you for that sin, once and for all,
you will go to hell." That's not cool—but it *is* loving—*if* you can pull it
off in the proper way.

If you don't, you probably won't be getting an invite to the next BBQ.
However, if we look to Jesus, He warned us more about hell than He
talked *positively* about heaven. He spoke about hell all the time because
He doesn't want *any* of us to go there.

I believe the main problem with telling others about hell is the
approach most Christians have, myself included. There is a fine line
here. One of Jesus' closest disciples, Peter, advises us to tell others about
the hope we have in Christ, but to do so with *gentleness* and *respect* (see
1 Peter 3:15). I've never won anyone over to believing in Jesus by being

rude to them about the gospel. We don't make Jesus look good to unbelievers (which He *is* good) by acting snarky, self-righteous, *or* by trying to
make them petrified of hell.

Sure, I think Jesus wants us to make it known that there *is* a place
He has *nothing* to do with—a place specifically reserved for those who
reject His free forgiveness—but we are to make that place known about,
with *grace*.

Let's do some 101 stuff here about hell, and then let's try to see if we
can get people to not so much be afraid of hell—although, heck yes we
should be, it's a bad place—but let's try to get people to see the easy way
out of *going* to hell: Jesus' death on the Cross and our belief in that event
as true for our own personal sin—not others' sins—but our own. We
have to believe *we* need it (keep the focus on ourselves), and then receive
it freely by grace through faith *in* that event (see 1 John 1:8, Romans
3:23-24, Ephesians 2:8,9). The worst part about hell is that it does not
end, but the best part about heaven is the same. So let's refocus!

I like to make lists when I study God's Word, as well as in other areas
of my life. An organized break-down makes things more memorable.
Itemizations of steps to take, goals to strive for, things I want to learn
more about (or expound on), *lists* have always helped me *further* myself.
So here's a list of some of the facts about hell, what we can do to help others not go there, and why it even exists. Let's start with that last subject:

1. **Why is there a hell?** Jesus said that hell is a place of fire, and
   that it was created for the devil and his demons (see Matthew
   25:41). Some people claim we are currently *in* hell, but we're
   not. There are *three* different realms. Heaven, hell, and this
   physical universe. God is a part of *two* of these realms (heaven
   and earth), and so is Satan and his demons (hell and earth). As
   humans, currently, you and I are a part of just *one*—the physical universe (earth). But one day we will die physically, and
   spiritually, we *will* go on to be in heaven *or* hell. Heaven is sin-
   free, a place where God's love is completely undiluted. That's

why it's so wonderful. Hell is *only* sin and love is not allowed. It is a place of torment where *evil* is completely undiluted. In hell, God's presence is void, *that's* why it's so terrible—because He is not there. This physical universe (the planet you are on) has a mixture of the option of both good *and* evil—in order to have free will. Our free wills are finalized in heaven *or* hell. You will become *one* with either place.

2. **God is here with us, on earth. In hell, He is not there.** I just touched on this, but I want to go a little further. In heaven, God's presence is magnified completely. In heaven, His will is done *completely*. He is so prevalent there that He *is* heaven. When we get there, we will actually get our light *from* Him, just like we currently get our light from the sun. This is why the Bible says, "The city does not need the sun or the moon to shine on it, for the glory of God gives it light, and the Lamb is its lamp" (Revelation 21:23).

3. **"Nobody will be in heaven who doesn't want to be there."** This was something Grandma used to always say to me. The fact of the matter is that it is *our* choice whether we go to heaven or not. God doesn't decide, *we* do. Our loving Creator doesn't *send* people to hell, we go there by rejecting the gospel. The Bible says, "If you declare with your mouth, 'Jesus is Lord,' and believe in your heart that God raised him from the dead, you will be saved" (Romans 10:9). As you can see, God has made it simple to go to heaven...BELIEVE IN JESUS AS YOUR LORD. The religious Christians have made it so much more difficult than simply *believing* He *has* forgiven us (past tense). Should we repent of sinful behavior and attitudes? Should we get baptized in water? Abso-freakin-lutely. BUT, repentance of incorrect actions and attitudes, nor water baptism, will get you to heaven. These are the carts *behind* the horse. These are the things you do to build *up* your relationship with God—*after* being saved for free—in order to *show* Him how much you love

Him. These are the things which allow you to *have* the abundant life Jesus spoke about! (See John 10:10).

4. **A "terrible person" who didn't get baptized or prove to God through his actions (behavior repentance), is currently in heaven.** That person is the thief on the cross. When Jesus was hanging on His cross, a man next to Him was being executed on his own cross. This man told Jesus he believed him, and Jesus said, "On this day, you will be with me in paradise" (Luke 23:43). Jesus didn't get down off His Cross, run to the closest well, get a bucket of water, and then come *back* and toss it up on him— neither did anyone else. And, this man didn't even have a *chance* to turn his life around. Yes, the earthly consequences of his sin was killing him, but he *still* believed in Jesus. This happens to Christians every day. So it is our *belief* which saves us—our *heart condition* toward Christ! Now THAT'S good news!

5. **As a Christian, you must stop being afraid of hell.** "STOP BEING AFRAID?! Matt, you can't say that! People are going to hell every day!" I know, but *we* aren't. I'm not saying don't be afraid of hell if you don't believe in Jesus as your Savior, that's a very healthy fear. I'm saying, once you *do* believe in Jesus, stop being afraid of hell. Sure, be afraid of what your unrenewed *thinking* will do to your life, but stop being afraid of eternal punishment. You ain't going there once you believe Jesus has forgiven you—I repeat—once! As in, THE VERY FIRST TIME! (See Hebrews 10:10, Romans 6:10). The very moment you believed He forgave you, He actually *did*. And He forgave *all* your sin— past, present, and dare I say, *future*. YES! This is the gospel! Keep in mind, when Jesus died, *all* of your sins were in the future. He is not bound by time. I know this immeasurable forgiveness is impossible to grasp in our finite minds, but it's true! So stop being afraid! You've been adopted into the family of God, and as long as Jesus lives you will *stay* saved from hell! (See Ephesians 1:5, Hebrews 7:25).

Of course, I could continue on with this list, but I believe this will help you understand hell better. Remember, God doesn't *want* you to go there! That's why He sent Jesus! He's made it so easy for us to be *sure* we don't end up there after we die: BELIEVE IN JESUS AS YOUR SAVIOR. The legalistic people will say, "Even the demons believe and shudder" (James 2:19). That's true, but they are already damned, we aren't. And *they* aren't asking for forgiveness, *we are.*

So repeat this prayer with me, believe it in your heart as true, and you will not go to hell:

Jesus, I am a sinner. I have sin in my life that I need you to take care of for me. I do not have the ability to remove the sin punishment of hell FOR my sin, only you do. The Bible says that God is patient with us because He doesn't want any of us to parish, and I'm grateful for that. Thank you for your patience with me! I don't want to go to hell. I want to go to heaven and be with you forever. Please, forgive me of all my sin. Past, present, and future. Make your home in my heart. I want to live my life for you. Please live through me and show me how to do this each day. Please begin to mold my life into what YOU want it to be. Always remind me that you are here. Remind me that you love me, and remind me not to be afraid. Thank you for saving me. Now help me to do your will day by day, and help me to help others find you too so that they can enjoy their life on earth, and in heaven with us! Thank you! Amen.

DAY 19

WHAT TO DO WHEN YOU FEEL FAR FROM GOD

*"But now in Christ Jesus you who formerly were far
off have been brought near by the blood of Christ. For
he himself is our peace, who made both groups into one
and broke down the barrier of the dividing wall..."*

EPHESIANS 2:13, 14

D o you ever feel like a Christian who is far from God? Man, I sure
did. It was a constant feeling of dread:

"Am I doing this right? I don't think I am."

*"Oh no, I messed up. God is gonna be so mad. I better make up for this
tomorrow so He doesn't punish me."*

*"Dang it. I lost my temper, again. WHY CAN'T I JUST BE A
GOOD CHRISTIAN?!"*

*"The heck with it. I keep messing up, God is already mad at me, I'm
just gonna drink. What more harm could I possibly do?"*

"If I'm really saved, why do these bad things keep happening to me? That's it, I'm making SURE God treats me right. I'm never missing another church service, I'm never gonna cuss again, and I'm going to read my Bible at least 30 minutes a day, THEN God will answer my prayers."

Or even, *"WHY DO I FEEL LIKE THIS?! AM I EVEN A CHRISTIAN?! I CAN'T GET THIS RIGHT!"*

...I could easily continue writing such statements as these for an hour, but I won't because I don't think this way any more. All of those thoughts do nothing except create distance between me and my Creator, *in my mind*—and I've already *un-learned* them. How?...Oh you're gonna love this:

By getting to know Jesus, personally, daily! Yep! This is the secret to removing incorrect thinking as a Christian. GET TO KNOW JESUS, over *time*.

"But Matt, I thought I *did* know Him. I asked Him into my heart, I told Him I believe, so why do I keep feeling like I'm so far away?"

Friend, over the course of my mind-renewal with Christ, I've learned that you can't just go off of your feelings, you have to learn to go off of His truth as well; and *that* takes time. To enjoy *any* relationship, it takes time because you are getting to know the other person—same with God. The process of getting to know Him, and actually becoming *like* Him, will not end on this side of heaven (See Philippians 1:6). So be easy on *you*.

Sure, Christ *in* you has now *given* you new desires to make different choices in thought, word, and deed—because *when* you're saved, God writes new desires on your heart (see Hebrews 8:10)—but you're just a baby in your spirit; freshly born (see John 3:7). At first, babies need to be coddled and hand-fed. But after they grow, they need to learn to stand, then walk, then run! We should always be moving forward *growing* in our mind renewal, while also understanding it is *not* our state of mind which saved us—only our faith Jesus did that.

Never confuse your salvation with the process of allowing Jesus to renew your thinking! No matter *how* you feel! Your feelings didn't save you, Jesus did!

Accepting Jesus as the Savior of your sin gives you a *rebirth*, spiritually. Once you believed, that moment, it happened! More than likely you didn't feel *anything* happen (although you could have), but supernaturally an event occurred. The *spirit* part of you was made perfectly brand new! By faith, your spirit was crucified *with* Christ, and now He lives *in* you, actually *infused* with *your* spirit forever! (see Romans 6, Galatians 2:20).

"*Gasp*! BLASPHEMY! Matt, we aren't perfect! We are dirty, rotten sinners!" That's what the religious Christians will say. But I beg to differ. We *were* imperfect, we *were* dirty rotten sinners—but not now. At our core, our spiritual DNA says, "Child of God"—we're the *exact* same as Christ!

Jesus told Nicodemus in the most famous Bible passage of all time, found in John 3, the very thing that I'm telling you: You MUST become perfect, spiritually. No if, ands, or buts. *How?* Rebirth, spiritually—become *exactly* like Christ!

Please allow me to repeat this for emphasis because *I too* had to have my mind renewed: ONCE YOU PLACE YOUR FAITH IN JESUS YOU ARE PERFECT—SPIRITUALLY. God the Father now sees you in the same light as Jesus because of your faith in the Cross. A new agreement happened between the Father and Son, and *we* are the beneficiaries! (See Hebrews 8:13). We did NOTHING to create this agreement, we can't enforce it, or sustain it—we simply reap the benefits. The innocent, perfect, Godly blood, which was shed for you—and *because* of your acceptance of it for your sins—*that* has made you *exactly* like Jesus in your spirit, the eternal part of you! You've been supernaturally baptized *into* Christ! (See Romans 6).

THAT'S CALL TO CELEBRATE!

The gospel means "good news" for a reason! You've become exactly like Christ, spiritually. So your identity is now in Jesus and not in yourself any longer. Paul, a former bounty-hunter of Christians said it best:

"I have been crucified with Christ and I no longer live, but Christ lives in me. The life I now live in the body, I live by faith in the Son of God, who loved me and gave himself for me" (Galatians 2:20).

Spiritually, you *are* Christ. Stop doubting that. Say it with me, and believe it as true:

"Spiritually, I am Christ."

Again.

"Spiritually, I AM CHRIST."

AGAIN!

"SPIRITUALLY I AM CHRIST!"

YES!!! Your feelings will catch up to this truth later! But keep saying it!

Believe this! PLEASE! Why? Because once you do, you'll not be so hard on yourself any longer. You will STOP doubting. You will stop feeling far from God, because you're not! GOD IS *IN* YOU, COMPLETELY! And even YOU can't make Him go away because this agreement between the Father and Son will never end! (See 2 Timothy 2:13, Hebrews 7:25).

Once you get this fact down pat—embedded in your soul—the actual *truth* about your identity, everything changes. You stop being so mean to yourself, you stop calling yourself a sinner, *and* you stop believing the lies of others. Only now, you deal with yourself *and* others, in a loving, confident way, like Jesus does.

Jesus is *in* you. The Holy Spirit, the *spirit-version* of your Creator resides in your sprit, *with* you. You're not far from God no matter *how* you feel, because you and Him are one.

The problem is you still have this pesky little thing called *flesh*. God didn't change this part of you when you got saved. It's still the same as it's always been. *You* have to begin to reign in the actions of your flesh by the power of your *spirit*, who is Jesus, by allowing Him to renew your mind day by day.

Plainly stated, your flesh likes what it sees, and wants it now. It has no moral compass. It is simply a tool for your soul to *use*. Your flesh previously led your life, but now Jesus does. Your flesh is necessary and God-given because it is what allows you to live out this life on planet earth with free will.

SO BE EASY ON YOUR FLESH! One day it will be gone, and when Jesus comes back you'll get a *new* body—a perfect one (see 1 Corinthians 15:52). Your flesh does *not* define you, your spirit does! Your spirit now *leads* your flesh! Not the other way around!

Here's where this comes full circle: By getting to know *Jesus*, day by day, a *relationship* begins to form with Him. Therefore, changing how you *feel*.

How do you build up this relationship? Through prayer, worship (which is *anything* about your life you offer up to Him), and His Word. By simply waking up each day, saying, "I'm available. Use me. Live *through* me." Make no mistake, He will!

A prayer for you: *Wow, good morning Heavenly Father, it's good to be alive! You chose US to wake up today, to have life, and to have it abundantly. Thank you! Right now, I lift up all who are reading this, directly to you. Many of them are way too hard on themselves, and live by how they feel. Please, help them. Help them to realize that it is Jesus who resides in them spiritually! Help them to realize that their true* *identity is found IN Christ! Once they understand this truth, their words and actions will THEN begin to reflect this fact, little by little, as it did me. Thank you Jesus for making us a part of your Family! We love you! Amen.*

DAY 20

JOEL OSTEEN HELPED SAVE MY LIFE

*"If anyone acknowledges that Jesus is the Son
of God, God lives in them and they in God."*

1 JOHN 4:15

My ministry used to be very aggressive towards religious Christians. Over the years, I've grown in love for them—but, the hurt that self-righteous Christians caused me left a huge open wound in my soul. When I say "religious Christians," I'm not trying to disrespect anyone, but instead, pull the curtain back and expose a cancer in the Christian community. I'm talking about Christians, yes, they could even be believers (although, I'm guessing some are not), but these Christian have certain characteristics that keep the lost, lost, and new believers stuck in fear and condemnation.

Religious Christians have a heart of extreme coldness and judgment, not just towards non-believers, but other Christians as well. "*Gasp*! Did you see what she wore today?" Or, "How *dare* they talk about that in the pulpit!" And even, "They skipped church, again? I bet they are going to hell now. I'd never miss a service! Backslider!"

They think it is their calling in life to pick apart the lives of others in such a way that there is no breathing room, or room for growth in Christ's ways. These are the people who say, "You are getting what you deserve!" when all you want is some mercy. They have no grace, no unconditional love, no true forgiveness, and no hope for the lost; just judgment and a set of rules for everyone to abide by.

Religious Christians want to give lessons to everyone on how *not* to sin. This is maybe their favorite thing to do. Oh, and if you *do* sin, you've insulted *them*. "Don't you dare curse in front of me!" "You're gay? You better stop that immediately, or you are going to hell!" "You didn't get baptized? Well then you're not really a Christian!" They act as if they *have* a heaven or hell to throw you into. And when *you* sin, you've insulted the "godliness" in them.

Which, sure, as Christians we have a buzzer that goes off in our hearts that notices sin—and the Holy Spirit is pressing that button. Now, the *real* us doesn't *want* to sin because Christ died to remove the punishment *for* our sin, and He lives in us. That event at the Cross hurt Jesus greatly, so we *should* take sin seriously, but not focus on it. Instead, we should focus on who is now *in* our spirits—Jesus Christ Himself!

For the religious Christians, their ratio of sin-inspection-to-grace is 90/10. It's all out of whack, and this is a repellent to a new believer. It doesn't convict, but condemns. They are trying to do the work of the Holy Spirit and they can't—none of us can. When this happens, all this does is create tremendous fear and frustration in a weak, or new Christian.

But their judgmental attitude is not just for new believers—it's for current Christians as well! And when they have that same attitude towards the mature Christians it creates severe conflict. For the religious Christians, NOTHING IS DONE OUT OF LOVE, it's all conditional, based on *you* "shaping up," like them. This is why we must remember what Paul said when he wrote to Timothy: "He has saved us and called us to a holy life—*not because of anything we have done* but because of his own purpose and grace" (2 Timothy 1:9, my emphasis added). Yes, we are holy—we restfully strive to do what God approves of—but only because of *His* purpose and grace! WE'VE NOT EARNED ANYTHING…this is all free, because of what Jesus *has* done.

Religious Christians also enjoy showing off their "level" of repentance, church attendance, and church work. Listen, I'm all for these things. Do them, please. These are a huge parts of my life. REPENT OF INCORRECT BEHAVIORS AND MINDSETS! GO TO CHURCH! DO STUFF FOR JESUS! These are *good* things! But we must ask ourselves a question when doing anything for God: *"Why am I really doing this?"* The answer should always be, *"Because I love God."* If there is a hint of anything else, water it down. Keep things in perspective. Remember, *where* you are at in your faith is not because of YOU. It's *God* who has worked *in* you (See Philippians 2:13). Never let anything you do or don't do take precedent to showing Christ your appreciation of what He's done for you by allowing Him to live *through* you.

Further, religious Christians attack other churches and preachers who aren't like them. Oh my goodness this is such a bad thing. Sometimes they even call others "non-Christians," "false teachers," or "anti-Christs." This might be one of the most dangerous things to do as a Christian— which is placing yourself on God's level by judging the hearts of others. We don't have this ability, *either*.

This act of religious Christians actually caused me to get asked to leave my former church. How? Here's how: As a Christian alcoholic who was also addicted to porn, money, video games, and was living a life completely abusing the grace of God, I needed some *gospel baby food*—badly. The full on, hard core teaching of having someone tell me how horrible of a person I was—a "steak dinner" teaching—I could not eat. I had not grown any Christian teeth. It was impossible to listen to a mean preacher (back then, that's what I'd call them). I needed some serious grace in my teaching! I already knew I sucked at life! I didn't need some dude with a tight suit and comb-over beating that into my head! *"YOU CAN KEEP THAT CRAP TO YOURSELF!"* was how I thought.

My problem was pride. I took absolutely *everything* personal when it came to Christianity and how *I* needed to change my life. Then one

Saturday morning, I woke up hungover, *again*, and I felt like I needed to read a Christian book (in hindsight, this was the Holy Spirit nudging me). The problem was, I didn't have one. So I got off the couch, after binge-eating Chinese food (that's the best hangover remedy—SALTY FOOD—then you get fat and swollen; what an awful, demonic cycle); I dragged myself to Wal-Mart and picked up a book called *Everyday a Friday* by Joel Osteen.

This book was *just* what I needed. Oh my goodness, if you only knew. This single book was the spark that God used to light the fuse in me which set off *who* I am today! You would *not* know who I am, or ever heard of this ministry, had I not been obedient to the Holy Spirit that Saturday morning!

Heck, even I wouldn't fully know who I am in Christ and the potential on the inside of me if I didn't get my butt up that day and began to read Joel's book. Joel made God look good again. He made me *want* to change—everything. He made me *want* to get to know Jesus better. Why? Because he never said how bad of a person I was, but instead, how good! And why was I good?…Simple, because of my faith in Jesus. He made it *so easy* to understand. And that's what the gospel is, easy to understand, *good news*.

Joel's simple, encouraging teaching, nursed me back to life—*saved* my life, actually. His teaching made me want to go back to church! It made me want to forgive absolutely everyone! It made me want to begin seeing the *good* in life, and in myself, not the bad! His teaching made me want to begin using my gift of writing *for* God, rather than against Him! It made me want to have a goal of being an author! It made me want to pray for those who've harmed me, and actually bless them! Oh so many wonderful things his style of teaching stirred up in me!

His simple, baby-food-style-teaching, made me want to change my *entire* life—absolutely everything! It also calmed me. That roaring, aggressive, frustrated person on the inside of my soul, *he* was learning a new way of living from this smiling preacher with corny jokes. Joel was helping me to renew my mind with *who* God really was, which is a loving, *good* Father.

In the process of this life change I even started to go back to church! Here's the problem: I voiced how much Joel had done for me one day to my former pastors, and they immediately began to rip him apart. This upset me greatly because it was Joel's teachings, not theirs, that made me want to change my entire life for God. After they knew I was learning from Joel, they began to attack him in their sermons. They started to tell the congregation about how "non-gospel" he was. This hurt me, and it was starting to cause a rift in my soul because Joel had helped me get out of a deep, dark pit—these two preachers did not—they only made things worse. Instead of encouraging me, they barked things at me like, "You ain't living right!" Or, "Any man of God would get his house in order!"

Eventually one of them asked me out for coffee, and while he was sitting across from me at the table, he said, "Why don't you get plugged in at another church?" Isn't that crazy? How the devil works even in the inner-circles of church? Here I was, someone on the brink of suicide, everything around me is falling apart, and I start to enjoy Joel's teachings and the local pastor of my church tells me to leave? Yeah. That happened.

The devil wanted me to hate that man, and the other preacher too, and I almost fell for it! But then God taught me what was really going on. Religion. Not relationship, but religion. This preacher was blind to what the lost really need, which is unconditional love and grace.

The fact of the matter is that I love Joel, but I also love Billy Graham, and I love David Jeremiah, and Joyce Meyer, and John Piper, and Phillip Yancey, and Tim Keller, and Todd White, and Charles Stanley, and Andrew Farley! I LOVE *ALL* OF THESE TEACHERS! God has lead me to each one *just* when I needed them! They all believe in Jesus, they just have a different style than one another! WHICH IS A GOOD THING! It's the religious Christians who pick apart other teachers, preachers, and people who are simply trying to be who God called them to be!

God gave *each* of us a unique style, voice, and testimonial for a reason—to REACH others for Christ in different ways! Just because Joel is so positive doesn't mean he's not preaching the gospel! HE IS! There is nothing *not* positive about the good news of the gospel! The religious Christians attack him all the time, and I'm tired of it! Sure, we are gonna be wrong sometimes, so what. That's why we need Jesus. As fellow believers, we are supposed to cover up those wrongs with grace and love, not have a sermon on how wrong they are, or write a hate-filled article on them comparing their preaching to atheism—that is such crap! THE LOST ARE WATCHING! STOP IT!

Peter says, "Above all, love each other deeply, because love covers over a multitude of sins" (1 Peter 4:8). My friends, we *have* to love each other deeply, we have to. We have to remember who *is* perfect. It's not us because we still have a thing called *flesh*. It's Christ *in* us. Joel is not the anti-Christ, and he's not taken anything away from the gospel. He just teaches differently, just like we all do. Here's the biblical way of how you *know* if someone is preaching the gospel, or not: "If anyone acknowledges that Jesus is the Son of God, God lives in them and they in God" (1 John 4:15).

Joel acknowledges that Jesus is the Son of God, and he does this all the time. I began to read a book once, where the man started off the introduction by saying the opposite—that there *is* another way besides Jesus—I immediately tore it up and threw it away. The *true* Christian teachers are the ones who say, "Yes, place your faith in Jesus to be saved," it's just, we all have a different flavor of teaching this message. We must celebrate that! Imagine if we all had the same way, look, voice, and expression of Christ's Good News! That'd be boring! So be glad that the different teachers are doing what they are doing, and *how* they are doing it! If you don't like it, start your *own* teaching and then let's talk about *your* style.

Because of Joel, I am a life that was changed. If you are too religious to understand that, then I'd double-check my faith in Christ if I were you. I'm not saying that's *you*, but there *are* people out there who believe if you've learned from Joel, you're not saved. Hogwash.

I began reading, watching, and listening to Joel in 2011, and my life started to change dramatically. With gentleness, respect, and encouragement, he helped *renew* my mind. For the first couple years, I read all his books, watched him on TV each week, and soaked up everything he had to say. At that time, my life was absolutely crazy and I thought my heart was rotten. I couldn't believe how nice this guy was as a preacher, I had never seen that before. I was used to feeling like I just got beat up after a sermon, not healed up! He was so soft, confident, and inspirational…I needed that desperately. When I began to learn from Joel, I was like a parched flower in the middle of the desert and a tsunami of God's goodness had just washed over me…it was amazing. If I ever met Joel face to face, I'd say, "Thank you. You've helped me greatly." His easy-to-understand, truthful, digestible gospel, helped me to grow.

After a few years, I no longer listened to Joel on a regular basis. I had a firm foundation of God's goodness, and it was time to move on to deeper teachings. But make no mistake, he was the one who got my roots planted in the soil of how *good* God really is, and I'm forever grateful.

He inspired me to start my own ministry. Sure, my style of teaching is more aggressive in getting people to take a deep look within themselves as to how to make positive changes—to actually begin to live *out* Christ—but, I'm not Joel Osteen, I'm Matt McMillen. A person who is an absolute failure without Jesus, yet, infinitely successful with Him. But I still like to think that I have a little bit of Joel in my writings, each time I say the word, "friend." He's who I got that from. It always made me feel good, so now, I do it as well. Sometimes I'll still flip him on Sirius XM, once or twice a week, just to hear his country accent and kind voice—but I've already got his friendly foundation of the gospel built deep into my soul.

I've learned just how important I am to God, because of Joel.

So if you are reading this, and you dislike Joel, you may as well dislike me because he's helped me become the man I am today. Be easy on Joel. Pray for him. *Think* of him with love (that's one thing he taught me). But really, be easy on *all* teachers of Christ's wonderful news! And please, begin to remove any religious Christian judgments, if you've got some, and just *love* them.

That's what we are all called to do.

A prayer for you: *Heavenly Father, I want to thank you for leading me to Joel's teachings. And not just his, but all of the teachers you've used to get me to the point I'm at today. I pray that I can do the same for those who are reading this, those who want to make an impact on this planet for you. Strengthen them with your love and confidence! They can do it! If I can do it, through Christ, so can they. Amen.*

DAY 21

RELIGION BLINDS YOU. RELATIONSHIP HEALS YOU.

"They still did not believe that he had been blind and had received his sight until they sent for the man's parents."

JOHN 9:18

There is a story found in John 9, where Jesus gives sight to a man who had been blind since birth. I wrote a devotional about this event in February 2016, which has been viewed by tens of thousands of people on my Facebook page. But today's devotional *isn't* about that healing, in itself, but what happened with the religious people *afterwards.* You're gonna love this!

To set this up, I need to summarize the event of the healing. Jesus and His crew were strolling along and saw a man who was blind from birth. Jesus heals him—but not how you would think! He made the man do something which *seems* demeaning. You'll have to read the story in John 9 to see what I'm referring to, however, HE GOT HIS SIGHT! A MIRACLE! He had never seen a thing in his life, and then Jesus showed up and gave Him a brand new vision—literally! That's what He does! HE GIVES US OUR SIGHT—not just our physical sight, but also, our *spiritual* sight.

Back then, there was a group of people called *the Pharisees*. They were just like today's religious Christians—no different. They picked apart everything that was good, they judged everyone harshly (believers and non-believers), and they were *extremely* self-righteous. They compared "how long" they've been religious to others, as well as what they "did" and "didn't do," in order to be acceptable to God. They were nasty, and couldn't *stand* Jesus.

Once the Pharisees heard that this man had been healed by Jesus, they called him in for a meeting. They asked him, "What do you have to say about him (Jesus)?" (see John 9:17).

This guy had no clue who Jesus was, just yet. So he replies, "He is a prophet." The religious people still didn't believe that Jesus healed this man, even *after* he sat in front of their faces! Determined to get to the bottom of this, they called in his parents.

"Is this your son? Is this the one you say was born blind? How is it that now he can see?" (John 9:19). They were scared of the Pharisees, so they said, "Yes, that's our son. He was definitely born blind, but he's old enough to speak for himself, talk to him about this" (see John 9:20-23).

THEY *STILL* DIDN'T BELIEVE THAT JESUS JUST HEALED THIS MAN! EVEN AFTER HE *AND* HIS PARENTS TOLD THEM THE TRUTH! Why? Because of their religious pride! They were *more* blind than that man was, when he was feeling around in the dark!

How many people do you know like this? Something absolutely wonderful happens in the life of a lost soul, and the religious Christians pick it all apart! They totally snuff out the new sight of a baby Christian, *or* a Christian who has *finally* decided to allow Jesus to live *through* them! And even *after* they get "proof" of the change, they *still* judge others crudely!

THIS IS RAMPANT IN OUR CHURCHES AND IT MUST STOP!

...So, the Pharisees called the man in *again*, hoping he would change his story. Trying to force him into discrediting what Jesus had done, they said, "Give glory to God. We know this man is a sinner" (John 9:24).

The newly-sighted fellow replies, this is so good, "Whether he is a sinner or not, I don't know. One thing I do know, I was blind but now I see!" (John 9:25). HOW AWESOME IS THAT ANSWER?! C'MON SOMEBODY! "My proof of Christ is my changed life! I CAN SEE!" That's what he said!

They didn't like that answer. "What did he do to you? How did he open your eyes?" (John 9:26). Oh my goodness, these people were *more* blind than a baby bat! I've dealt with this a lot in my ministry, but have you ever told your testimonial to a legalistic Christian, and they didn't believe it? Instead, they judged *you* and your turn-around? Called you a phony?

THIS IS *NOT* A NEW THING! This started with the blind man over 2,000 years ago, so if this happens to you, you should feel honored!

Tired of their questions, the man says, "I already told you and you did not listen. Why do you want to hear it again? Do you want to become his disciples too?" (John 9:27) HA! How great was that?! This is golden! He says, "Do you want to become his disciples too?" In essence, saying, "Do you want your blindness to go away, too?" After he asked them if they wanted to follow Jesus, here's how the story ends:

Then they hurled insults at him and said, "You are this fellow's disciple! We are disciples of Moses! We know that God spoke to Moses, but as for this fellow, we don't even know where he comes from."

The man answered, "Now that is remarkable! You don't know where he comes from, yet he opened my eyes. We know that God does not listen to sinners. He listens to the godly person who does his will (my note: this man was still going off of Old Testament Law, not Jesus' New Covenant of grace—He hadn't yet gone to the Cross). Nobody has ever heard of opening the eyes of a man born blind. If this man were not from God, he could do nothing."

To this they replied, "You were steeped in sin at birth; how dare you lecture us!" And they threw him out (John 9:28-34).

Do you see that? Jesus had just made this man's life better, and rather than celebrate that, they insulted him, belittled him, and then they kicked him out. They simply did *not* like the experience he had with Jesus. Why? Because it wasn't religious enough. It wasn't "just like" them. It didn't match up with their style, or earn their approval.

What's most sad is that this still happens *today*. In our churches, all across America and throughout the world—people are rejected. We gotta change that. The spiritual blindness these religious people had, really, just kept *them* from enjoying a wonderful miracle—the *sight* of a new believer in Christ. However, what I like best about this story is that once Jesus found out they treated him poorly and kicked him out, He hunted the formerly blind man down, and spoke to him. Here's what happened:

Jesus heard that they had thrown him out, and when he found him, he said, "Do you believe in the Son of Man?"

"Who is he, sir?" the man asked. "Tell me so that I may believe in him."

Jesus said, "You have now seen him; in fact, he is the one speaking with you."

Then the man said, "Lord, I believe," and he worshiped him. (John 9:35-38).

He believed, and he worshiped Him. That's it. That's *my* life. Friend, Jesus will never throw you out, ever. You are a part of His family for eternity *once* you place your faith in Him. He will remove your spiritual blindness, today, if you want Him to—but you gotta want it. Just ask Him to and He will! It's a good life when you begin to see so clearly!

A prayer for you: *God, today I want to thank you for opening up my eyes. I was blind as can be, and then Jesus brought a brand new vision into my life. THANK YOU! Right now, I lift up all who are reading this, directly to you. For those who have been so beat down by graceless Christians, and their enthusiasm snatched away, open up their eyes* *again! Help them to refocus on Jesus! For me, once I began to do this, you gave me the confidence and spiritual tools needed to combat such harsh criticism, and in the right way. Although sometimes I fail—when I'm not obedient to the Holy Spirit—I'm 1,000 times better than I used to be when it comes to HOW to deal with those who find their identity judging others. Give these dear readers a brand new confidence IN Christ! Amen.*

DAY 22

Do You Keep Secrets?

"And they have defeated him (Satan) by the blood of the Lamb and by their testimony..."

REVELATION 12:11

I used to be a very private person. I could keep secrets with the best of them, and not just secrets about others, but about myself. Deep, dark, nasty secrets. That would soon change.

When I decided to finally allow Christ to live through me, I mean *really* give Him full access to every part of my soul, I no longer had the ability to be secretive. It just was not in me. Jesus and secrets don't mix, they are like oil and water. Had I known this, and what God was about to do through me being extremely candid about my past, Old Matt might have fought New Matt a lot harder than he did, because he was a very determined chap!

If you aren't familiar with my writings, in my first book, <u>*True Purpose In Jesus Christ*</u>, I dedicated nearly an entire chapter talking about myself in the third person, about "Old Matt." Not in an arrogant way, but in a way that makes me seem like I'm fighting myself; the version of me who hadn't yet allowed Jesus to begin renewing his mind. My spirit was saved, but my soul was still full of pride and lots of secrets.

That dude did whatever the heck he wanted to, "So shut up!" Old Matt would have said that, especially if you called him out on how he was living. I was not happy with him, but he ran my life.

Honestly, Old Matt still tries to peak his head out now and again, but he's way too weak, that part of my soul has *no* power. New Matt, my *renewed* soul—by the grace and strength of Christ *in* my spirit—has put his boot up Old Matt's rear. The Bible says that "I am a new creation in Christ! The OLD has gone and the NEW has come!" (See 2 Corinthians 5:17, my emphasis added). And that's the truth! I AM A NEW MAN. PERIOD. You can't *un*-convince me of this!

Sure, this has been a process, and it always will be as long as I'm alive in this body, but that's okay. We are to enjoy the *journey* of letting Jesus reshape our inner-man—actually *enjoy* it! This process of reining in the *flesh* part of you, through your spiritual *new* self, which re-forms your *soul*, takes time. So have a goal of starving the *old* you, but give *new you* some slack in the process. As long as you stay focused on Christ *in* you, coming *out* of you, it will happen! At first, the new you starts out as a little seed, but then you will begin to grow into someone very big and strong in Christ!

The fact of the matter is once you believe in Christ, you are instantaneously brand new on the inside! (See Romans 6). Your spirit is crucified with Him, and He then comes to live in your body *with* you (see Galatians 2:20). Jesus calls this one-time event "born again" (see John 3:3). Just like physically we were born *once*, spiritually, we have a new birth as well. This birth happens the very *moment* we believe that Jesus is the Son of God and that He has forgiven us of our sins! That's it! Anything less is not enough, and anything more is trying to add *to* it. Your new birth is a free gift from God, by grace, through faith in Jesus (see Ephesians 2:8,9).

The legalistic Christians want to make it harder than that—this is *not* good enough for them. They say that's *way* too easy for us. Why are they like this? Because they want to hold our *complete* forgiveness hostage… so "we don't sin." Well that's not fair because we *will* sin, because we still have flesh—and so do they. They are lying if they say that they don't, therefore, becoming hypocrites of their own standard, by not telling the truth. The problem is, they are simply too focused on sin, rather than on Christ. They've got it backwards.

Friend, listen, if you are balking on fully giving your all to Jesus because you still sin, don't do that. You won't last long that way, and that's not how living out the gospel works. If you keep straining not to sin, you'll either give up quickly, or worse, become extremely self-righteous. Your goal should now be to simply allow Christ to live through you. He will never lead you into sin. But know this, you aren't the one who will keep yourself from sinning anyway, it's Christ *inside* you (see Philippians 4:13). It's His grace which now empowers you to constantly fight sin, but without fighting at all—this is the sweet spot! Sounds strange, but you'll find it! (See Titus 2:11-12).

The author of Hebrews said it best, "Let us therefore strive to enter that rest" (see Hebrews 4:11). Do you see that? *Strive* to *rest*?…How do you strive to rest?…Yeppers. Oxymoron. It's not you, it's Jesus *in* you.

When the religious Christians judge you so harshly, that's just their way of comparing what they do and don't do, to you. Ignore that if they aren't doing it in a loving way. If you don't, you will stay shackled to their religious bondage—but YOU hold the key—not them. Stay focused on Jesus. He's the one who knows the truth about you, as well as the direction your soul is growing. Show them love, show them respect, pray for them, and bless them—but understand the truth about yourself! YOU ARE SPIRITUALLY PERFECT!

What you do and don't do will change organically as you allow Christ to come out of you. This includes some of the stuff the graceless Christians are magnifying. And these things begin to change because you *love* Jesus! Everything we do and don't do, now, is because we love Him! It's not to earn anything or to make sure we don't lose anything, but because we are so appreciative! LOVE IS A VERB! IT'S SOMETHING WE DO! We love Jesus, so we change!

Now, let me tell you, killing off the old version of yourself is a major process. They ain't going away easy! Remember: You've fed and clothed him, or her, for this long, and they like their life! But so what! They don't run the show any longer, Christ *in you* does!

THEY ARE DONE! THEY ARE ABOUT TO BE PUSHED OUT OF THEIR LAZY-BOY, SLAPPED IN THE FACE, AND THEIR COLD DRINK KNOCKED OUT OF THIER HAND! YOU AIN'T HAVING IT ANY LONGER! YOU ARE NOW STRONG IN SPIRIT BECAUSE THAT'S WHERE JESUS IS!

And you allow Christ to become stronger *through* you, how? Little by little. Little by little. Paul said we go from "glory to glory" (see 2 Corinthians 3:18). As you get to know who you truly are in Christ, and as you come to understand just how special you are to Him, He will supernaturally give you the ability to choke out Old _____ (insert your name here).

For my old self, Old Matt, he was strong, but New Matt is stronger. My *soul* is stronger, because I'm allowing Jesus to *make* me stronger. Old Matt was also extremely deceptive, manipulative, and *secretive*. Secrets ruled his life! Soon enough, Old Matt had a new, huge problem. *New* Matt asked God a question that forever changed the course of Old Matt's destiny. I said, "God, please use me, no matter what."

BOOOOOOOOOOOOOOOOOOOOM!!!!! An atomic bomb just landed on Old Matt's lap! "YOU'RE TOAST, BRO! GET THE CRAP OUTTA HERE!"

When I asked God that, to use me, little did I know He actually would—and in an *unfathomable* way—internationally. If I told you the number of people I reach each day through my ministry, you wouldn't believe me. And let's keep things in perspective, *I'm just a regular guy*. I'm just like 99% of the population out there, but *look* what God has done for me "ministry wise"—it is mind-blowing! I didn't plan this but God *did*! YOU CAN DO THIS TOO!

I haven't done anything special, all I've done is simply given my heart to God. I began to seek out *who* Jesus is each day. I gave Him my trust, my talents, and my time. I didn't do a 12-step program, I did a one-step program: *I began to show Jesus how much I loved Him!* And He told me, "I don't want you drinking," so I stopped.

I didn't go to seminary, I went to the school of the Holy Spirit! *HE TAUGHT ME!* And if you are truly seeking, listening, and applying the love of Jesus to your life and the lives of others, He will teach you too!

Now I'm not secretive anymore. I've learned that the only secrets that can hurt me are the ones I don't bring out into the open. These are the secrets that the devil attempts to make me feel ashamed about. But God *never* wants us to feel ashamed—convicted, yes, but never ashamed. So let it all out, you'll be amazed at what happens. Your misery can become your ministry if you let it, and if you have the right attitude. An attitude of love, joy, peace, patience, kindness, gentleness, and self-control—no matter what is happening in your life! (See Galatians 5:22,23).

The devil wants you to always feel horrible and *keep* your secrets. God simply wants you to continue doing your very best while resting in His grace and knowing that you are loved unconditionally because of Jesus. Your victory will come once you get focused on who you are spiritually—Christ! So get rid of your secrets. Tell God *sorry* when you mess up, and then keep moving forward! You are already *completely* forgiven!

A prayer for you: Heavenly Father, b*ecause of your grace I get to live out another day of life, and I'm so excited to do so. Help me with every situation I face. Right now, I lift up all who are reading this, directly to you. For those who are trapped in a self-made prison of secrets, BREAK THEM FREE! Show them there is a new life on the outside! Give them that extra boost of confidence to escape! I know that you don't waste any part of our past, so whatever it is they bring out into the light today, begin to quickly use it to help others who are struggling with the same things. You did this for me so I know you'll do it for them! In Christ's awesome name I ask these things, amen.*

DAY 23

WHY SHOULD I HUMBLE MYSELF?

"He must become greater; I must become less." ~John the Baptist

JOHN 3:30

Growing up, we are taught to be the best. In grade school, at the end of the year, certificates and awards are handed out the the over-achieving pudding-cup people. In middle school, our social life turns toward having the prettiest girlfriend or most athletic boyfriend. We are *pushed* to have the best. Sports and activities, which you are also driven to be the best at by coaches, teachers, students, and parents—these things start to take off as a new goal. BE THE BEST! DON'T BE AT THE BOTTOM!

In sports, you wanna be cheered for at the games and included as an important part of the team. So you begin to practice your heart out, so that you *can* be good in the games; so that you can...*be the best.* We are driven to be the best! Not be lowly, not be humble, but elite.

For some, it's band or school clubs, but in junior high, the notion of being the *top person* begins to take precedent. High school takes it to a whole other level. You are nudged to be the stud athlete, or the most beautiful girl. Grades? Forget about it. The pressure to get all A's is astronomical. WE ARE DRIVEN TO BE AT THE TOP! Not the bottom, but BETTER than the rest!

It doesn't end there. College is simply high school without teachers and parents pressuring you, but instead, *yourself*. The school doesn't care if you show up or not, you'll just have to keep paying them if you fail. So the pressure to be the best is on *you*.

After college, the job market is the most severe when it comes to being the best!

"Make the most money!"

"Get the biggest house!"

"Drive the best car!"

"Take awesome vacations!"

"Have big bank accounts!"

"MAKE. MORE. MONEY!"

"DO. MORE. THINGS!"

"BUY...MORE...STUFF!"

Oh, and if you decide to go into entrepreneurship, my goodness, the gut-wrenching pressure from the world to be *the* very best is monumental! BE ON TOP! OR DON'T HAVE A BUSINESS! PERIOD!

There is *so* much pressure to be the best, to be better than others. From the time we are just little kids, our hearts are molded toward high achievement. And don't even get me started on the pressure of the loveless Christians, to be "the best" like them.

With all this pressure, it's no wonder so many people have a difficult time living out the Christian life. Why? Because the entire premise of Christianity is based on *humbling yourself.* Humility is Christianity 101, the entry-level course.

Until we finally admit that we are extremely flawed—on our own—Christ can't fully use us. Even as a Christian, until we do as John the Baptist said, "He must become greater; I must become less" (John 3:30), we will never fulfill our deepest God-given destinies.

Jesus said that if we never "change and become like a little child, we will never enter the kingdom of heaven" (Matthew 18:33). James, the half-brother of Jesus reiterated Scripture when he said, "God opposes the proud, but gives grace to the humble" (James 4:6). *Opposes* the proud! The best! The ones on top without Him!

Humbling ourselves is the only way we can *become* exactly like Christ in spirit! That is, saying, "I'm not above this. I can forgive the unforgivable. I can love the unloveable. I can do all things through Christ, *He* strengthens me." *That's* humility! Humbling ourselves to Christ *in* us is simply changing our habits, choices, and lifestyles to the point of near-excruciating pain!

And this pain is coming from KILLING OFF our old, unrenewed mindsets! That arrogant, "I know what's best for me" version of ourselves! I WAS THE WORST AT THIS!

It wasn't until I finally said, "Okay, God. Use me, no matter how much it hurts," that *everything* changed. It was *in* my humility that God gave me a brand new life. What's funny is, I'm more confident now than I've ever been.

So today, my friends, know this: Humbling yourself to God, through Christ, is a courageous thing! Allowing His Spirit to live through you is the highest achievement ever! This is where your new confidence begins! This is where you learn your value! This is where you get a backbone! This is where you learn how to overcome evil with good, and hate, with love! Begin to humble yourself today. Just say, "Jesus, I'm ready. Let's do this," and you're off!

A prayer for you: *God I want to thank you today for knocking the stool of pride out from under me. It was a good thing. And although I fought you for so long, thank you for never giving up on me. Right now, I lift up all who are reading this, directly to you. HUMBLE THEM! SHOW THEM WHAT TRUE HUMILITY IS! SHOW THEM WHAT REAL STRENGTH IS! Do them like you did me, and remove everything in their lives that would keep them from coming to know Jesus on the deepest level possible. They might not know it now, but this will be the best thing that ever happened to them! In Christ's name I pray, amen!*

DAY 24

JESUS FEELS YOUR PAIN

"Jesus wept."

JOHN 11:35

Someone once told me, "You're not allowed to use definitions from Webster's Dictionary when trying to get your point across about God." Well guess what? I'm gonna do it anyway.

"Jesus wept" (John 11:35), the shortest verse in the Bible, to me, may have the most meaning. A god, crying? Gods don't do that, they're gods! All-powerful! Nothing can hurt them! But, the one *true* God, Jesus, He actually wept—not just cried or sniveled a little—but boohooed, He bawled like a baby. How do I know?

Webster's Dictionary defines *wept* as this: "to cry because you are very sad or are feeling some other strong emotion." OUR GOD CRIED AND GOT EMOTIONAL! Imagine that! And *we* are created in His image! (See Genesis 1:27). So now we know that we never have to hide how we *feel*, but instead, look to how Christ handled *His* feelings.

He actually cried, hard. Weeping is crying hard. I'll get to why Jesus wept in just a minute. But as we can see in this short verse, God created us to be emotional because *He* is emotional! It's okay to be sad. Jesus was sad, *very* sad that day. So when we feel sad for whatever reason, God simply wants us to, yes, feel our emotions, but then bring those emotions *to* Him. His Holy Spirit will then comfort us and guide us as to what to *do* with our emotions.

Don't be afraid to feel. Feeling is good. Express your feelings, and then don't feel bad about expressing them. Just don't sin *while* expressing them—that's the key.

And why did Jesus weep? Did He stub His toe in the middle of the night? I've wept before because of that. Did He burn His pizza? Again, such sadness I've felt after the oven overcooked my pie. No, Jesus wept because He felt the pain of His loved ones. He wept because He is so full of empathy. Let's do another definition here from ole Webster. He defines empathy as this: "the ability to understand and share the feelings of another."

The ability to understand and *share* the feelings of another...Wow...I don't know about you, but that gives me goosebumps. *My* God, The Omnipotent One, CREATOR OF HEAVEN AND EARTH, He actually understands and *shares* my feelings—THAT'S JUST CRAY-CRAY!

Jesus wept that day because one of His best friends, Lazarus, had died; and Lazarus' two sisters, whom Jesus was very close with as well, they were in a serious state of mourning. But let's be clear here, Jesus didn't cry *because* Lazarus died (his death was part of one of Jesus' planned miracles, which is *power over death*), but He cried because of the *pain* Lazarus' sisters were *feeling*. Empathy.

Let's back up for a sec; four days earlier, Mary and Martha had sent someone to get Jesus because Lazarus' health was quickly declining—they were afraid he was gonna die and knew Jesus could stop this. "So the sisters sent word to Jesus, 'Lord, the one you love is sick' (John 11:3)."

But Jesus purposely waited and didn't rush over to heal him. Why? Because Jesus had a much better, *future* purpose for this pain! The Bible says so, "When he heard this, Jesus said, 'This sickness will not *end* in death. No, it is for God's glory so that God's Son may be glorified *through* it' (John 11:4 my emphasis added)."

Most of us Christians know the story of Jesus bringing Lazarus back to life, but this message is *not* about Christ's amazing power over death. Oh no, this devotional is not about how Jesus *allowed*—didn't *cause*—Lazarus' death. It's not about how Jesus let this tragedy happen so that maybe His greatest miracle ever, other than bringing *Himself* back to life, *could* happen! NO! THIS MESSAGE IS ABOUT JESUS FEELING *OUR* PAIN!

But if you're not familiar with what happened in that story, Jesus walked up to this dead man's grave and then spoke to one of the latest cast-members of *The Walking Dead*, saying, "LAZARUS, COME OUT!" And He did! Stumbling out, looking like a mummy, pulling cloths off left and right, JESUS BROUGHT LAZARUS BACK TO LIFE! JUST IMAGINE THE STORIES HE HAD TO TELL! Myyyyyyyy goodness! I get so excited about the things Jesus does! Don't you?! How *awesome* is our God?!

But this message isn't about that. It's about how Christ *feels* for those whom He loves—which is all of us—yes, all of us. Gay, straight, black, white, rich, and poor—Jesus feels your pain! NEVER, EVER, *EVER* THINK THAT NOBODY FEELS YOUR PAIN, BECAUSE JESUS DOES!

AND HE IS *THERE* FOR YOU! He is longing to enter into a close, personal relationship with you! Do you feel all alone? YOU'RE NOT! Jesus is with you always! He said it, not me, "And be sure of this: I am with you always, even to the end of the age" (Matthew 28:20).

If you don't have this relationship with Him yet, simply say, "Jesus, help me," and He will...He promises. I'm proof of this. I've personally been comforted by Him so I know it's real.

So today, my friends, know this: God weeps. And what makes Him weep? Hurting people. Why? Because He loves us so much. Jesus showed us in this story as He listened to the sisters saying, "If you were *just* here, this wouldn't have happened" (see John 11:21, my emphasis added). They were in such a deep sadness and Jesus felt that.

He feels *your* pain, too. And if you will draw near to Him, He will comfort you, and then show you the good plans that will come out of this. It might be on this side of heaven, or it might *not* be, but either way, Jesus *will* eventually reveal it to you. For the sisters, they got to see a miracle which made it to the pages of the Bible. And because Christ is still with us today, in Spirit, He still performs miracles *today*! He will do so in *your* life! Just like Mary, Martha, and Lazarus' lives! So don't focus so much on *what's* causing your pain, but instead, begin to focus on a God who *feels* your pain deeper than you do—and can do *amazing* things.

A prayer for you: *Heavenly Father, I want to thank you today for my good health. I was just thinking this morning how blessed I am to not have a single ailment in my body, what a blessing. Right now, I lift up all who are reading this, directly to you. For those who are in tremendous pain, I ask that you comfort them with your Holy Spirit. EASE their pain, Lord, please. And as you ease their pain, help them to go even deeper into their relationship with you. Help them begin to understand your unconditional love, and thank you so much for Jesus! What a wonderful gift! Help us to walk out each day as He does, doing good things, being confident in you, and loving others with empathy. Amen!*

DAY 25

HOW TO KILL YOUR WIFE'S HUSBAND

"And the two will become one flesh. So they
are no longer two, but one flesh" ~Jesus

MARK 10:8

Today, August 23, 2016, is my twelve year wedding anniversary!
TWELVE YEARS OF MARRIAGE! Take *that* marriage statistic
keeper! As of today, my marriage is good, my family is getting stronger,
and Jesus is the center of it all!…But it wasn't always like this.

As most of you know, I talk about my addiction to alcohol and the
negative effects it had on my family quite often. That part of my testimonial is a huge piece of my ministry. The devil wants me to hide it, God
wants me to expose it. If I was not in recovery, I *would* hide it, but I've got
nothing to be ashamed of because that is the *Old* version of myself. I'll
explain "Old version" shortly.

I want absolutely everyone to know that I *never* thought I could
break this addiction—even as a Christian. I had just succumb to the
"fact" that I drank. But that was a lie from hell because Christ set me
free! What always started out as an innocent way to relax or have fun,

was obliterating every part of my life—my marriage included. I've now been sober over 25 months! BOO-YA! Take that devil, ya idiot!

As a result of this new freedom, I'm no longer shy to publicly talk about how Christ helped me overcome that stronghold. I got to this point by starting to care about what *God* thought of me, rather than what *people* thought of me. That wasn't easy, but it was worth it! I'm not ashamed to say that I'm a Christian alcoholic in recovery, or that God didn't bless me with an off-button when it comes to enjoying a couple beers like other people. And that's okay.

I'm at peace with the fact that I can't drink. And not just *at peace*, but I've actually let God *use* my past for my purpose! He wants to do the same for you! That deep, dark secret you're keeping? God wants to shine a big spot-light on it, He wants to clean it up, and *then* He wants to have you *purposefully talk about it*. Why?…To help others who are struggling with the same things. YEP!

The Bible says that it's the blood of Jesus *and our testimonies* that help us defeat the enemy! (See Revelation 12:11). SO SPEAK THAT OUT LOUD! This is how you fight back! This is how you win! But one thing I've wanted to use for my ministry, but haven't *yet* been able to, is my severely difficult marital problems. I've prayed and asked God to show me the time when it's okay…today is that day. So here we go. God bless this writing. I'm not ashamed.

My wife, Jennifer, and I met each other in 7th grade science class. She was one of the popular kids. She was (and still is) beautiful, sweet, and friendly–to everyone. Me, I was the shy, poor, new kid. At this time of my life, Dad had just been awarded final sole custody of us kids, and we had settled in a little town about an hour south of St. Louis, Missouri.

Let's back up even further. My brothers, sister, and I had been wards of the state while Dad battled hard in the court system to get us back. Mom was on drugs and didn't care about us kids at that time of her life. What's worse than that, she didn't want Dad to have us either, so she had accused him of some serious false allegations. Just *thinking* about it, the enemy tries to tick me off to this day. I gotta remind myself that the past is the past, and God used all of it for good. I've forgiven Mom, she has expressed her sincere apologies, so there is no reason to get riled up. It's over.

But what ensued during those dark years of my childhood was Mark, Luke, John, Faith, and I, all being split up into different foster homes and children's shelters. It was a nightmare. The tear-soaked pillows in those places, I'm sure, still remain today, but by other kids dealing with the same heartbreaking situation. It was devastating.

I tell you about this because when you are in the custody of the state you go to whatever school they send you to at that time, based on whatever place, or "home," you are staying at. So we kids were shipped around to many different schools.

This was *extremely* painful because once we finally got comfortable and made friends, we had to start all over again. The fear, anxiety, heart palpitations, and shaking, was near-crippling each time I was brought into a new school classroom, as the teacher said, "Class, this is our new student, Matt."

You get picked on a lot, made fun of, and mostly rejected as the new kid. Nobody wants to be your friend. You are considered weird. And if someone *does* act nice to you, it's not normal, and you almost don't trust it. So I quickly learned to just be quiet, keep my head down, and mind my own business.

HOWEVER! In Mrs. Bates' 7th grade science class, for some strange reason this beautiful, popular girl was genuinely very nice and respectful to me! Her name was Jennifer Meador. Come to find out, she was *really* like this. I had actually made a friend—a hottie—a *nice* hottie.

That was the only class I had with her, so each day I looked forward to sitting behind her and asking if I could borrow her pencil, or anything, just to talk to this beauty…and she *talked* back to me! This was huge!

Fast forward to a year after we graduated high school, Jennifer and I finally started dating. We had stayed friends all throughout our school years, but never "went out." Since Central was the school that my brothers, sister, and I finally got to stay at permanently, I began to develop a confidence in myself, I gained friends, played basketball, got good grades, and overall my schooling experience at Park Hills was a very pleasant time of my life.

In the beginning, yes, middle school was difficult, but nobody messed with me in high school. We were all friends and it was fun. Central, Class of 1999, we all got along quite well. I have very fond memories of everyone from my graduating class.

Let's fast forward even further, to August 2004, the month Jennifer and I got married! So young! So dumb! So in love! But most of all, we were so excited about the life we were about to begin together! WE HAD BIG PLANS!

When we got married we didn't have any money. We didn't even have enough to *have* an actual wedding, or even a cake. We just wanted to make it official so we went to the church privately and had our pastor marry us: Mr. and Mrs. Matthew McMillen was here.

Oh what a day! It was rainy with a dreary overcast, but we were so happy! *"WE JUST GOT MARRIED!"* *"I'M YOUR HUSBAND!"* *"I'M YOUR WIFE!"* *"WHAT?!"*...So giddy. I remember that day like it was yesterday. Both of us were 23 years old.

We moved into my father-in-law's basement for a year so we could save up money. As my home security business began to grow, we moved out into a townhouse for another year, and then I built us a nice home in a very nice neighborhood. In August 2006, we moved into the house where we currently live at. Here's where things began to change.

Because we had a nice, big house, and a little money now, we started to *entertain* at our house quite often. So, I began to drink more frequently than normal, and it snowballed. I had *also* developed a terrible addiction to video games. I'm talking marathon sessions of 6-8 hours per day; sometimes not even crawling into bed with Jennifer until daylight.

God was blessing us, and we were ignoring Him.

We began to argue a lot, not communicate, and it almost felt as if we were not even married. She did her own thing, and I did mine. We had money now, so we pretty much did whatever we wanted to. We stopped going to church, I never read my Bible or had devotional time and I had actually become very afraid of God. I turned into a bad husband, and a bad dad. Arrogant. Selfish. Greedy. Full of pride, excuses, blame, rage, cursing tirades, and then self-pity.

But in the midst of all of this my business was booming, and publicly my life *looked* like it was something to be envied.

I kept hearing God say to me, "Pray." I heard this all the time in my heart, but my life was so darned sinful that I was afraid to pray. I *knew* there was more to life than what it had come to, and my drinking in the midst of this had gotten out of control. I wanted to *feel* different, and the devil had me convinced that alcohol would do this for me.

I can remember actually arguing with myself, out loud, as I pulled up to the liquor store towards the end of my drinking, "*NO! You are NOT going in there!*" But I did it anyway. Once I got a few sips in me, that part of me, which was the Holy Spirit *in* me, was bound and gagged—"grieved" is what the Bible says (see Ephesians 4:30).

I was living a fake life. I needed a change. So one night I finally just prayed, "God, help me," and I went to sleep. What He did was give me a dream that I went to hell...I'm not gonna talk about that, but I woke up screaming and sobbing...I slammed my face into the carpet and begged God to never show me that place again.

Jesus was calling me to a deeper purpose...

So I decided to just be a fun, drinking Christian. I would talk about God all the time with a beer in my hand. I'd post selfies with my Corona and barbecue on Saturday, and then on Sunday, I'd check-in at church on Facebook—usually hungover.

"Jesus turned water into wine!" was one of my best excuses. That lifestyle didn't work either, as both the devil and Jesus were fighting to take control of my mindset. Christ had made it very clear that He didn't want me drinking, not even one drop...So what came next was a few years of *trying* to stop drinking.

The secret was I *couldn't* stop…but I *could* begin. Begin what? A new life in Christ! One that actually exuded His character *through* me! (I'm getting excited just typing that!).

And then one day, hungover, for what seemed like the millionth time, I began reading a Christian book by Joel Osteen called *Every Day a Friday*. I mean, who doesn't love a Friday? This preacher wanted to teach me how to make every day of my life *feel* like a Friday! Sounds good to me!

So I began to read this book, and I couldn't put it down. He wasn't like other preachers, he was kind, and extremely humble—*gentle* even. I've never experienced that from a preacher before. I usually cringed and waited for them to beat me down. I *know*—without a doubt—God lead me to that book! It was just what I needed! Christ *through* Joel, set a brand-new fire inside me! Because of his teachings, I now had new goals to change *for* God, rather than drive myself nuts trying to earn anything *from* God. It felt great!

At that time of my life, the last thing I wanted to hear was how bad of a person I was—I ALREADY KNEW THAT! Joel began to tell me how *good* of a person I was, and that no matter how many times I failed, I could always start again…today…because of Jesus' great love for me.

He taught me how much God loved me, despite…*me*.

I now *wanted* more than ever, to change everything! I now *wanted* to begin to seek out *who* Jesus is, on a very deep level! As a broken man, he planted the seed of God's goodness in me. That was January 2011.

So here's the part about killing my wife's husband (from the title of this devotional). Old Matt's incorrect mindset (based on 2 Corinthians 5:17, stating that the OLD has gone and the NEW has come), was starting to die off. As I sought to get to know Jesus better and better each day, I was learning new life skills from the Holy Spirit!

Jennifer didn't understand this new version of me, who I call, *New Matt*. But little by little, day by day, month by month, I was allowing

Jesus to *renew the mind* of the old version of myself—the weak part of my soul who the devil played like a puppet!

I was becoming New Matt! I say this humbly, but I really liked this guy! He handled his problems so much differently than Old Matt! He had a good attitude! He stopped blaming everything on everyone else! HE FELT HIS FEELINGS, AND BROUGHT THEM TO GOD FOR *HOW* TO HANDLE THEM! He took responsibility for his own actions! He forgave! He showed mercy!

…He had love, joy, peace, patience, kindness, gentleness, and most of all *self*-control! Unbeknownst to me at the time, I was organically growing *fruit* of the Spirit! (See Galatians 5).

The problem was, Jennifer didn't know this person—yet. This was *not* the man she married. This was *not* the Matt McMillen she had known since 1993. I had killed that guy. Dead.

Further, and I say this respectfully, Jennifer had some serious changes to make as well. Old Matt was extremely codependent. He allowed things to go on and on that he shouldn't have, just to keep his marriage and fake reputation intact. Also, because of the blatantly sinful life *he* lived, he allowed a lot of totally unacceptable behavior to happen—after all, who is he to correct someone else?

New Matt however, would NOT allow things to stay as they were. He actually began to establish healthy boundaries that others must respect in his relationships, business practices, parenting, *and* in his marriage. I know it's strange talking about myself in the third-person, but this is the best way I can describe this change.

Frankly, it just wasn't *in me* any longer to overlook certain things. I tried. I even attempted to make excuses for Jennifer, giving it my best effort to cover up her actions with the love of Christ. But Jesus soon taught me that He was *not* an enabler, so I no longer had it in me to be one either.

"GOD, I LOVE JENNIFER SO MUCH, BUT I CAN'T LIVE LIKE THIS ANY LONGER!!!!"…It got bad. We decided that we should divorce and just move on with our lives separately. We were just too different. She didn't know me any longer.

Because of me learning about my value in Christ, that I'm *so* loved He would actually *die* for me, *as* a sinner (see Romans 5:8), I, in turn, developed a backbone to be able to stand up to certain behaviors which were not okay. Only now, I was attempting to enforce these needed changes with love and respect—I didn't throw fits any longer.

I had become humble *and* confident. This is possible through Christ! I stopped putting my identity in my marriage—which was something I could lose—and I started to put it solely in my relationship with Jesus! He was now the center of my life, and He no longer allowed me to sit idle when it came to how I was being treated.

And just in the nick of time, God saved my marriage! Not when *I* wanted Him to—despite my constant pleading—but when *He* was ready to! HE SAVED IT! JENNIFER AND I ARE NOW CLOSER THAN EVER!

But I must say this as well, Jennifer is new too. This wonderful woman in my life, she is not only absolutely stunning on the outside, but her soul now matches that as well! In the beginning, I pressured her way too much to seek Jesus like I was, and she rebelled because of that. I learned my lesson to *not* to try to do the work of the Holy Spirit, but instead, simply set the example for her and *show* Jennifer the good life in Christ.

God has taught me to just love her like Christ loves me, and that *He'll* take care of reshaping her mindset. He's blessed us both for that.

My wife is going to be reading this, so I want to say something to her directly:

Happy anniversary, baby. Look at how far we've come! We were just kids trying to play house in the beginning, but God has molded both of us into Christ's image—and I *know* that He will continue to do so until we both go Home to be with Him. What a blessing. I thank God for you every day and for the protection He's had on us and our family. I love you more than I can possibly express in typed words. Even though this is my gift, my most finely-crafted sentences would fall short in attempting to explain just how much you mean to me. I'm so glad we never gave up! I'm so glad we pushed through! I'm so glad God taught us *both* how to forgive like Jesus! I promise you that from this day forward, I will do my best, every single day, to show you how much I love you. I already know that I will fail at times, but I promise that I'll never, ever, *ever* stop trying to make you understand, and feel, just how special you are to me. New Matt and New Jennifer are going to do amazing things together! I love you so much! Not just today, but always and forever!

Day 26

Do You Listen To The Devil?

*"The evening meal was being served, and
the devil had already prompted Judas
Iscariot, son of Simon, to betray Jesus."*

JOHN 13:2

I'm not gonna lie, I used to think that it's weird to talk about the devil—even *as* a Christian. "That's just creepy." And also, I didn't want to be known as someone who blames the devil for everything. BUT—as God really began to open up my eyes to this spiritual instigator, I began to realize just how real he is, how he works best, and *where* he works best... in our *minds*.

Sure, the devil has physical powers as well—both, on his own, and through people (see Acts 19)—but his main conduit of tyranny is through the spiritual part of us which is connected to our thought life. We are always thinking *something*!

If you will glance at my opening verse of this devotional, the devil even had Judas "mentally ready" to betray Jesus. And, he had been working on Judas all day long! It wasn't until dinner time that he finally had his mind made up to tell the Pharisees where Jesus was at in private, so they could arrest Him under the cloak of night.

WE MUST BEGIN TO RECOGNIZE THE DEVIL'S TACTICS—
IN OUR MINDS! Jesus said Satan only has three main goals: *Steal, kill,
destroy* (see John 10:10). Apply one, or all three, to any situation in your life,
and if it's falling apart or strenuous, the devil is hard at work!

But be careful. Don't call *people* the devil, that doesn't do any good.
Jesus did this to Peter (see Matthew 16:23), and I've tried it...I did NOT
get a favorable result. Learn from my mistake, and keep that to yourself
(it's not the truth anyway). Some things only Jesus got to say, because
He saw the spiritual world crystal-clear. So even if you *think* (remember
the mind) a person is unknowingly walking hand-in-hand with the devil
because of the rotten fruit in their lives, zip that up and pray for them
instead.

Remember: WE DO NOT JUDGE. We simply speak the truth
with love, have discernment, and look at our *own* sin as the worst sin
we know of. BUT MOST OF ALL WE ARE TO LOVE OTHERS
UNCONDITIONALLY, like Jesus does us.

Here are a few tips I've learned over the past few years when it comes
to noticing our main enemy, his tactics, and what we can do to fight back
against this pathetic butt-wipe:

1. **THE DEVIL AND HIS CRONIES ARE EXTREMELY
   NEGATIVE.** "This is never going to work out, just give up."
   "You've failed a thousand times, what makes you think you are
   going to be successful this time?" "You'll never get out of debt."
   "You'll never be a good enough Christian." "You'll never break
   that addiction." "You're not really saved because you still sin, just
   look at you." "You are a terrible Christian, give up." "Your marriage is done, stop trying." "You'll never find a spouse." "They've
   hurt you too many times, forgiveness won't help anything."
   "Your child will never straighten up." "You are gonna die." "You
   have too much anxiety to function." "You are going to lose your
   job." "They hate you." "Your business will fail." "You are a joke."
   "You're ugly." "You're fat." "You're not smart enough." "You are
   the wrong color." "You come from the wrong family." "Nobody

likes you."…I could continue, but you get the gist. This demonic moron wants you to be extremely down-in-the-mouth, defeated, depressed, and negative—all day long. In order to be able to do this, he will bombard you with lies in your thoughts. Why? Because he knows if you will actually *begin* to be hopeful and positive, your entire life will change for the better! He knows if you will begin to speak out the promises of God, and just how SPECIAL you really are, you will start to exude the character of Christ! *Then* you will begin to grow fruit of the Spirit (see Galatians 5)—and people will actually EAT some of it—in turn, *they* will begin to grow strong in Christ too! So when a negative thought comes your way, simply ask Jesus, "What do you think?" and He will begin to transform your mind into His!

2. **THE DEVIL WILL TEMPT YOU, SEVERELY.** This turd-wagon has been studying the life of man for a loooooooooong time, it started with Adam and Eve. He saw what tempted them the best, and he presented it to them. They didn't *have* to eat that *one* piece of fruit that God said "Don't." It was their choice! This continues today! Satan understands very well how to bait and trap us through *temptation.* And make no mistake, he knows YOU, personally, as well. From the womb he's been trying to kill you, and temptations are one of the things he baits you with. He even enticed many of your parents to get an abortion. The temptation of not having to go through a pregnancy, or the difficulty of raising a child; this was something that many of you readers' parents battled against. BUT HERE YOU ARE, LIVING! HE DIDN'T WIN! And now, he's watched you closely since you were little. He understands your actions, reactions, likes, dislikes, tendencies, and he knows your temperament. The good news is, when it comes to temptation, YOU ARE IN GOOD COMPANY! The devil even tempted and tested Jesus! And he did this for 40 straight days! I have a hard time passing up Krispy Kreme once a week, and Jesus was stuck with this moron at a

temptation retreat for over a month, dealing with his crap (see Matthew 4). What's very interesting to me is that *as* he was tempting Jesus, the devil quoted Scripture *out of context*, just to get Him to break! Satan has even memorized the Bible! And he wants to use it against you by twisting it! But what did Jesus do? He didn't argue or get upset…Instead, He quoted Scripture right back, and in the proper way—in the CORRECT CONTEXT. That's what you gotta do! Begin to speak the Word of God *at* this dummy in the midst of your toughest temptations! HE'S A JOKE!

3. **THE DEVIL WANTS YOU TO LIVE IN FEAR.** This might be his best weapon. If Lucifer and the demons of hell can make you afraid, you will stop dead in your tracks. I speak from experience. You won't want to change your life. You won't want to spread the gospel. You won't want to help others. You won't want to allow Jesus to live through you. FEAR WILL KEEP YOU STUCK IN A SORRY, FLIMSY LIFE. Fear is the opposite of faith! This is why the Bible says "don't be afraid" 365 times! Once for each day of the year! And I've learned that just because I might *feel* fear, or I have physical manifestations of fear that I have no control over, such as sweating, shaking, heart palpitations, stammering, etc., I can *still* move forward while afraid! That's called courage! COURAGE IS MOVING FORWARD WHILE *FEELING* AFRAID! This is where YOU end and CHRIST begins! This is called "doing all things through Christ who strengthens you! (See Philippians 4:13). And lastly, try to remember that fear is not just part of our natural reflexes to danger (that's a fleshly fear), but fear is also a spirit from hell. And "God did not give us a spirit of fear, but of power, love, and a sound mind" (see 2 Timothy 1:7)—and that Spirit, is Him. JESUS LIVES IN YOU!

Of course, there are many other destructive tactics which I've learned about in regard to this spiritual dingle-berry named "Satan"; but I believe by becoming educated little by little through God's Word, you'll start to see him in the crowd—then you'll be able to point him out, and overpower him!

WE HAVE THIS ABILITY! Jesus said that He has given us POWER to overcome our enemy! (See Luke 10:19). So stand up to him today! Don't believe his lies! Don't be negative! Don't fall into temptation! And more than anything, DON'T BE AFRAID! You got this! Christ *in you* has GOT THIS! PUT YOUR CHIN UP, YOUR SHOULDERS BACK, LOOK FORWARD, AND KNOW YOUR STRENGTH!

A prayer for you: *God I want to thank you today for exposing the devil's tactics to me. Your Word says that Jesus' main objective for coming to earth was to destroy the work of the devil, and I'm grateful! So now, help us to do the same! Help us to exude the confidence of Christ and STOMP on this snake's head by doing your will! We know that we can do the same as Jesus by simply loving others unconditionally, overcoming evil with good, doing our best to turn from sin each day—but only through your grace—and by showing mercy, empathy, and forgiveness to absolutely everyone. We love you. Amen.*

DAY 27

ARE YOU STUCK IN THE PAST

"Then David got up from the ground."

SEE 2 SAMUEL 12:20

G od seemed really harsh in the Old Testament. Thankfully, Jesus came and took on that harshness of punishment *for* us—once and for all. *In* the Old Testament, there was a man who made some mistakes, which, without his love for God, would have ruined his entire life because he'd be *stuck* in his terrible past. His name was David, *King* David.

King David was one of the most blessed and influential people of the Bible. Nobody chose him to become who he became except God. He was laughed at, belittled, and overlooked by everyone, even his own family. His rise to biblical superstardom would make for an awesome Hollywood movie!

He is called many things, including "a man after God's own heart" (see 1 Samuel 13:14), and Joseph, Jesus' earthly father, is a direct descendant of David (see Matthew 1).

This is the same David who killed Goliath with a slingshot and a stone.

But just because he is a Bible rockstar doesn't mean he was perfect—far from it! David had an affair with a married woman and got her pregnant. Oh yeah…but it doesn't end there. Then he tried to cover up this affair by having her husband come home from war, sleep with her, then he sent him *back* to war (on the frontline, on purpose) and got him killed!

Doesn't seem like a man after God's heart to me! Sounds like he needs his own show on the *E! Network*, rather than taking his time to write out the Psalms, which we still read to this day!

To make a long story short, David got called out on this terrible cluster of sins by a messenger, and he immediately repented. He said, "I have sinned against the Lord" (2 Samuel 12:13). As a king, he didn't *have* to do this. He could have been arrogant and said, "I can do whatever I want," and then had the messenger of God killed. But no…David *loved* God, so he humbled himself and admitted his sin, even in his position of great power.

What happened next was God's punishment coming down on David's life. The child from this affair became sick. Remember, we are still in the Old Testament here, the punishment Jesus on took for us was still being doled out left and right to the people who went against God's laws. King David was no exception.

So David fasted and prayed. He begged God to not take the life of his child, but unfortunately, the child died. Bear in mind, God is sovereign. He does not have the ability to be incorrect, even if we think He is—and *even* if we don't agree with Him.

What did David do after this tragedy? Did he blame God? Did he sit in self-pity for months? Did he stay *afraid* of God or not get out of bed? Did he beat himself up each day, or decide to live in the shadow of his mistakes forever?…NO! HE GOT UP! The Bible says "He got up from the ground, changed his clothes, worshiped God, and got something to eat!" (See 2 Samuel 12:20).

This is what made David different. He knew God still loved him and that he had a purpose for his life, so he didn't stay stuck in his past! HE MOVED FORWARD! This is what we all gotta do!

Friend, we've all made bad choices and have done things we wish we could change, but can't. I've made some of the worst mistakes possible and the devil kept me shackled to those mistakes along with the consequences which came *from* them. God, on the other hand, has a better idea...LEARN from them and MOVE *FORWARD*! Since we now have Jesus, we can let *Him* take the brunt of those mistakes, ask for help, and then look to Him as to how to get back on track!

Jesus has set the example and given us the guidelines and Spirit needed to get *on* with our lives! We have *nothing* to be ashamed of! God actually wants to *use* our past mistakes *for* our future purpose! BUT YOU GOTTA GIVE IT TO HIM AND STOP BEING ASHAMED! Just look at the example David set for us, we are *still* talking about it! He messed up! So what! We need to have that same attitude and remember our value, which is priceless! So priceless, God became a man and took on any and all punishment *for* our sins! Awesome! You are *not* your mistakes! You are a co-heir with Christ! (See Romans 8:17). GET UP AND GET GOING!

So today, my friends, know this: God doesn't want you to stay stuck in your past—not even *yesterday*. The devil sure does, but God doesn't. The Bible says that "*Today* is the day the Lord has made, we will rejoice and be glad in it" (Psalm 118:24). TODAY! Not yesterday, not tomorrow, but today! It also says that God's mercies renew *every* morning! (See Lamentations 3:22,23). So when that sun came up, He immediately served up a brand new batch of mercy, just for you. Enjoy it and live out your purpose *in* Christ!

A prayer for you: *Heavenly Father, today I want to thank you for your daily dose of mercy. We don't deserve it, but you freely give it! You don't hold grudges against us, but instead, you see us as your beloved, cherished children. Thank you for teaching me this fact so that I could get over my past. Once you taught me how full of mercy you actually are, I finally stopped being ashamed of my past, and you've used it for my purpose! Thank you! I ask that you do the same for all who are* *reading this. For those stuck in shame and regret, help them. Give them a new mindset. Begin to move in their lives on a whole new level, and teach them how to REFUSE to stay stuck in the past. YOU MAKE ALL THINGS NEW! We are grateful! In Christ's name, I bring this prayer to you. Amen.*

DAY 28

ARE YOU READY TO GROW, SPIRITUALLY?

*"When I was a child, I talked like a child, I
thought like a child, I reasoned like a child. When
I became a man, I put childish things behind me."*

1 CORINTHIANS 13:11

I used to be a pretty pathetic Christian. Like a baby, *I wanted what I
wanted, and I wanted it now*! During that stage of my journey in coming
to know Christ deeper, God allowed my tantrums and He gave me what
I wanted quite often. Then came the growing up part. He wasn't going
let me stay in diapers any longer.

Let me back up a step here and say something: Being a bratty
Christian doesn't make you any *less* of a Christian. Being a Christian is
not a verb, it's a noun. You *are* a Christian. That is, if you've accepted
Christ's forgiveness.

Just like a crispy new $100 bill is worth $100 when it leaves the mint,
it will always be worth $100. No matter how many sweaty pockets it gets
shoved into, severely crinkled it gets, or dirty hands it exchanges—its
value is always $100 US dollars. *Your value* in Christ stays the same from
day one of your belief! It is instantaneous and eternal!

Side note Love* however *is* a verb—*not* a noun. It's something that you do! It's action! Love is *not* simply a feeling.

But anyway, back to me being a "little baby believer" even as a grown man. Why did God allow these fits? Why did He protect me so often while I did so much dumb stuff? Why did He place angels around me during my excuse-filled, blatantly sinful life? Simple.

Because He was giving me time to grow.

He wants to do the same for you!

God knew all along that the really hard stuff was coming; and like a kindergartner who still gets to take naps in class, I too, was about to get a rude awakening as I graduated up to the first grade, then second, third, middle school, so on and so forth, until I was finding myself studying for my Master's Degree of Grace.

I was growing, *spiritually*.

What I didn't understand in the beginning was *when* I asked God certain questions, such as, "Will you use me? I want to reach millions of people for you," or if I made statements to Him like, "God, give me patience." "God, make my ministry grow." "God, show me how to love like you do." "Lord, please teach me unconditional forgiveness." "Show me how to control my temper." "Help me understand you on the deepest level possible." "Show me how to love the religious Christians, and church people."—*WHEN* I said such things, God perked up.

Like a dad who just got asked to go play catch in the back yard by his son, He was about to give me the *opportunities* to achieve new growth... new *skills*...

By requesting such maturity, God was sending a hurricane of trials my way in order to work me out, and make me stronger. Nowadays, I'm careful about what I ask for. So let me ask, do *you* want to become strong in a certain area of your life? More skilled? Well...prepare yourself, because if you do, God will sign you up for a marathon of that particular *thing*.

Jesus had to do the same, before *He* fulfilled His personal ministry, so we are in good company! (See Matthew 4).

James, the half-brother of Jesus, actually said that we should be JOYFUL when we face tough times. Joyful? WHAT?! Oh yeah! Here is what he wrote:

> *"Consider it pure joy, my brothers and sisters, whenever*
> *you face trials of many kinds, because you know that*
> *the testing of your faith produces perseverance. Let*
> *perseverance finish its work so that you may be mature*
> *and complete, not lacking anything" (James 1:2-4).*

And do you see *why* we should be joyful during trials? It is so that we can become MATURE, COMPLETE, AND NOT LACKING ANYTHING!

I don't know about you, but I'm not a person of lack! It's just not in me! So like James said, we are to "not lack anything," I *want* the best, I want to *be* the best, and I *expect* the best from others! And we get rid of *lack* by *growing* in the maturity process of allowing Christ to live through us! C'MON SOMEBODY! WE GOTTA *WANT* TO GROW! *I* want it! Don't you?!

Don't you want these trials?! Don't you want these tests?! Don't you want to become strong in your faith?! *Don't you want to let Jesus live through you?*

YES! WE WANT IT!

Don't you want the best from yourself? Don't you want God to be proud of your attitudes and actions? Don't you want to become mature, complete, and not lacking anything? Sure you do. If the Holy

Spirit resides in you, *He* does, even when *you* don't—and He carries you through those times.

So, we grow, spiritually. How? We look forward to new tests! We look forward to new opportunities to strengthen our faith! WE LOOK FORWARD TO BECOMING STRONGER IN CHRIST! We look forward to graduating from being babes.

So today, my friends, please do this: Ask God to make you grow. Don't be afraid, just ask Him. You were *meant* to grow, not just physically, but also spiritually. Just like God didn't plan on you being in your mom's belly forever, or eating Cheerios out of your little cuppie—He doesn't plan on you sitting still or complacent in your relationship with Christ either. Ask for growth today, and then prepare yourself...BECAUSE YOU *WILL* GROW, little by little, day by day, He promises!

A prayer for you: *God, today I want to thank you for the extreme trials you've sent my way. While going through them, it hurt, VERY BADLY. But you've always brought me through at just the right time. Each trial has made me grow up and become stronger in Christ! So thank you! Thank you for teaching me to trust you and not blame you. Thank you for teaching me to not question you during my seasons of extreme trials, just like I don't question you during my seasons of extreme blessings. Right now, I lift up all these dear readers directly to you—STRENGTHEN THEM! So many of them are in the midst of difficult trials and tests, give them that extra BOOST they need to develop a new confidence in your ways! If I can do it through Christ, anyone can do it! HELP THEM TO GROW IN YOU! CHANGE THEIR ENTIRE LIVES! MAKE THEM STRONG! MAKE THEM ENTHUSIASTIC! HELP THEM DO GREAT AND MIGHTY THINGS THROUGH YOU! In Jesus' name, amen.*

DAY 29

WHY I DECIDED TO QUIT DRINKING

"Be sober-minded; be watchful. Your
adversary the devil prowls around like a
roaring lion, seeking someone to devour."

1 PETER 5:8

The title of this devotional is "Why I Decided To Quit Drinking," but to be honest with you, I almost titled it, "*How* I quit drinking." I went with the first, because I can include the *how* in with the *why*…So let's go.

I heard it once said, "The 'ISM' in 'alcoholism,' stands for: Incredibly Short Memory." That little nugget of wisdom is true. We forget. We forget how bad the episodes can get *when* we drink. Either because we've blacked out—therefore *forgetting* what happened—or, we forget on purpose. Forgetting on purpose is better known as *denial*.

Another one-liner that us veteran problem-drinkers know is, "Denial is not just a river in Egypt." That could not be further from the truth! For me, I was the Michael Phelps of "Denial." I swam through it like a fish, I was the best, and I was the fastest.

I was the best at ignoring what my "casual" drinking was doing to my health, my parenting, my marriage, and my relationship with God.

As I type this, it's very early Saturday morning, the sun has barely peeked out. For some strange reason—which, if I think about it, it's not really strange, it's the Holy Spirit activating my ministry gift—on Saturday mornings, I always want to write about my alcohol recovery.

I guess it's because I can still feel the remnant hangovers from Old Matt's life, the most debilitating ones being on Saturday mornings. Why were my hangovers so painful on Saturdays? Because my alcohol addiction flared up the most on Friday evenings. To celebrate a successful workweek (or any other excuse I could come up with), I'd drink more heavily. *And* the devil always placed the excuse in my mind, "You don't have to work tomorrow, so you can drink more." So, I would. Saturday mornings *hurt*...bad.

I would try to act like they didn't, but truth be told, I wasn't just in pain physically, but also mentally, emotionally—and because I was grieving the Holy Spirit with my binges—I was in pain, *spiritually*.

As a Christian alcoholic, because I was blatantly ignoring the Holy Spirit each time I put a bottle up to my lips, I *grieved* Him. Just in the same way a loving parent grieves their child's behavior who is on heroin—or any other drug—God still loved me infinitely, but it hurt Him each and every time I pounded beers and shots.

The Bible says, "Do not *grieve* the Holy Spirit of God, with whom you were sealed for the day of redemption" (Ephesians 4:30 my emphasis added). Another version says, "Do not bring sorrow to God's Holy Spirit by the way you live. Remember, he has identified you as his own, guaranteeing that you will be saved on the day of redemption."

That one is easier to understand. *"Do not bring sorrow to God's Holy Spirit by the way you live!"* That's exactly what I was doing each time I popped a top! I just *kept* ignoring Him!

Now, I want you to notice the second sentence in that verse because it's very important—it will help *anyone* recover, because it proves that we can always try again—ALWAYS—as long as we are alive, no matter if we are 9 or 90, God let's us begin again: "Remember, he has identified you as his own, guaranteeing that you will be saved on the day of redemption."

Do you see that? My addiction, my alcoholism, did *not* remove my guarantee of heaven! And it doesn't remove *yours* either, if you have an addiction of any type as well! OUR ACTIONS—GOOD *OR* BAD—DO *NOT* CHANGE OUR POSITION WITH GOD! Had I *never* stopped drinking, I'd still get to go to where He is when I die—the day of redemption!

Because of my faith in Christ, I've been "identified as his own" and "guaranteed" that I'd be "saved." It's right THERE! The grace of the Cross supersedes EVERYTHING! This is the only way!

The religious Christians won't agree with this. They'll say that if you keep sinning, or if you're stuck in a sin-pattern—because of a tendency—you will lose your spot in heaven, or, you're not really saved.

Well, the Bible says that is incorrect. They've not earned a THING. It's all been free for them as well, the devil simply has them convinced their religious actions *makes* them acceptable to God...they are in for a big surprise.

On that day of redemption, when they walk in with their barrel of religious works, set it down in front of our Creator, and say, "Look at what *I* did," I believe God will say, "So what. Tell me, *why* did you do these things?"

WE DO EVERYTHING BECAUSE WE LOVE GOD! Nothing added, nothing taken away!

That's why I'm here to help the alcohol—addict! The drug—addict! The sex—addict! The _____ (fill in the blank)—ADDICT! I'm not here to stroke the egos of the religious Christians, or fall in line, just so they'll approve of me or say nice things about me. I'M HERE TO HELP THE LOST FIND THEIR WAY OUT OF THE DARKNESS! I'm not here to be a good little Christian boy so I'll get patted on the head! I'M HERE TO SHAKE UP THE RELIGIOUS WORLD FOR JESUS!!!!

The Christians who REFUSE to get out into the world and help people find what WE have, *they* are more lost than the lost! DO SOMETHING! DO *ANYTHING*! THIS LIFE AIN'T ABOUT US "GOING TO CHURCH" or getting dunked in water! It's about us getting off our polished butts, getting our hands dirty, and SAVING PEOPLE'S LIVES! THEY *NEED* US!

ahem...Sorry about that. I get worked up when I think about religion, how it's destroyed so many lives. All the rules and judgment and members-only clubs. COUNT. ME. OUT. I'm all for the truth, but I'm also all for *love*. Jesus spoke both at the same time, that's my goal. And I'll rest in His grace with confidence as I speak this out.

I want to get in with the people who are hurting; the ones who have been lied to about Jesus. I want to *show* those who don't really understand His grace...His grace. And if that takes me upsetting some religious Christians in the process, so be it. If it takes me airing out my own dirty laundry, to make me relatable, so be it.

My friend, if you're addicted, your addiction does not define you, your Creator does. I want to tell you something that is really neat: You *look* like God. Yep. You look like Him. The Bible says we were created in *His own image* (Genesis 1:27). So that fact should make you feel at least a *little* better, if you are struggling today.

But this Good News (that's what *the gospel* means) doesn't stop there! God not only created you in His own image, but He loved you so much, that He joined you here on His own created planet! (See John 1). Why? For many reasons!

First of all, He wanted to pay off *all* of your sin-debt with Him—personally. Imagine if you were standing in front a judge in a court of law and you are guilty and you know it. Convicted of the crime, the judge says, "Guilty," but *then* he stands up and pays off your fine...that's exactly what Jesus did! HE LOVED YOU SO MUCH HE TOOK THE PUNISHMENT OF DEATH FOR YOU! And you have access to this gift, by grace, through simply...*believing* (see Ephesians 2:8,9).

Besides our free sin-punishment-pay-off, Jesus also lived the life that *we* should try gracefully to live. Why? Because He was perfect! Because He was, and is, God in the flesh! He laid out all the principles, ways, and truths we should follow! He set the standard for all humanity! He saw that we couldn't get it right, so He came down and showed us how to live, forgive, and love others properly! And by faith *alone*—through *His* Spirit—we can do the same.

Will we still mess up even after we place our faith in Him? Yes. And God knows that. That's why Jesus completed *all* of the required work, laws, and commands of God *for* us (see Galatians 3:13, Romans 10:4, Matthew 5:17). It is now our job to simply live by faith in Him, through His Spirit, and *enjoy* this awesome gift of being adopted into the family of God! HOW EASY! HOW SIMPLE! HOW AMAZINGLY GRACEFUL!

SO! Let me answer the question that is the title of this devotional, "Why I decided To Quit Drinking." Simple: Because I love Jesus...absolutely everything I do, or don't do, is because I love Him. And I love Him because I can't stop Him from loving me, *even* if I was still binge-drinking all the time. And then the next question, "How did I stop drinking?"

Simple: *Because I love Jesus.*

A prayer for you: *Well good morning, Lord! MAN, I have a lot of energy today! I know that this energy is a gift from you through me being obedient to the Holy Spirit by NOT getting plastered last night. With over two years of sobriety now, I can see this is what you wanted for me all along! THANK YOU! Right now, I lift up all who are reading this, directly to you. I understand that everyone reading today's devotional is not an alcoholic or addict, but some are. First, for those who aren't, help them to understand that us addicts are just in need of some serious mercy and grace—but also, we need firmness. We need people who will call us out, and stand up to us! If there is any hint* *of codependency or enabling in ANY relationship here, please begin to give them the tools they need to set healthy boundaries for the addicts in their lives—and give them the strength they need to enforce those boundaries with love.*

And for those who are hungover right now, or who may have made some terrible choices while drunk or high last night—in the name of Jesus—I REBUKE SATAN'S GRASP ON THEIR MINDSET AND LIVES! I DEMAND that he leave them alone! BREAK THEM FREE! RIGHT NOW! Give them the extra grace needed to simply begin. Not quit, but begin a new life in Christ! And most of all, show them that you will USE this difficult season for their purpose! Thank you in advance! I SPEAK FREEDOM OVER THEIR LIVES! In Christ's name, amen.

DAY 30

How Can I Make My Life Better?

"Be made new in the attitude of your minds"

EPHESIANS 4:23

I used to have a very poor attitude. I blamed everyone for my problems, I held grudges, and I constantly *talked* about my problems and grudges. To top it off, I'd then feel *guilty* about having problems, grudges, and a poor attitude! Why was this? Why couldn't I *make* my life get better?! It took me a while to finally grasp what the problem was…it was my mindset. I hadn't yet allowed God to begin renewing it!

God has a great plan for each and every one of us, He doesn't have favorites—I didn't know that. I thought I had to be a "good Christian" before my life would get better, when all along all I had to do was get to know Jesus better…more *closely*, and then allow Him to live *through* me.

The religious Christians want you to think that unless you do the things *they* want you to do, you are "less than" in God's eyes—YOU'RE NOT! The prostitute and the preacher are both loved by God the same. They both need to have Christ in the proper position in their hearts and minds—the *same*. And when they do, *then* their lives will begin to get better!

Just like there are tons of miserable drug dealers, wife-beaters, alco-holics, and addicts—there are also tons of miserable preachers, mission-aries, faithful church-goers, and worship leaders.

The only way to change our lives for the better is to begin to show Jesus that we love Him through our words, thoughts, goals, and actions—there is no other permanent, *eternal* way. This begins as you allow Him to renew the *attitude of your mind.*

Here are some key guidelines that helped me along the path of renewing my mind, which, in turn, renewed my life, therefore making it *so* much better! Sure, there are many more, but these five things helped me, and I believe they will help you too:

1. **READ ABOUT JESUS.** I can remember as a kid, picking up a big, leather Bible, and then holding the pages against my thumb as I fanned through it from front to back. I specifically remem-ber thinking to myself, "Wow. That's a lot to read and know." Unbeknownst to me at the time, the enemy was already placing doubt and discouragement in my mind. What I came to find out was that my *life change* would happen by simply taking *little bites* of God's Word, day by day. As I did this, I began to understand the personality of Christ. THIS IS THE ENTIRE GOAL OF READING THE BIBLE. Once you know Jesus, how kind, mer-ciful, patient, and powerful He is—*then* He begins to teach you your value. That *value* instills a new confidence *in* you—hence, making your life *better*. But this all began by having a daily goal of simply reading about Him. So don't feel intimidated or pres-sured, just read. The Holy Spirit will do the rest!

2. **WATCH YOUR MOUTH.** This is not natural for me because I've always had a foul mouth. When you are in foster homes and children shelters as a little kid—as well as being forced to go from school to school—you not only pick up really bad lan-guage, but if you *didn't* swear, you were looked upon as weak. So my sailor-mouth was a way to look cool, fit in, and be tough.

This habit continued on into my adulthood, but as I got to know Christ more and more, He began to convict me of my foul language. "Matt, that's not okay. I don't talk like that and neither should you. You need to start watching your mouth." So I have. No I'm not perfect by any means when it comes to my language, but I do my best to be conscious of what I say, as well as speak in a manner Christ approves of most of the time.

3. **PRAY FOR THOSE WHO CAUSE YOU HARM, GENUINELY.** This was one of the most difficult things for me to begin. To be perfectly honest with you, I actually began to seek out God in the beginning, deeply, so that He would make my enemies pay...HA! I chuckle at that *now*, but only because I've learned He doesn't work that way! DUMB! You see, I'm a very competitive, passionate person, so asking God to bless my enemies did *not* come natural. However, as I got to know Jesus more and more, I started to see just how much *I* did in my life that *He* did not approve of—yet, He still blessed me! Because of that, I started to do the same, even though in the beginning it was like eating glass. It's not difficult any longer. God has taught me that as soon as I begin to feel resentment towards someone to immediately say, "Jesus, please bless them," or "Please help them to come to know you deeply." What happens is this frees *me*, because I release *them* from what they owe me—I'm not saying that it's okay, but instead, I'm simply letting that debt go. When I do this, I get to keep my peace and this also unlocks God's power in *their* lives because they'll see Christ doing this *through* me. Remember: He loves all of us! Not just those who treat us right!

4. **DON'T TRY TO FIGURE OUT ALL OF THE RELIGIOUS STUFF.** I get messages from people who seem to be in utter turmoil about trying to understand every single facet of the Christian religion. When honestly, all you really *need* to know is that you are a sinner who needs to place your faith in Jesus as your Savior, that He is the Son of God, and that He loves

you unconditionally...That's it. No, you don't want to *stop* there, but that's the kindergarten class. With that knowledge and belief in Christ, you are a Christian and you are going to heaven. But so many people are trying to make sure they do everything exactly right, or that they never mess up—*and* they want to understand all the *hows* and *whys* and *what's gonna happen next.* They are driving themselves crazy. They want to be able to know what every single scripture means, RIGHT NOW, and if they don't they are very upset! To top it off, they want to make *you* upset about it as well! They have no peace. I used to be like this, and God taught me to just relax and enjoy Jesus. He has given us *just enough info* to establish belief in Him, as well as be able to understand what He expects from us. The devil wants us confused, Jesus wants us to *rest.* Rule of thumb: if you can't figure it out, don't worry about it. God wants you to simply relax, live by the Spirit, and enjoy your relationship with Him!

5. **PRAY.** If these steps were in order, this would probably be number one. It is vital that you get in the habit of continual "chatter-prayers" all day long. Your prayers should eventually be something that you don't really even notice—like breathing. Little one-liners or a few sentences, you know, like you talk to *people*? You talk to God the same. Prayer is just talking. You don't have to throw in the "thees" and "thous"—you don't live in the 1600's—just speak like you always do. God gave you your mouth, so just use it *normally.* Just talk. Talking builds up *any* relationship. God hears you at *all* times—He even knows your thoughts—your unspoken words. So you may as well begin to include Him, and be real. Yes, we should have a time or two each day where we bow our heads in awe and respect to Him—spending a few minutes (or much longer, or much less, there is no law in prayer) in a longer conversation with Him. But overall, you just chit-chat with your Creator from sun up to sun down! Some of my main prayers are, "Help me," "Thank you," and "Show me how!"

A prayer for you: *God, I want to thank you today for changing my entire life for the better! It hasn't been easy, but it's been worth it! Thank you for changing my attitude and renewing my mind through simply seeking Jesus' will each day, and doing my best to show you that I love you. Right now, I lift up all who are reading this, directly to you. For those who have been struggling to make life changes for a very long time, and just feel stuck, LIFT THEM UP AND OUT! It could be obvious stuff in their lives that you want changed, and it could also be a religious, judgmental soul—BOTH ARE INCORRECT! I'm asking today that you infuse in them a brand new resolve of your grace! PUSH THEM THROUGH! Teach them! Guide them! Mold their minds into Christ's, gracefully! If you can do this for me, you can do it for anyone. Begin to show them just how much better life truly is, by having the mindset of Jesus. In His name, amen.*

MONTH 2

"Teacher, which is the greatest commandment in the Law?"

"Jesus replied: 'Love the Lord your God with all your heart and with all your soul and with all your mind.' This is the first and greatest commandment. And the second is like it: 'Love your neighbor as yourself.' All the Law and the Prophets hang on these two commandments."

MATTHEW 22:36-40

DAY 31

GOD HAS A MINISTRY FOR YOU TO START!

"For God's gifts and his call are irrevocable."

ROMANS 11:29

There is a ministry inside you, something that only *you* can do. Ministries are no longer bound to the four walls of a church building, but instead, they are walking all over this planet...everywhere. Let me explain how to unlock *your* ministry.

When I get off work each day and head home, I park my car in the garage, walk through the mudroom door and get greeted by my dogs, Harley and Charlie, as well as my wife's kisses. I always look forward to this. Also, I look forward to *relaxing*. Relaxing does not come natural for me, I have to do it on purpose.

I'm the type of person who doesn't sit still. And if I do sit still, something has to really have my attention. From very early in the morning I'm goal oriented. I want to be accomplishing *something* at all times. I used to think something was wrong with me because of this, but as I got to know Jesus more and more, He taught me that this was actually a good thing! But only if I could keep it *in balance*.

The Bible says for us to be "well balanced" (see 1 Peter 5:8), but for years, I didn't understand how to do this because my mind never stopped. Used to be, I not only didn't know *how* to be well balanced, or, "shut my mind off," so I'd drink. Not anymore. Instead, the Holy Spirit has taught me to relax *on purpose*. That is, to consciously make myself sit still, and focus on *not* focusing. So part of my relaxation ritual is simply sitting on the couch with my wife in the evening, and watching TV. One of the shows we like to watch is *The 700 Club*.

I don't agree with *everything* they teach, but like any other ministry, preacher, or teacher—I don't have to. Instead, I simply eat the meat, and spit out the bones. My favorite segment of this show is the testimonials. So many people whom Jesus has changed their entire lives! Drug dealers, prostitutes, prison inmates, legalistic preachers, so on and so forth. But what I've noticed over the years is that *each* of these people in these testimonials, now have a ministry…a *personal* ministry.

Sure, some of them have become pastors and evangelists, but most of them are regular folk, like you and me, just living out their lives—only now, they are making a HUGE impact for God!

As I watched the show one day, there was a man who was caught up in the street life. He was selling drugs, gang banging, and whatnot—but then he had an encounter with Christ! Now, he has a ministry directed toward helping others get *out* of that lifestyle! How? By pointing them to Jesus, and using his own past for his purpose! NONE OF IT WAS WASTED!

Another testimonial of a personal ministry sprouting to life, was a man who was in prison, ready to commit suicide, and guess what? *He* had an encounter with Christ! What resulted was a personal ministry for those dealing with *his* same struggles—A MINISTRY BIRTHED IN A PRISON CELL! GOD IS SO CRAY-CRAY! But I like it! The Prophet Isaiah was right when he said, *"His ways are not like our ways"* (see Isaiah 55:8).

I also watched the testimonial of a man who was a director of porn movies. He had actually been attacked by demons while living that life, but God saved him! Now, he reaches out to those in the porn industry for Jesus! A ministry started in *filth*.

Another one: I saw the story of a man and a woman who were *both* incarcerated, and while in prison a little bitty white Christian lady with an English accent, helped them come to know Jesus through her non-judgmental kindness—she was the prison chaplain. This man and woman got married after they got out, and were so moved by this lady's sweet soul that they started a transitional house for newly released inmates—and then named it after her! Another ministry! BOOOOOOOOM!

I've also witnessed a stripper who was on the brink of giving up on life, but her *mom* had become a Christian and she was so inspired by her mother's amazing life change, that she too, came to know Jesus! This lady now has a ministry that reaches out to women who are stuck in the stripper life!

C'MON SOMEBODY! IS ANYONE OUT THERE TODAY?! CAN YOU *FEEEEEEEL* IT?! God *uses* what was meant for our harm for our testimonies! You didn't go through it for no reason! IT HAPPENED SO YOU CAN HELP OTHERS *WITH* IT! Don't sit still any longer!

SO MANY MINISTRIES! SO MANY DIFFERENT TYPES OF PEOPLE! So many ways that God uses what Satan meant to destroy our lives, FOR GOOD THINGS!

Friend, God wants to do the same for you. Yes...YOU! Those gifts on the inside of you are irrevocable, they've been specially designed and placed in there by God Himself (see Romans 11:29). There is *something* about you that is very rare to this planet. Something extremely *unique*. Only *you* can do it! Only *you* can accomplish it! I don't know what it is, but God sure does! And if you will begin to ask Him, He'll reveal it to you!

The secret to unlocking your own personal ministry is this: You gotta want it. Notice I didn't say, "You just gotta straighten out your life first." Nope. No way! That's what the religious Christians want you to believe, but God wants you to begin your journey...now...today...*right now*—this moment!

The Bible says that "God *chose* the foolish things of the world to shame the wise; God *chose* the weak things of the world to shame the strong" (1 Corinthians 1:27 my emphasis added).

Do you see that He *chooses* the foolish and the weak! THAT'S ME! WITHOUT CHRIST! AND AS YOU CAN SEE, WE ARE CALLED

TO DO GREAT THINGS! Jesus chose the "dumb" fishermen, not the "intelligent" Pharisees! Why? Because He was looking for humble people who would get to know *Him*. Jesus was looking for those who would make themselves *available* to Him. That's it.

So today, my friends, know this: Your life is a ministry. You have something *in* you that God wants to get *out* of you—and it's gonna change the course of history for the better, forever. Begin today!

A prayer for you: *Good morning Heavenly Father. Thank you for another day. Thank you for another shot at life! What an honor it is to be alive on planet earth! I feel so blessed to get to do what I do for you! Right now, I lift up all who are reading this, directly to you. For those who want to begin their own personal ministry, I ask that you infuse them with your strength! If they are afraid, teach them how to do it afraid—that's called courage! For those who don't feel qualified, teach them that they ARE qualified, because Jesus lives IN them! Help them to change many lives for the better, and to stock the halls of heaven with souls! In Jesus' magnificent name I pray this, amen!*

DAY 32

WHO'S OPINION MATTERS THE MOST?

*Elijah came near to all the people and said, "How
long will you hesitate between two opinions? If the
LORD is God, follow Him; but if Baal, follow him."*

SEE 1 KINGS 18:21

I used to be a slave to the opinion of others. If I heard that someone was talking bad about me, my heart would immediately sink, I'd scramble and fret—*then*, I'd do my best to try to *make* that person like me—or, I'd resent them, hold a grudge, and do my best to make sure *other* people didn't like *them*. That is, if I couldn't change their mind about *me*.

I was a puppet, the devil's puppet, completely blind to the fact that the opinion of people did not define me, at all. If the enemy can get us to worry about everyone's opinion of us, then he can keep us upset. Staying upset keeps us weak. Weakness then makes us *powerless*...if we are powerless, we won't be able to enjoy the abundant life Jesus came to give us! *And* we won't be doing anything good for the Kingdom of God!

So as Christians, there is a question we need to ask ourselves: *"Who's opinion matters the most?"* and then a follow-up question, *"Why?"* Once we establish the true answers in our hearts and minds, absolutely *everything* in our lives changes for the better!

The first answer is, "God's opinion matters the most!" But, do we *really* believe that? YES! HECK YES! This mindset will not happen instantaneously, it will take a lot of time and practice, but it *can* be developed! And it is developed by answering a follow-up question: "*Why* does God's opinion matter the most?"

Your mental and spiritual breakthrough will happen *after* the "why" question was answered, and here it is:

"God's opinion matters the most because He created me. And not just created me for no reason, but because He has a purpose for me being alive. He created me because He loves me! And He doesn't just KINDA love me, but He loves me so much that He would become a man, take on MY sin punishment, PAY IT OFF PERMANENTLY, and then give me access to a powerful life and heaven for free by grace through faith."

That's why God's opinion matters more than anyone's, it's because your value is so high to Him! So high, He just *had* to create you! Your parents did not *create* you, they were simply the vessels from which you came! YOU WERE GOD'S *PERSONAL* IDEA! OH MY GOSH, THIS SHOULD MAKE YOU FEEL LIKE A MILLION BUCKS! This should make His opinion SMASH everyone else's! This should make you put your chin up, your shoulders back, and be extremely confident!

The reality is, even the very *best* opinion of you should seem like a golf-clap to God's opinion! Why? BECAUSE GOD KNOWS YOU DEEPER THAN EVEN *YOU* KNOW YOU—AND HE *STILL* LOVES YOU, AND *WANTED* TO CREATE YOU!

YEAH BABY!! THIS MAKES ME WANT TO RUN AROUND THE HOUSE!!!

THIS is the seed that needs to be planted in you, which is... UNDERSTANDING YOUR FULL VALUE. And it is my goal with this ministry to plant that seed.

Friend, God loves you *despite* you. That means, no matter what you do or don't do—or how many *people* like or dislike you—God's love remains. *That's* where your identity is, because you *can't* lose this. *Nothing* can change your value to Him, not even your incorrect attitudes and actions. He loves you *so* much, He gave His Son to save you (see John 3:16).

If I could just get this fact embedded in your soul, this seed of your infinite value, *then* you will begin to take on the attitude of Christ! And that's what the Bible says we are to do!

"You must have the same attitude that Christ Jesus had" (Philippians 2:5).

So if we have the same attitude of Jesus then we are allowing Him to live through us, in turn, we will begin to love even those who have a negative opinion about us—because this is what Jesus does for everyone—yes, *everyone*.THIS MINDSET CHANGE WILL NOT HAPPEN WITHOUT *CONTINUING* TO ALLOW JESUS TO LIVE THROUGH YOU. Having a positive opinion about negative people is something you have to *practice* (as in "do repeatedly to get better at") *through* your faith. Your mind has to be renewed, little by little (see Romans 12:2).

But once you get this down pat, by understanding *who* lives in you, your *exuding* of Christ will be on a very high level as time goes by! You will then begin to enjoy your life to the fullest!

After that, negative opinions will be like a fly landing on your arm—it doesn't really bother you—you simply brush it off.

"But Matt, how do I do this?! What if I feel hate towards those who try to publicly and privately destroy me?!"

Friend, I understand. I know very well what that feels like. To overcome this, you must remember that the enemy wants you to *act* on your feelings in ways that the Holy Spirit doesn't approve of. He's attempting to set you up for failure. Jesus, on the other hand, wants you to instead *bless* those, and *pray* for those, who cause you harm (see Luke 6:28).

"BUT HOW?! I DON'T EVEN LIKE THEM!" Simple...begin to *think* of them with love. Just *think*...your feelings don't have to match up with your thoughts. Imagine if Jesus only went off of *His* feelings, we would not have our free salvation today!

So pay close attention to your thoughts and be on guard! The very moment the enemy places a *hint* of dislike or resentment in your mind toward someone, just say, "God, bless them," and mean it. Even if it's like eating a rotten lemon. Trust me, this works. Just say, "Jesus, help them to come to know you deeply," or, "Lord, show them how much you care for them," or, "God, give them the desires of their heart."

As you do this, you will be doing as the Apostle Paul said and "*Not being overcome by evil, but overcoming evil with good*" (see Romans 12:21, my emphasis added). This is the key! Don't take the bait, don't retaliate, but instead, OVERCOME EVIL WITH *GOOD* THINGS! The more evil that comes against you, the more *good* you should be exuding!

Little by little, by overcoming evil with good, and as the seed of your value in Christ grows in your heart—*and* as you respond like the Holy Spirit wants you to—you will begin to have a knee-jerk reaction of blessing those who try to hurt you, because you are letting Jesus live *through* you. But at the same time, you will begin to establish healthy boundaries in your life which will protect you. This happens when you finally understand your *extreme* value to God!

So today, my friends, know this: God has a very positive opinion of you! And even better, that positive opinion will never change! Even *you* can't change it! As you begin to realize this and *believe* this, as time goes by, you'll get to know Jesus better. In turn, you'll allow Him to live through you even more! After that, the opinion of others won't matter because you know who you are in Christ. Sure, we all like to be well-liked, but we can't control the opinion of people. Jesus teaches us to not be upset about anything we can't control—or, to find our identity in anything we can lose.

You will *never* lose God's love for you in Christ, and He will *never* have negative things to say about you! Begin to enjoy this confident, loving, positive opinion about yourself today! Because it's the truth!

A prayer for you: *Well good morning, Lord! Man, I slept GOOD last night! As I got up in the middle of the night to use the restroom, I was just thinking to myself, what a blessing this nice, cozy home is. Thank you so much for my home for. And thank you for teaching me my value in YOUR opinion of me. It's changed my life. Right now, I lift up all who are reading this, directly to you. For those who struggle severely with worrying about the opinion of people, deliver them from that strangling mindset. That used to be me, and it was pure torture from hell. Who cares what people think, when YOU think good, hopeful, positive things about us—EVEN IN OUR DARKEST HOURS! So, PLEASE, begin to teach these dear readers the amazing value they have to you—no matter what! Make it to where NOTHING and NOBODY can change their minds about how much you love them! In Jesus' confident name I pray, amen.*

DAY 33

ARE YOU LIVING FOR TODAY

*"I have learned the secret of being
content in any and every situation…"*

SEE PHILIPPIANS 4:12

For so many years I lived a life of discontentment. I was never truly happy, I never felt accomplished, and really, I was never satisfied with anything or anyone—myself included.

The *overall* picture of my life was always changing and getting better, but my *mind* was not. If you zoomed in to my life even closer, the main crux of my discontentment was the fact that I didn't know *how* to enjoy what was presently going on around me—I was always wanting to go on to something else.

My problem was I didn't know how to enjoy "the moment."

What's strange is I can remember this pattern beginning even as a kid. I'd think to myself:

"If I could just have my own room, then I'll be happy."

"If I could be popular in school, then I know life will be good."

"If Mom and Dad would get back together, then life would be great."

"If I could just turn 18! Then I can move out, and I can finally enjoy myself!"

This continued on into adulthood:

"If I could just get Jennifer to date me, then life would be wonderful."

"If I could just move out of my father-in-law's basement, I'd be happy."

"If I could just build my own home and live in a nice neighborhood, then things would be so much better."

"If I could just get in shape, then I'd be satisfied."

"If I could just get my company to grow, then we'd have money, then we'd finally be happy."

I was never satisfied. Ever. Period. The enemy had me convinced that something *always* needed to be different before I could enjoy my life. Eventually, I thought porn, drinking, and video games would fix this. Nope.

After none of that worked, I thought that becoming a religious Christian, shutting off the world, telling people, "STOP SINNING OR GO TO HELL!" while placing all my time and energy in making sure I *never* messed up (and if I did, I would beat myself up for a week)—or if I read my Bible at least an hour each day—MAYBE, *FINALLY*, this Christian stuff would fix this terrible longing in my heart!…No way.

Religion only made things even *more* miserable because it's impossible to live up to so many Christians' "idea of perfection"—which is *their* own works, or their works *added* to Jesus' finished work. What they don't understand is they haven't earned anything. All they have, has been given to them for free—just like you and me. They are in for a surprise when they meet Jesus and He reveals their works won't buy them a fancier spot in heaven. In Christ, we are all equal.

The devil even had me sold on the incorrect idea that if I never missed church (while getting mad at people who wouldn't *go* to church)–*this* would finally take care of the "never satisfied feeling" inside me! And *worse*, I thought if I *never* sinned again, I'd finally be able to reach this dangling carrot of contentment!

But it didn't...none of this gave me what what I was looking for. I soon found out that I couldn't *not* sin—that only Jesus had this ability, and that it's simply my job to rest in His grace, do my best, and enjoy this free gift of spiritual perfection in what He did *for* me—for free. The preachers who are telling everyone they will never sin again if they are truly saved, need to be smacked...gently, of course. It doesn't work like that. They are damaging the souls of believers by keeping their *complete* forgiveness hostage. This method also rejects the lost. They are making Jesus look like a loan-shark—someone we *can't* pay back and He's gonna hurt us bad for it. So if that's you, please, stop.

I could sit here and type up pages and pages of stuff that I thought would fix the emptiness on the inside of me—that one "*thing*" to make me *finally* feel content! All I wanted was to *not* always be wanting more—or longing to be somewhere else!

Who could teach me how to enjoy the moment?! Who could teach me how to live for *today*?!

Jesus.

By Him teaching me my value, through what He's done for me, Christ began to reveal *in* me how to see the beauty of *every* moment in my life! EVERY moment! Not just when things are good, or when I accomplish a feat—BUT RIGHT NOW! TODAY! THIS SECOND!

So I'm no longer saying such dumb things as, "I wish I was living in the good old days"—NO! TODAY is the good old days! TODAY! I'm no longer looking ahead, relying on TOMORROW to make me feel content on the inside. NO! "*TODAY* IS THE DAY THE LORD HAS MADE! I WILL REJOICE AND BE GLAD IN IT!" (Psalm 118:24). TODAAAAAAAAAAY!

We *must* begin to thank God for today. "But Matt, what about—" No. TODAY. My friend, no matter what…today. Jesus has taught me how precious every *breath* is, how blessed I am to even have a *beating heart*, and how *honored* I am to be alive on His awesome Creation.

He wants to do the same for you.

So *today*, my friends, know this: Jesus wants to teach you how to have an abundant life, a life of complete contentment. Like the Apostle Paul said, "I have learned the secret to being content in any and every situation. I can to all things through Christ who strengthens me" (see Philippians 4:12,13). Your strength, your enjoyment, for today, is Christ in you—the Holy Spirit. He's there. Once you begin to combine everything *you* are, with everything *He* is, right now, this *very* moment…you'll have it!

A prayer for you: Say this with me, "*Jesus, help me. Help me to begin to understand you better. Help me to remove anything in my life that creates stress, discontentment, grumpiness, or removes joy from my soul. Help me to shake off these loose articles to where all that is left is YOU, and what YOU want in my life! And for the things, people, and situations which still attempt to cause discontentment and trouble—that you are ALLOWING in my life to strengthen me and hone my faith—show me how to handle everything and everyone, with grace. Teach me how to exude the same grace that you exude towards me. I want to be just like you in all of my actions and attitudes. I want to enjoy the miracle that is my life, each and every day. Thank you. Amen.*"

Day 34

I Command You To Love Me!

"This is my command: Love each other." ~*Jesus*

JOHN 15:17

Most of us have seen the Disney movie *Beauty and the Beast*, which was originally released in 1991. In one scene, the Beast is standing outside Belle's bedroom door in his mansion, after kidnapping her, *commanding* her to come downstairs to eat dinner with him.

He slams his fist on the door, *WHAM! WHAM! WHAM* "Hurry up and come down to dinner!" Lumière, the French candle-stick, tries to help him woo Belle, "Master, I could be wrong, but that may not be the best way to win the girl's affections."

However, the Beast isn't having it! He *needs* her to love him so that the curse can be broken, and he can return to being a normal man. He slams his fist on the door again, and yells at her, only in a fake, *softer* voice, "WOULD YOU PLEASE JOIN ME FOR DINNER?"

Belle, petrified, says, "I'm not hungry," from the other side of the door.

"FINE! THEN GO AHEAD AND STAAAAAAAARVE!!!!!!" the beast screams, and storms off.

Do you remember that scene from this classic cartoon movie? Sometimes I want to say that very same thing to Grace when she doesn't want to eat what Jennifer has cooked for dinner. But the Beast so desperately wants the girl to love him, he tries to *force* her to. We see the results of how that works out—it doesn't.

Love cannot be forced. If love *could* be forced, then it wouldn't be called love—it would be called *duty*. Duty is not love, and love is not duty. There is no other way! Jesus knew this, that's why he put all of the rules and regulations aside, and instead, He focused on teaching the *root* of a good, abundant life...love. Love for God, love for others, and love for yourself. We must have all three!

If we can begin to position love in the proper place in our hearts, by making it the very bedrock of our lives, then everything else falls right into place! Paul said no matter what he does for God or for people, without love, none of it means anything (see 1 Corinthians 13). When we *choose* to love, God's will is being done on earth as it is in heaven.

In Matthew 22, one of the religious people, a Pharisee, a person who didn't care about love but still knew every rule and law of Old Testament Scripture, he tried to trip up Jesus with a trick-question, "Teacher, which is the greatest commandment of the Law?" (Matthew 22:36). Jesus replied with the best answer ever:

"'Love the Lord your God with all your heart and with all your soul and with all your mind.' This is the first and greatest commandment. And the second is like it: 'Love your neighbor as yourself.' All the Law and the Prophets hang on these two commandments" (Matthew 22:37-40).

THAT'S IT! That's how you do what Jesus did, and still does! This is how you allow Him to live *through* you!

1. Love God with all of your heart, soul, and mind.
2. Love your neighbor as yourself.

And as you can see, if you love yourself as God loves you—*which is a lot*—only then can you truly fulfill the second command, which is to love your neighbor *as* yourself! You can't hate yourself, and *love* your neighbor! It's impossible! You *must* understand your value! And your "neighbor" is *everyone*—not just your next-door neighbor. YOU GOTTA LOVE YOURSELF AND *SEE* YOURSELF AS VALUABLE! BECAUSE YOU ARE! Not in an arrogant way, but in a way that is *important*. You ARE important!!!

So after Jesus was asked, what's the "best law" of God, He *then* does something which made this arrogant, stiff, know-it-all religious person want to pull out his hair! HE SUMMED UP *THE ENTIRE OLD TESTAMENT*–IN ONE WORD!

LOVE!

LOVE!

LOOOOOOOOOOOOVE!

It was LOVE that compelled God to CREATE US! (Ephesians 1:4). It was LOVE that compelled Jesus to come to earth! (John 3:16). And even more than that, God doesn't *just* love us, but LOVE IS WHAT HE IS! (1 John 4:8).

...And He lives in *you*, in full, if you believe in Jesus as your Savior. So you have this *same ability* on the inside, which will sprout up and out...on the *outside*...the more you allow Christ to live *through* you each day. As you get to know Him more and more through His Word and Spirit, your mind will become renewed, and *then* you will *exude love* easily and organically.

So today, my friends, do this—and please do it authentically and genuinely: Love. *Choose* to love. Make a decision, right *now*, to love God, love others, and love yourself. After all, Jesus loved *you* so much, He made a way for you to become spiritually perfect in our Heavenly Father's eyes—at the Cross. Place your faith in His blood which was shed for *your* sins—yours—and enjoy that love! And after that, begin to give this love away to everyone, absolutely everyone! Not just to those who love *you*, but even to those who don't! Do this, and you'll be *just like Jesus!* Who is confident, hopeful, and *always* loving!

A prayer for you: *Heavenly Father, today I want to thank you for your everlasting love for me. Through Christ, you made a way for me to be spotless, and I'm forever grateful. Thank you for teaching me how to love others, like you love me. Help me to do this in even greater ways. Right now, I lift up all who are reading this, directly to you. For those who don't understand your love, please teach them. Begin to send new people into their lives who will help them with this. Begin to teach them that love is not just a feeling, but something we practice all day long. Teach them Jesus' type of love, which is unconditional; but also, because we are so valuable to you, teach us how to refuse to allow others to abuse us. Teach us how to set healthy boundaries, and enforce those boundaries with love—like you do for us. I ask that you instill a brand new life of love, in each and every person who wants it today! In Christ's loving name, amen!*

DAY 35

WHY WAS JESUS BORN?

"For to us a child is born, to us a son is
given, and the government will be on
his shoulders. And he will be called
Wonderful Counselor, Mighty God,
Everlasting Father, Prince of Peace."

ISAIAH 9:6 (WRITTEN 700 YEARS BEFORE JESUS' BIRTH)

"SANTAAAAAAAA!!!!" Most of us know this line from the movie *Elf*, as Buddy squirms with excitement, thinking Santa is in the mall. Most of us can also picture the squirrel on the back of Clark Griswold's jacket, as his dad yells out, "Squirrel!" while the entire family runs crazy throughout the house trying to get the squirrel outside—or, to "smash it with a hammer," as Clark says. In the madness, eventually the squirrel leaps onto the shallow, annoying neighbor, Margo, RIGHT IN THE FACE, as the front door is opened up and Clark quickly closes it with a smile of contentment.

The Christmas season is such a great time of the year! It's cozy! It's extra friendly!…It's…*giving*. Even some of the most greedy people open up their pocketbooks, hearts, and homes for others during the holidays.

And I believe this time of year is so giving because God's Spirit hangs extra heavy over planet earth during Christmas time. God is a *Spirit* of giving, He loves to give! There's nothing we can do to imitate God more *authentically* than when we give, with love. And that spirit rubs off on people who don't even believe in Him, during the month of December.

That *something* you feel in the air?…It's your Creator. He's giving you a taste of His character—a smell of heaven. And *why* is God so giving? Because He is loving—and not *just* loving—but the Bible says that He actually *is* love (see 1 John 4:8). LOVE IS WHO GOD IS! And love, *gives*.

God loves us *so* much, He created a place for us to have life! PLANET EARTH! He loves us so much, He *created* us—actual *HUMAN BEINGS*—and He took it a step further, creating us in *His* image! We look like God! (See Genesis 1:27). HE JUST *HAD* TO HAVE US! And God loves us *so* much, that He gave us His only begotten Son, Jesus, to save us, and to make us just like Him in spirit! (See John 3:16). *Begotten Son*, as in, *from His very own spiritual loin!* Jesus is the only man to ever have the DNA of the Creator of the universe!

The reason why Jesus was born is because God *also* wanted to give us…*rest*. God came to earth in human form to give all of humanity, rest. For myself, as a person who didn't understand *how* to rest, how to just sit still and relax, I needed this badly. As someone who always had to be doing something, accomplishing a goal, working—SOMETHING, SOMETHING, SOMETHING—AT ALL TIMES—more than anything else in my life, I needed rest! We all do. We all need *internal* rest. Jesus gives this to us, freely, at our taking.

God knew we were going to need rest; not just rest from sin, addictions, stress, and fear—but rest from religious expectations, church work, and impressing others. That's why Jesus came. He said so Himself, "Come to me, all you who are weary and burdened, and I will give you *rest*…My yoke is *easy* and my burden is *light* (Matthew 11:28,30 my emphasis added).

As you rest in Him, you will then produce an abundance of spiritual fruit—the Bible calls it "fruit of the Spirit." Galatians 5 and 1 Corinthians 13, give you a full list of this fruit. Here are a few pieces of it:

Love, joy, peace, patience, kindness, gentleness, SELF-control; you won't be jealous, you won't brag on anything that doesn't really matter, you won't be disrespectful or dishonorable, you won't stir up trouble, you won't gossip or be happy when bad things happen to other people—and you will even love your enemies.

This organic spiritual fruit growth *only* happens in a *state* of rest—in a state of resting in God's *grace*—you cannot force it. His grace is Christ *in* us, infused *with* our spirits. When you finally realize everything in your relationship with God has been free from the beginning of you *simply believing* in Jesus as your Savior—and that it will always *stay* free—no matter what your flesh may do, you've got it!

We didn't "work" to get anything from God, so we can't "work to keep" what He's freely given. From the very millisecond you believed, your adoption into the family of God was given to you out of love, *from* your loving Heavenly Father (see Ephesians 1:5, Galatians 4:4-7). The only thing you should now be striving for is to *enter the rest of God* (see Hebrews 4:11), and that rest, is Jesus.

Fruit of the Spirit grows in abundance, *naturally*, from entering this place of rest in His grace—because it's happening from the inside *out*. When you try to force it, you will not produce fruit of the Spirit. But when you find rest in what *Jesus* has done, *only*, you will then produce, give away, and trip all over *His* fruit! *Then* you will go on to do more work for God than you've ever done before! And in the proper way—His way.

This is why Jesus was born! To give you, yes *you*, rest! Any pressure that you may be feeling in your life is *not* coming from God, but instead, from others, yourself, or the enemy. So begin to relax in Christ and enjoy what He's finished for you! And be sure to thank the Father today, for such a wonderful gift of love! JESUS!

A prayer for you: *Today is Christmas! Happy birthday Jesus! I know this isn't the actual day you were born, but it is the day we celebrate it! So thank you! And thank you Father for sending us this little baby who would grow up and save the world. WOW! I CAN'T FATHOM*

THIS! And thank you, Jesus, for teaching us how to live, love, and forgive—AND HOW TO GIVE! Thank you for giving us your Spirit, and continuing to live inside us after we invite you in. Right now, I lift up all who are reading this, directly to you. For those who may not be having such a great day, wrap your arms around them and help them to feel your love. Let them know you are with them, and that you have good plans for their lives. Reassure them in their spirit that everything will be okay, one day soon. I also pray for those who may be stuck in a pattern of religious works, those who don't know how to rest; those who think they gotta keep striving to earn your approval—GIVE THEM THE REST THEY NEED! Give them a sense of peace, comfort, confidence, and a sound mind, which is found in knowing Jesus has finished everything; and now we can simply enjoy that gift. In His name I pray, amen.

DAY 36

How Can I Become Wise?

*"If any of you lacks wisdom, you should ask
God, who gives generously to all without
finding fault, and it will be given to you."*

JAMES 1:5

For most of my life, I've lacked wisdom. Even though I thought I was wise, I wasn't. I was simply "wise in my own eyes." Sure, I had special gifts and talents (which I mostly hid from God, and used for myself); I was good at managing money, rather big or little (but I was greedy); I was self-motivated (self-motivated to sin a lot, and have excuses for those sins). On and on, I was "this" or "that," and *bragging* was a big part of my life.

"Look at what all *I've* done!"

"Look at what *I've* got!"

"Look a how smart *I* am!"

"Blah, blah, blah...and blah." Old Matt thought way too highly of himself and his abilities. Most of my bragging was *on* myself, that is, *my* accomplishments, and not on God. And to top it off, I would get mad at *you*, if you didn't acknowledge my triumphs! I was dumb! I was not wise.

The great Christian writer, A.W. Tozer, said in his book, *The Pursuit of God*:

"Whoever defends himself will have himself for his defense, and he will have no other; but let him come defenseless before the Lord and he will have for his defender no less than God Himself."

Ain't that the truth! When we are *not* wise, we place *ourselves* in our defense. The problem with this stupid method is that *we* are extremely flawed—God is not. Eventually, as we continue on in this manner, a great crash will happen in our lives—a crash that I've personally experienced.

This *crash* comes to everyone who doesn't build their lives on Christ—rich, poor, male, female, old or young—it's gonna happen one day. Why? Because God wants us to *choose* to build our lives on Jesus! IT'S A CHOICE! Unlike other religions, the one true religion, Christianity, our God lets us choose to love Him back. He never forces us. **Side note: Our God actually died *for* us, He doesn't require that we die for *Him*, unlike other fake gods that Satan has established in this world.**

So we must choose to *not* build our lives on ourselves but instead on Him. In return for this choice we get wisdom. My previously arrogant lifestyle was wisdom-free. It took God pulling back everything (and everyone) I had formed my identity in—other than Him—for me to finally realize this! But I *still* had to choose this.

Some people will have absolutely every part of their lives shaken up by God—because He's trying to get things prioritized—and they *still* reject Him. I was *nearly* that person! I had the very best excuses! And I blamed God and people for *all* my troubles, just like a bratty teenager blames their loving parents and siblings!

"God, if you're *so* good, then why won't you fix this?! I'm doing all this stuff for you, and it's not working! Fix it and hurry up!" This was how I thought!

The reality was, God *was* fixing things, mainly my mindset. He wanted me to begin allowing Christ to live *through* me, and that's what hurt so much because I didn't want to. *"I know better than Him,"* was one of my "secret" thoughts. I always had a dumb back-up plan, and I refused to trust His ways.

When God kept saying, "Let me build you a new life," I threw a fit. That was *un*-wise of me. Jesus talks about wise and foolish "builders" in Matthew 7:24-27—those who did and *didn't* build their lives on Christ, and the results of that:

"Therefore everyone who hears these words of mine and puts them into practice is like a wise man who built his house on the rock. The rain came down, the streams rose, and the winds blew and beat against that house; yet it did not fall, because it had its foundation on the rock. But everyone who hears these words of mine and does not put them into practice is like a foolish man who built his house on sand. The rain came down, the streams rose, and the winds blew and beat against that house, and it fell with a great crash."

There's the crash! MY HOUSE, MY LIFE, MY *EVERYTHING*, FELL WITH THE GREATEST CRASH *EVER!* It got so bad, the devil had me convinced that *suicide* was the best option!

But it was in the rubble of that great crash, where Jesus cleared the ground away. He got out His supernatural shovel, and started to dig. Once He had dug down very deep, Jesus began to pour new footings. HE MADE THEM STRONG. He made sure they'd never move by simply teaching me my value in His unconditional love! Next, He poured the *best* concrete—His Word—*into* this foundation, and then reinforced it with the strongest rebar ever…The Blood of The Cross. Lastly, He *personally* hand-crafted a brand new structure that my entire life is now built upon—HIM!

Just Jesus!

HIM! HIM! *HIM!*

We gotta get this right, *first!* CHRIST IS THE STRONGEST FOUNDATION YOU CAN POSSIBLY HAVE! NOTHING ELSE IS MORE STURDY! HE IS OUR CREATOR IN THE FLESH! HE IS OUR SAVIOR, OUR WAY TO HEAVEN, AND OUR GUIDE TO AN ABUNDANT LIFE, RIGHT NOW!

Your ability to even *have* an ability is because of *His* choice to make it possible! YOUR EXISTENCE IS IN HIS HANDS! Just as a baby is cradled in their mother's arms, *everything* about your next heartbeat depends on Christ's desires!

WE ARE HERE BECAUSE OF HIS WAYS, HIS TRUTH, AND HIS LIFE! So when we finally begin to do as He said and "practice like a wise man who built his house on a rock," *then* everything changes! This is where true wisdom begins. Not in ourselves alone, but in Christ, fully. Everything else in our lives cascades from Him *in* us.

Here are a few tips I've learned over the years about godly wisdom, I believe they will help you too:

1. **You must destroy your pride.** This was a major overhauling in my life. Although I'm so much better than I used to be, I'll never be 100% pride-free until I'm with God in heaven, and out of this body. Due to my God-given overly-competitive, aggressive personality, I have to be *deliberately conscious* of pride—and I realize that. It is a daily thing (if not hourly) for me to WILLINGLY accept, that I need God's grace to overcome my pride. Because I don't like to be told what to do or how to do it (because my flesh thinks he knows it all, and my mind is still being renewed), when such things happen, I have to STOP for a moment and weigh my options. The Holy Spirit usually says, "Is this worth it?" Sometimes it is, but 9 out of 10 times it's not. So through God's

grace in me I try to do my best to become the *opposite* of prideful while still staying confident (this *is* possible). I *consciously* become humble, to destroy a prideful moment. To do this, I'll simply say, "God, help me," and He does! He always doles out extra grace when needed!

2. **Be teachable.** Again, this is a branch of *humility* (the opposite of pride) that you must develop if you want godly wisdom. If you think you know it all, you are once again relying on yourself. And no, I'm not saying that everyone is always right, but neither are we. Because of this fact—that we are all *flawed creations*—we can always give other people respect and listen to what they have to say, even if we don't agree. Ultimately, it is the Holy Spirit who will be the one to instill *His* truths on our hearts and in our minds. In the meantime, don't get infuriated with those who don't believe exactly like you. Instead, keep your chin up, look people in the eye, be respectful, and show them grace and love. Always listen to others with a gentle mindset, no matter who they are.

3. **Don't gamble on your future.** What I mean by this is make good choices which will benefit you and your loved ones for *tomorrow*. If you are smoking cigarettes all day long, getting drunk, getting high, overeating, refusing to get regular exercise, living with a short fuse, cheating on your spouse, watching porn, refusing to get married after years of dating, blowing money, being legalistic, or _____ (you fill in the blank)…you are risking the joy, fulfillment, and security of your future, not just for you but for those who *love* you. Begin to ask God for help with all of these situations, and He will send new people into your life who will help you change these things, as well as give you new desires to *want* to change them. Also, begin to seek out Jesus' ways daily, in prayer and study, and He will start to transform and renew your mind into something strong, beautiful, and prepped for the future! You will begin to have a wise mind!

4. **Be decisive.** Wisdom begins with humility; humility in yourself (not disrespect), and *trust* in God. So when you trust in God, by allowing Jesus to live through you—to the point of severe pain through growth—this builds your confidence in your Creator! And confidence in your Creator…*drumroll*…makes you a *very* decisive person! Because of your trust in God, you will rarely second-guess yourself because you know that God always has your back! So even if you *do* make a dumb move, or take an incorrect step in the wrong direction (like I do all the time), God will somehow use it for good! *SO BE DECISIVE AND MOVE FORWARD! YOU'VE GOT NOTHING TO WORRY ABOUT! EVER! YOU ONLY HAVE WISDOM TO GAIN! LET'S GOOOOOOOOO!!!*

A prayer for you: *Heavenly Father, thank you for your wisdom. I ask that you continue to teach me how to handle all of my life situations with YOUR wisdom, until you call me Home. Thank you. Right now, I lift up all these dear readers, directly to you. For those who are extremely frustrated with everything and everyone around them, give them peace in your wisdom. Teach them how to grow in your humility, which, in reality is actually STRENGTH! Guide them as they begin to walk OUT Christ in them, and change the world for the better through your wisdom! In Jesus' name I pray, amen.*

DAY 37

FORGIVING OTHERS, REPENTANCE, AND SPIT

"Come and let us reason together…"

SEE ISAIAH 1:18

Wat does God really say about "forgiving others," "repentance," and being "spit out of His mouth"? Here is a conversation I had on social media that I believe will help you understand all three subjects much better:

"Matt, are you saying after you give your life to Christ and your sins are forgiven and forgotten that when we stumble (and we will as long as we live in this human body), we don't need to ask God for forgiveness?…Jesus' example of prayer, specifically the one called, *the Lord's prayer*, teaches us to ask God to 'forgive us our debts (trespasses) as we forgive our debtors their debts (those who trespass against us), and to pray this daily. Jesus says He is our intercessor who sits at the right hand of God. My relationship with Christ is based on wanting to please Him in the living of my life. What's your opinion of those who harden their hearts and no longer care about pleasing Him? Where do they stand? Some theologians say 'Well, they never knew Christ to begin with or they would feel convicted.' Others say 'They are in danger of being spewed out of His mouth on the day of judgement if they don't recognize their their sins and repent.' What is your take on this?"

"Good morning. First off, sure, we *should* ask God for forgiveness, just like if you do another person wrong, you ask *them* for forgiveness—it's just the right thing to do. But asking for forgiveness doesn't make you any *more* forgiven, or not asking, makes you any less forgiven. We are forgiven once and for all. That's what Hebrews 10:10 says. Our asking doesn't save us anyway, but faith in Jesus' blood *as* our saving (see Hebrews 9:22).

As for your next question, I went ahead and read all of Matthew 6, where your first verse is taken from. It's a very legitimate question. You mixed two verses together, from two different books, you said, 'the Lord's prayer teaches us to ask God to forgive us our debts (trespasses) as we forgive our debtors their debts (those who trespass against us), and to pray this daily.'—That's Matthew 6:12; and Jesus doesn't say to pray this daily. But He does say 'give us our daily bread' in the previous verses.

However, if you read this in context, and you start from the beginning of the chapter, Jesus isn't speaking to those who believe in Him, but instead, to the hypocritical Pharisees—those who had religious pride in their hearts, and the only reason why they did anything was to get attention.

This is 'pre-Cross,' so Jesus is still teaching Law, to show how impossible it is to live up to—that we need someone to do it *for* us, a Savior. Remember, God doesn't grade on a curve. Christianity is not a self-improvement program, but a spiritual death and resurrection. It's "obey ALL LAW," or you are a complete failure (see James 2:10, Romans 3).

And not only does He say, 'And forgive us our debts, as we also have forgiven our debtors,' but in verses 14 and 15, He goes on to say, 'For if you forgive other people when they sin against you, your heavenly Father will also forgive you. But if you do not forgive others their sins, your Father will not forgive your sins.'

This is obviously not true for Christians because *after* the Cross, Paul teaches us the opposite; he says we *should* forgive, because we are *already* forgiven:

> *'Be kind and compassionate to one another, forgiving each other, just as in Christ God forgave you.' (Ephesians 4:32)*

> *'Bear with each other and forgive one another*
> *if any of you has a grievance against someone.*
> *Forgive as the Lord forgave you.' (Colossians 3:13)*

Both times he says, *'forgave,'* that is past tense.

When Jesus said that in Matthew 6, He was speaking to the wolves in sheep's clothing who looked at *themselves* as their *own* righteousness; all you gotta do is read all of Matthew 6 from the beginning, and you'll be able to discern that. He wasn't talking to those who had faith in Him.

God doesn't forgive us because *we* are great forgivers, but because *He* is. So much so, that He gave us His best in His Son to pay off our forgiveness sin problem once and for all. Just imagine if God had a stipulation of not letting us in heaven because of some hidden resentment? There would be millions of Christians not make it—if not billions. So that verse you referenced is a law which was being taught by Christ to set up the Pharisees, this is not meant for Christians, but for those who think they can forgive their way into heaven—we must have a Savior.

The second half of your comment, 'Jesus says He is our intercessor who sits at the right hand of God,' is from Romans 8:34, and here is that verse in full:

> *'Who then is the one who condemns? No one. Christ Jesus*
> *who died—more than that, who was raised to life—is at*
> *the right hand of God and is also interceding for us.'*

This is once again proving that we are *not* condemned *because* of Jesus—so this is in favor of the fact that we don't live by a law of 'forgiving others so God forgives us.' Should we forgive? ABSOLUTELY! But we don't always pull this off. Thanks be to Jesus who no longer condemns us, but represents us at God's side.

Next, you asked my opinion on people hardening their hearts. God can decide to do *anything* to achieve a much greater, *eternal* purpose—He's God, He can do whatever He wants—but I don't believe God purposefully hardens anyone's heart, and this is just my opinion. Because if He did, then free will would be gone. Instead, He gives us opportunities to *not* harden our hearts; this is why the Bible says 'CHOOSE this day whom you will serve' (see Joshua 24:15), and, 'I set before you life and death, CHOOSE LIFE' (see Deuteronomy 30:19). It's up to us to choose.

However, God sees the beginning from the end because He is not bound by time—we are—so He knows what will happen before it happens, just like we know what will happen if we record the Super Bowl and watch it the next day, already knowing the end result. Does us watching that recording cause the players to make different choices? No. It already happened and they freely made their own choices. But *we* are not bound by the *time* of that actual event *on* that recording. Same with us and God. Time can't contain His greatness, even though we *are* still contained by time, ourselves.

You then combined several Scriptures together toward the end of your comment: 'they are in danger of being spewed out of His mouth on the day of judgement if they don't recognize their sins and repent'. So part of that is found in Revelation 3:16:

> *'So, because you are lukewarm—neither hot nor*
> *cold—I am about to spit you out of my mouth.'*

First off, this is not referring to God spitting Christians out of His mouth on the day of our judgment—and honestly, even if God *did* spit us out of His mouth, because of Christ, He would slurp us right back up. If you read this in context, you can understand what it means. And the movie *War Room* has a great demonstration of it as well, when Miss Clara hands Elizabeth a lukewarm cup of coffee. Nobody likes to drink anything lukewarm. You either want a hot drink, when it's cold—or a cold drink, when it's hot—both are satisfying and make changes to how you feel. A lukewarm drink does nothing.

However this is not saying that Christians will be rejected by God because Jesus says that He will *never* leave us—and that, even if we are faithless, He remains faithful (see Matthew 28:20, 2 Timothy 2:13). The New Covenant is between the Father and the Son, NOT US. It's a promise between *them*, and *we* are simply the beneficiaries who receive it by grace through faith. We don't create it, or sustain it, we simply *accept it* as the truth for our sins (see Hebrews 8:13, Ephesians 2:8,9, Romans 10:9).

And 'as long as Jesus lives He is able to save us completely' (Hebrews 7:25), and He is *not* dying again. So we can rest assured that we will be forever saved, through HIM, not ourselves.

The next part of you comment is another verse, you say, 'on the day of judgement if they don't recognize their sins and repent…' This is quite a few verses all mashed together. But first of all, once you die, and you're in God's presence, it's too late to repent. Second, NO CHRISTIAN will be judged, but instead, Jesus has already judged us NOT GUILTY, because of our faith in Him. Jesus tells us this in John 3:17,18—that only unbelievers will be judged, not us:

> 'For God did not send his Son into the world to condemn the world, but to save the world through him. Whoever believes in him is not condemned, but whoever does not believe stands condemned already because they have not believed in the name of God's one and only Son.'

There is not a single verse in the Bible that says a *Christian* will be judged. Those are lies from Satan to try to make us afraid of God, or to think that we can possibly do something to remove our guilt. We can't. Only Jesus can—and did.

As for repentance? Again, the modern legalistic churches have turned this word into a law—as if we can possibly keep track of every sin, and then repent, and if we don't we are still condemned. This goes against the gospel and is a lie. Are we forgiven or not? Is Jesus a liar, or not? We gotta make up our minds.

The truth is *He* finished everything for us (see John 19:30). In our spirits, we died *with* Him, and was *raised* with Him as well, in spirit (see Romans 6, Galatians 2:20). We are *new* Creations *in* Him (see 2 Corinthians 5:17). We don't STOP sinning to be saved, we believed that Jesus has saved us (see John 3:16, Romans 10:9). So we don't STAY stopped sinning, to STAY saved. This is madness and creates fear. God's love for us is perfect and casts out all fear because fear has to do with punishment (see 1 John 4), and because of Jesus, we are *not* going to be eternally punished.

The Cross, and our *faith* in it as the truth, is the only sin that is required to be repented of in order to be saved. The only unforgivable sin is *not* accepting Christ's Spirit into yours through believing (see Matthew 12:31). So repentance is a two-step process—and one *follows* the other, they are not combined:

1. We repent of unbelief in Jesus as our Savior in order to be saved.
2. *Because* we are *already saved*, by grace through faith, we repent of incorrect attitudes and actions so that Christ can live *through* us (see Galatians 5:22, 23)—not to be saved again and again, or to stay saved.

I hope this helps you understand my teaching a little better."

A prayer for you: *Heavenly Father, thank you for opening up my eyes to the truth of your loving, graceful, merciful gospel. Thank you for what Jesus has done for me! Thank you for teaching me the truth* *of my true identity, which is Christ IN me, forever! What a good God that you would become one with me! Right now, I lift up all who are reading this, directly to you. For those who have been incorrectly taught about WHO you really are, help them. Help them to stop focusing on what THEY do or DON'T do, and to START focusing on what Jesus HAS done—and continues to do—FOR THEM, which is save them COMPLETELY. Open up their minds to understand this truth, that you love us SO much, you paid off ALL our debts once and for all IN Jesus. And now, all we must do each day is wake up and say, "Thank you. Live through me. I'm ready." In Christ's name I pray, amen.*

DAY 38

BEWARE OF THE MEAN CHRISTIANS

"We are therefore Christ's ambassadors, as though
God were making his appeal through us..."

SEE 2 CORINTHIANS 5:20

Nobody likes to be told they *can't* do something. I was the worst with this—especially when it came to Christianity. "Who do you think you are, telling me what to do?!" was how I thought. And then I'd do the *opposite*, just out of spite. And guess what? I was *saved—although* I was a rebellious Christian.

My problem was, because I hadn't yet grown in my relationship with Jesus, or began to have my mind renewed, I didn't really love Him. I just used Him for His saving of my soul from hell. Believe it or not, this happens a lot. I'm proof. So many of us have had our faith established by the fear of hell, rather than on the good things that come from a loving relationship with Christ. I'm here to help you get this in order.

We must *stop* being afraid of hell, *after* we accept Jesus' forgiveness, and instead, *enjoy* an actual relationship with Him! How do we do this? By finally realizing our actions and attitudes don't *get* us saved—either *good* or *lack* of bad—only our faith in Jesus' forgiveness does (see Ephesians 2:8,9).

However, used to be, *I* was still too full of pride to understand this. That, and I needed my mind to be renewed through His God's graceful truth. This would be the only way I'd be able to make any serious changes in my life.

Sure, my spirit was saved, but my mind, mouth, and emotions had some catching up to do. The good news is, the Holy Spirit is a good teacher, and He's very patient with us.

Side note: *So many preachers teach that once you get saved, you will <u>immediately</u> change your ways, or else you aren't really saved. That's not necessarily true. Your SPIRIT is saved immediately, by grace through faith, but your soul and flesh need to learn how to live BY your new spirit, which is Christ in you—He is actually INFUSED with your spirit! (See Ephesians 3:16, Acts 2:17, Hebrews 13:5). For example, if you take a prostitute off the street who has been turning tricks for ten years and you give her a nice job, an apartment, and a bank account with some money in it—that won't immediately change her THINKING. She still has that prostitute mindset. By saying her old thought process "will instantly go away" is not fair to her, and it's a lie. She needs time to grow. Her mind has to be renewed, little by little, day by day. When we become a Christian, our faith takes our "spirits off the streets" (so to speak) and gives us a new identity—JESUS (see Galatians 2:20). But then the Holy Spirit (Jesus, in spirit form) begins to move WITHIN us, and teaches us how to live a healthy, spiritually fruitful life. Eventually we help others do the same! So be easy on yourself and give your relationship with Jesus time to mature!*

For me, I had a *lot* of maturing in Christ to do. Fighting was all I knew growing up, so trying to look "normal" and "behaved" was not natural for me. My upbringing was that of a nightmare: divorce, custody battles, 10 different schools, children shelters, foster homes, being abused by employees of the state—it was bad! I *had* to have my mind renewed, and it was *not* going to happen instantaneously! This is why Paul said, "Be transformed by the renewing of your mind" (see Romans 12:2).

Once this renewing began—through *my* choice—a relationship with Jesus began to develop because *I* chose it, not because I was being *forced*. So for the people who I considered "mean Christians," I just didn't understand at that time *what* I was being told to do, and *not* to do, was actually good for me. The problem was, their delivery was *very* forceful.

Of course, I take full responsibility for my poor choices, but back then, huge contributions to the religious frustrations in my life were flooding in from certain Christians who were *attempting* to teach me right from wrong. Their approach was all wrong. It was an approach of, "Be like me, or else."

That won't work. The world doesn't want that. What they want, is Jesus. We don't force-feed the gospel to anyone. Instead, we gotta get the world to *want* to get to know Jesus—not try to be "perfect like us." Let's try to get things in order here, please.

We haven't earned anything. Everything we have has been given to us for free. This isn't *about* you. This isn't about *me*. THIS IS ABOUT JESUS! Sure, we are partners in this mission; He wants us to use our personalities, gifts, talents, time, and resources for Him, but we must always have the spotlight on Christ *in* us.

It's not so much *what* we are saying to people, but *how* we are saying it. For example, I got a guy on my Facebook friends list who is a Christian, and he *really* wants to post stuff about God. I'm all for that. Facebook was not simply Mark Zuckerberg's idea, just like the telephone wasn't Alexander Graham Bell's idea—these were *God's* ideas, which were placed *in* man—FOR THE ADVANCING OF THE GOSPEL TO THE ENDS OF THE EARTH! (See Mark 16:15).

And now, because of all of this amazing technology, the Bible is coming true before our very eyes! This is why we need to use whatever outlet He gives us to spread the gospel. Social media ministries are booming! We are no longer confined to a building, or sitting in front of a radio, or even having to watch a television to hear about this Good News! The gospel will soon be global in the deepest parts of this planet's jungles, deserts, and ice-capped villages! Once this happens, Jesus is coming back! (See Matthew 24:14).

So sure, this is what we *all* need to do! Tell others about Jesus! But my Facebook friend's approach to doing so, is in a non-loving, very aggressive way—not just towards non-believers, but towards other Christians as well. Even *I* have to keep scrolling sometimes. I'm just like, *"C'mon man. Please. Start doing this in a loving manner."* His approach is wrong because it's extremely disrespectful—it's very self-righteous, graceless, and it makes Christianity look exclusive to do-gooders.

You see, each of us Christians are representatives of Christ. The Bible says, "we are his ambassadors," and that, "Jesus himself is making his appeal *through* us" (see 2 Corinthians 5:20). So when we are not being loving, even while being truthful, we are not truly representing Jesus. Instead, we are representing ourselves.

I believe one of the reasons for this terrible heart condition is because so many Christians have been taught to hate sin with *all* of their might— so much so, that *sin* is all they see in others. Because of this self-righteous teaching, sin gets magnified and love gets minimized. It's all down hill from there. Some preachers are just plain mean—downright ornery—so their congregations become mean and ornery as well. They've got *truth*, but no love. Any love they have is 100% conditional, based on people doing exactly what *they* want them to do.

Jesus doesn't do that, so we shouldn't either. Just imagine if He did?! We'd all be doomed! So our spiritually organic life-change *will* come, but *only* if we are focused on God's great love for us in Christ—*not* on our hate of sin.

Try to remember…Christianity is about…*relationship*…What kind of relationship's love is based on perfect behavior? Not any good one. Not any *intimate* one, or healthy one. The best relationships are based on grace, mercy, giving, and forgiveness. That's the same kind of relationship Christ wants with you!

Jesus is not looking for a religion with you, but instead, a *relationship* with you. One that is loving, spiritually fruitful, contagious, and prosperous! What's most sad about these religious Christians is that *although* they are bounty-hunters of sin, *they* have sin of their *own* which they overlook and belittle each day. They have ignored unconfessed sins which float away into the rear-view mirror of their lives, never to be talked about again. They act as if *those* particular sins are "no big deal"— yet at the same time, the sins of the gays, drunks, non-tithers, and drug addicts are so much worse.

They say such garbage as, "God will *only* save you if you've *truly* repented of *every* sin!" But that's wrong. They self-righteously have it out of order. The correct order is, "Because God *has* truly saved you, for free, by grace through faith—repent of wrong attitudes and actions to *show* Him how much you appreciate that. Begin to let Jesus live *through* you, because *He* is your true identity. When you sin, that's not even *who* you are inside any longer. It doesn't match up. So make healthy changes, so you can get the most out of your life in Christ.

Like the Pharisees, they are spiritually blind. They don't understand that *they* need to repent of their religious Christian mindset, which is sin as well.

And that word, *repent*, when my mind wasn't yet renewed, was a fighting word. It was like a button the devil pushed in me, each and every time I heard it! Even now, I have to consciously think about what I'm thinking about (which needs to be love), when a graceless Christian starts barking that word at lost people.

Sometimes have to say to myself *"Matt, relax. It's just a word,"* and it is! All repent really means is: *Turn around. STOP, go the other way. Do a 180. Change your life. Make different choices. Go to different places. Do different things! Let Jesus come OUT of you!*

We have to make people *want* to repent...*how?* Through our love and respect, and through our *testimonies.* The lost (who are the people who don't know Jesus, or why they even *need* to know Him) will take the gospel the wrong way if we don't tell them about the *good things* that come *out* of repentance. And we show them these good things through our own personal testimonies! We *all* have a testimony!

So we must *stop* telling people what to do, and instead, start talking about what *we've* allowed Jesus to do *through* us to get us to where we're at! We need to talk about what God has done for us *through* the changes we've made! We need to make repentance look attractive, not forceful!

We *must* begin to use our *own* lives as our worst examples, as well as our *best* examples! We don't have a heaven or hell to throw anyone into! We are *just* like them! WE ARE! The only difference is, we are saved and changed on the inside—for free—because we've accepted God's gift in Christ!

We must show them what the benefit of repentance is! Through our testimonies, we can show them what Christ-filled attitudes and actions look like. In order to be able to do this we gotta approach the lost with gentleness–not, "REPENT OR GO TO HELL! BACKSLIDERS!" Remember, *we* are responsible for representing Jesus. And Jesus said, "come and learn from me, for I am gentle and humble in heart" (see Matthew 11:29).

…Gentle…Humble in heart…That's what we gotta do. That's how we gotta be. On average, 105 people die on this planet every 60 seconds. Don't you want to be someone who *helps* people—not just make it to heaven—but also *live* an abundant life here on earth? If you do, then show them Jesus.

When we see ourselves sliding in the wrong direction from *that*, we must repent of it. We need to be doing the repenting as well. Not just the world, but each of us believers anytime we find ourselves *not* exuding Christ.

So today, my friends, know this: Nobody wants a set of rules to live by—but, absolutely everyone wants a loving relationship. Jesus gives us that. Let's all begin to show others *our* relationship with Christ, so that they will want it too.

A prayer for you: *Heavenly Father, we want to show others who you are, and you were personified in Christ. So as we get to know Him in Spirit, give us the graceful strength we need to let others come to know*

Him too. Reshape our minds from the inside out, as we learn how to love others as Jesus loves us. We know you'll do it, so thank you. In Christ's name, amen.

DAY 39

How To Be A Good Dad

"The Spirit Himself testifies with our
spirit that we are children of God"

ROMANS 8:16

Today is Father's Day! A day that is set aside, once a year, to pay homage to dads! A lot of people are waking up, excited to call up their dads, send them a text, Facebook something nice, or get prepped for a BBQ. Others, not so much.

For many, many, *many* people, this is a day of disappointment, frustration, anger, and sadness. Many people wish this day never came each year, because it's an awkward day. Conjuring up memories about their fathers is not a happy thing.

The relationship they *wish* they had with their dad is nonexistent. Many of them have nearly ruined their life trying to impress their dads, but their dads couldn't care less about what they do. Other dads have severely abused their kids, or caused them enormous amounts of pain.

Some dads have even abandoned their kids for their jobs or an addiction; and others, gave up on their wedding vows (or refused to even *make* wedding vows). Some dads have stopped caring for their kids to pursue the relationship of another woman, other than their mom. Some, might even still live at home, but their drinking or drugging, video-game-bing-ing habit, workaholism, or hobbies comes *above* being a loving, guiding parent.

There are even dads out there who completely ignore their *grown* kids all year long. They act as if they want nothing to do with them. Then, when they are with them face-to-face, they put on a smile, give hugs, and say "I love you," as if nothing is wrong.

Then again, you might have maybe the *worst* of the mix, a dad who left you without even saying good-bye. He never even acknowledges your existence. He has nothing to do with you, ever. Some have done this to their kids and they've passed away, leaving the kid (or adult) scarred emotionally.

For years, I was someone who refused to acknowledge that my own dad treated me poorly. Because of my codependency issues, I'd just sweep it under the rug, or white-wash it. But how my dad emotionally ignored me was wrong, and it still is.

As I got to know Jesus better, He wanted me to lift *up* the rug under which these feelings were swept, and scrape *off* the paint of my white-washed soul. TO HEAL, WE MUST CONFRONT UNFAIR ISSUES IN OUR LIVES–but do it how God approves. If we don't, then we will live in frustration and *severe* codependency, or, "dependency" in general (drugs, alcohol, porn, church-works, food, etc.).

Today, I want to give *you* the courage to confront your father, if he's hurt you. I don't care if you have to go to the local graveyard, I want you to voice how his actions have affected your life negatively. Religious people want you to just keep your mouth shut, and ball everything up inside. I'm NOT religious, I have a relationship with Christ. Jesus wants you to BE CONFIDENT! You *can't* be confident if you don't stand up to people's actions!

The enemy will continue to have his way with your emotions and torture your soul, if you don't confront your problems and issues, begin-ning with *yourself,* and *then* with the people who've hurt you.

Jesus has taught me to not be fake when it comes to my feelings. He made me to feel for a reason. So when we feel something, we need to acknowledge it, bring it to God, and then face it head on. Burying your feelings, especially about a bad relationship with your dad, will do some horrible things to your well-being. It's like having mold in your walls that you won't deal with.

If you don't break apart the walls and destroy it, it will fester, grow, and get worse. You *must* bring this stuff to God so that He can teach you how to handle it!

For years, I too, was a bad dad. Although I thought I was being a good one, I wasn't. I didn't have a good example of how to *be* a good dad—so I had to learn on my own. My dad was a chronic workaholic with a short fuse. His method of handling our relationship was to blow up on me, or ignore me. The silent treatment does some serious damage on a kid—*and* an adult, now that I think about it. I've had to forgive my dad for this, and release him from the relationship he's *owed* me, just so that *I* can be healthy on the inside. So when it came to *me* learning how to be a good father, this was how I learned: Trial and error. Trial and error. Trial and error, error, error.

When you have a dad who never thinks he's wrong about how he treats you, that doesn't mean they are *not* treating you wrong. It just means you are ignoring it, and that's not good for you.

In my past, when I actually stood up against how Dad is relationally, with us kids, I thought there was something wrong with *me* for doing so—THERE WASN'T! The Holy Spirit has taught me that that I can't *make* dad *want* anything to do with me, just like God can't make *me* want anything to do with *Him*. We must *choose* to have relationships.

The sad thing is, I not only had to learn this about my relationship with Dad, but also many other relationships in which I was going crazy trying to *make* someone to love me or be a part of my life. I DON'T HAVE THAT ABILITY. But the devil sure likes to try to make me *think* I do.

When you're a kid, you don't know any better, you think something is wrong with *you* because your father rejects you. And when you're an adult, you can stay in that *same* bondage if you don't allow Christ to teach you that there is *nothing* wrong with you for wanting a close relationship with your dad. If he rejects you, really, there is something wrong with *him*, not you.

To get to this state of good heart health, you must allow God to remold your mind as to *what* exactly, a good father looks like. Our Heavenly Father is a good father! HE SETS THE EXAMPLE PERFECTLY! When you get to know *Him*, then you understand how a good dad should be in word *and* action. Here are some things that I've learned about being a good dad, from Him:

1. **God will never abandon you.** Not only will He never abandon you, you don't have to keep pestering Him to try to have a close relationship with you because He lives *in* you. He's *already* deeply involved with *every* area of your life. The Bible says, "Though my father and mother forsake me, the Lord will receive me" (Psalm 27:10). So whether your father walked out on you, or has nothing to do with you, year-round, your *Heavenly* Father is still deeply involved in your life.

2. **I have no excuse to be a bad dad.** Just because my own father would rather work all the time, while I was growing up, (and I wasn't allowed to complain about that, it always fell on deaf ears) doesn't mean I have to do the same. And just because my dad has a bad temper and uses the silent treatment, that doesn't mean I have to as well. I'm responsible for my own actions in parenting, and *I* can be the one to break this destructive cycle. So whatever it is that your father did in your past, that *you* are currently doing, something that you *hated*, be sure not to do the same thing. We have no excuses because we've been on the opposite side of poor treatment. The Bible says that if you're sinning in the same way

as your parents, you can expect the same results (see Numbers 14:18). SO DECIDE TO MAKE A CHANGE!

3. **Don't be afraid to confront issues with your dad.** I was at a funeral not too long ago, sitting by my dad, and we started to talk about addiction. He absolutely refused to admit that there was any addiction problems in our family. I looked him in the eye and confronted him about this. All he cared about was whether or not the person behind us heard what I said. This is *not* okay. He should have taken what I said seriously! But he didn't, he ignored it, once again. The thing is, I'm not responsible for his actions. I said what I had to say. I was very proud of myself for being brave enough to say something to him. THAT WAS A VICTORY, an issue I confronted. Had I been doing this all my life, I'd be in a healthy state of mind much sooner. SO STAND UP! SAY SOMETHING! But let the Holy Spirit guide you as you do.

4. **Allow God to teach you how to be a good father.** Until I finally began to allow Jesus to live through me, I was a terrible father. Although, if you said such to me during that time, I would not have agreed with you. But the fact of the matter was I had *no clue* the amount of stuff that the devil had me fooled by. Sure, I provided financially for my family, but was I providing *spiritually?* NO WAY. Sure, I did my best to be a "Christian dad," that is, until I had a problem. Then 9 out of 10 times, I always handled things my own way, which was frustrated, forceful, and angry, *rather* than by Christ's Spirit in me. I was so full of self-pity, arrogance, and bull-crap. I blamed others for how *I* was, rather than allowing God to use harsh people and unfair circumstances to mold my soul into that of Christ's. God taught me that in order to be a good father, I can't have any excuses! So when I begin to think, "But...but...but..."—"NOPE!" The Holy Spirit interrupts me. We must get *this* right, *first*, then God shows you how to handle those butts. I mean, buts.

So just what is it that makes you become a good dad? That's easy. It's not a what, but a *who*.

Jesus.

You knew I was going in that direction, didn't you?

A prayer for you: *Heavenly Father I want to thank you for Father's Day, it's a good day! I want to thank you for the healing in my soul that you've given me, and the courage to express myself about my own dad. He's a good man. He taught me about your grace. I know that you use all things together for our good, even the parental vessels you choose to physically produce us. Give my father peace today, but at the same time, let him know that his kids desire a closer relationship with him, and so do his grandkids. Right now, I lift up all who are reading this, directly to you. I know some people will never understand what the difficulty of Father's Day feels like, and that's good! They are blessed! But for everyone who is in pain, I'm asking that you heal their hearts in regards to how they feel about their father. I'm asking that you give them the grace they need to forgive and release what their dads owe them, which is love. I'm asking that you reconnect lost relationships. I'm asking that you DESTROY resentment and unforgiveness. I'm asking that you give people COURAGE to finally say what they need to say to their fathers. Let the Holy Spirit guide their words. And lovingly convict the hearts of every dad who keeps ignoring you about their kids. TEACH THEM HOW TO CARE! I rebuke Satan's grasp on EVERY troubled relationship! MAKE THEM GOOD AND LOVING! In the name of Jesus I pray, amen.*

DAY 40

WHEN JESUS ASKS YOU TO DO DUMB STUFF

He said, "Throw your net on the right side
of the boat and you will find some." When
they did, they were unable to haul the net
in because of the large number of fish.

JOHN 21:6

Sometimes Jesus asks us to do things that seem "not so bright." In our own minds, and by our own reasoning, it's stupid. But if we will just go ahead and do it, Jesus can then work the miraculous *through* us! In order to be able to accomplish this feat, it's all based on *one* question: *Do you trust Jesus?*

If you do, and you're obedient to what *He* wants, a feast is coming!

Case in point, there is a story found in John 21, where the disciples are out in their boat, fishing. They fished all night long and caught nothing! I'm sure they were a little grumpy because of that, so when Jesus woke them up, yelling from the shore, "HEY! THROW YOUR NETS ON THE *OTHER* SIDE OF THE BOAT! THERE'S FISH ON THAT SIDE!" this probably didn't make them jump up and say, "Okay!"

I mean, this is a *small* boat! Why would there be fish on the other side of it, that's merely a few feet! *And,* they could have easily shouted back, "We're fishermen! We know what we're doing! Mind your own business!"

They didn't know it was Jesus standing on the shore, right then, but they did it anyway, although it seemed dumb. *After* they did, the Bible says, "they were unable to haul the net in because of the large number of fish!"

THEY COULDN'T EVEN GET THE NET IN THE BOAT! THEY HAD TO TOW IT TO THE SHORE! C'mon somebody, there's a message here! What seemed like a very dumb thing to do, turned into a huge blessing! Why? Because they were *obedient!* Because they had *trust!* This is the key to unlocking life's biggest blessings through Christ!

Here are some very dumb things that I've done in my life, which, at the time, made me look like an idiot. But all along, Jesus kept saying, "Just trust me."

1. **STAND UP TO THE RELIGIOUS CHRISTIANS.** First off, let me define "religious Christian" for you. This is someone who does NOT believe in the complete forgiveness of Jesus' sacrifice at the Cross—they have conditional love and semi-grace. They might *say* they *do* believe in complete, finished forgiveness, but their lives, teaching, double-talk (saved, not saved, saved, not saved, works, it's all free, works, it's all free), and their emotional manipulation of "I'm not having a Bible discussion with you!" along with attempting to instill fear and condemnation in the hearts of believers, and non-believers the like, say otherwise. They hold peoples' complete forgiveness hostage, because they don't want to give away "licenses to sin" (we are sinning just fine without licenses). They are focused on the wrong thing: SIN. Which, when we finally *know* that we are *completely* forgiven (and nothing can change this, not *even* sin), only then do we not *want*

to sin any longer, because we love Jesus so much, because He's removed *all* of our eternal sin punishment, for free. But to them, until we shape up and "be like them," we're no good to God (or to them for that matter). They say there must be *proof* of our saving. Really? Ephesians 2 says otherwise—that it's by grace (free, unearned) through faith (simply believing) alone, and that it's a free gift, so we *can't* say, "Hey! Look at what I did for God to get where I'm at!" We can't brag, ever, on ANYTHING we do, or *refuse* to do. Religious Christians also say you must confess *every* sin even *after* you get saved, that's double-talk. Make your mind up! You MUST ask for forgiveness for EVERY SINGLE SIN? C'mon. What about your *own* sins that you forget to ask for forgiveness for? The ones you belittle, cover up, overlook, and let float away into the rear-view mirror of your life? Do those just *go away*? No. That demonic method is madness, and incorrect. It keeps you focused on sin, and not on Jesus. There is a NEW COVENANT, based on a ONE-TIME sacrifice of Jesus' blood (Hebrews 8:13, 10:10). Your *asking* didn't get you saved anyway, your faith in Jesus' blood sacrifice did! If that weren't the case, then we could just sin away, and then ask for forgiveness once a week—or whenever. What kind of relationship is that? A terrible one. The truth is *once* you *believe* in His perfect blood, you are adopted into the family of God *as* God's own Child—just like Jesus! (See Ephesians 1). The Bible verse they keep taking out of context in 1 John 1:9, about confessing every sin, they need to realize John was speaking to *non*-believers who thought they had NEVER sinned. He was trying to get them to realize they *need* Jesus' forgiveness! So when you first stand up to the religious Christians, rather it be a church leader, legalistic friend or family member, it won't be easy—BUT BE CONFIDENT! You are no surprise to God! And your identity is *not* in proving or disproving, but the Cross! Remember to first THINK of them with love! Try to understand that they find *their* identity in what they *do and don't do for God,* so this will not go over well at first—they won't like this at all. Be brave. Understand that you've really got nothing to prove, but instead, something to share. Which is the free gift that Jesus gave *you*! Don't be afraid of them. They will try to get you to become fearful, or to feel condemned by this grace you are speaking of (they too, will be in desperate need of this *same* grace one day soon). Keep in the forefront of your mind that you've got NOTHING to fear because God's love for you is *perfect* in Christ, that there is *no fear* in His love, and that His love casts out *all* fear! (See 1 John 4). Further, you don't ever need to feel *condemned* because you have placed your faith in Jesus! (See Romans 8). When God first began to nudge me to do this, to actually stand up to them, respectfully, I didn't want to. I mean, *"Who am I?!"* is what I thought! This seemed like a very dumb idea! God taught me that I'm on the *exact* same level as them, because of my faith in Christ. So, I did it anyway, and by doing this I've been able to break free from religious bondage, fear, manipulation, and I've *actually* began to enjoy my complete freedom in Jesus' FINISHED WORK at the Cross! You can do the same!

2. **GO PUBLIC WITH YOUR WEAKNESSES.** My goodness this might have been the *most* difficult thing to do! We all *think* we have a reputation to maintain, but God wants to break that down, destroy it, and give us a brand new one! A reputation that is built on Christ! The problem is, nobody wants to air out their dirty laundry to get to this point—we don't want to look bad, weak, or wrong—this seems like a *very* dumb choice! BUT, the Bible says otherwise! It says "God's power is made perfect in our weakness!" (See 2 Corinthians 12:9). And with this mindset (our weakness is actually our strength), we can *now* put 1 John 1:9 in the proper context, "If we confess our sins, he is faithful and just and will forgive us our sins and purify us from all unrighteousness." There it is! We confess so we can *acknowledge* that God is right,

and we are wrong! We confess so that we can *get* on the proper path of repentance! Further, the Bible says that it is our "testimonies that overcome the power of the enemy" (see Revelation 12:11). YOUR TESTIMONY WILL HELP OTHERS! THE WORLD *NEEDS* IT! God allowed those things to happen (allowed, didn't cause) so you can break free *through* Christ's love, and *then* help others who are struggling with the same! None of it will be wasted unless you keep it all to yourself. The devil wants you to be ashamed of your past, but Jesus wants you to be confident in what He did to redeem you. So sure, it seemed like a dumb move when I first began to talk publicly about my addictions, my difficult upbringing, my anger problems, my greed, my marital issues, my bad parenting choices, and my codependency issues, but I trusted Jesus and I did it anyway. It hurt, bad! It was like I was being crucified on my very own cross! BUT JESUS HELPED ME THROUGH *ALL* OF THESE ISSUES—EVERY SINGLE ONE! And now He's using them for good, and for my purpose, all because I spoke up and stopped caring about what *people* thought of me, and started caring about what *God* thought of me. The fact is, people aren't looking to us Christians to see a clean, shiny person, who has never had a problem—NO! THEY WANT TO KNOW ABOUT OUR GRIT AND GRIME—AND HOW CHRIST SET US FREE! So don't be anonymous any longer. You have no reason to be. Anonymity is based on shame and fear—SO BE BOLD! SPEAK UP! SPEAK OUT! SAY YOUR FULL NAME! It's not a dumb move, it's called bravery! It's called doing ALL THINGS THROUGH CHRIST *IN* US! (See Philippians 4:13).

3. **BLESS THOSE, AND PRAY FOR THOSE, WHO CAUSE YOU PAIN.** Again, this seems very dumb. And when I first begin to really seek out Jesus through His Word, I was actually looking for Scripture I could use to sic Him on my enemies. What I soon found out is that Jesus does not do this, He loves all of us,

no matter what we do. And because He lives in me spiritually, I don't *want* to cause my enemies harm either. Instead, what Jesus asks me to do, is *genuinely* pray for my enemies to be blessed, to *think* of them with love, and to ask God to *help them* come to know Him, personally. Why? Because once they do, then their lives will change. Of course, this goes against my flesh's rules of tit-for-tat, so it is a conscious decision I have to make to allow Christ to live *through* me to be able to pull this off. Since God began to renew my mind, and teach me new life skills of breaking free from codependency, I can now stand up for myself *and* still love people. This is possible! The Holy Spirit will teach you how to establish healthy boundaries that others *must* respect for *your* well-being. You will get to this happy, non-enabling medium, by realizing just how valuable you are to Jesus! YOUR VALUE TO CHRIST WILL GIVE YOU WHAT YOU'RE LOOKING FOR! Once you get this down pat and firmly established in your soul, then you'll soon realize everyone else's value too—even your enemies'. Jesus died to make *all* of us right with the Father, even *while* we were far from Him in unbelief (see Romans 5:8). So yeah, it seems dumb, but ask God to bless your enemies! After that, your life will become much more peaceful!

A prayer for you: *God, I want to let you know today, that I love you. I know I say it a lot, but I really mean it. And the more I trust you, the deeper my love grows. Thank you for removing all fear and condemnation from my heart by teaching me my value, by showing me who I really am in Christ. And thank you for another day alive on your planet! Keep using me how you see fit! Right now, I lift up all who are reading this, directly to you. For those who might be on the brink of completely falling into you, pull them over the edge! Teach them who they really are in Christ's finished work! I BIND ANY HATE, RELIGIOUS MINDSET, FEAR OR CONDEMNATION IN THEIR SOULS, RIGHT NOW! BE GONE IN JESUS' NAME! Help them to make* *the moves you are asking them to make, THE MOVES THAT MAY SEEM DUMB! And give them the strength to ward off the angry, non-loving, judgmental, hyper-critical Christians, with their very own confidence, grace, and unconditional love! Show them how to keep their heads up high! ALWAYS! And how to have eye-contact with every-one—no matter what! Give them bravery as they walk out this life through Jesus! Amen.*

DAY 41

WHAT TO DO WHEN LIFE SUCKS

"For although they knew God, they neither
glorified him as God nor gave thanks to him..."

ROMANS 1:21

My life used to *really* suck. It never failed, no matter what I did to try to make my life get better, it was still terrible. And it was terrible because I wouldn't *allow* God to renew my mind. My life sucked because of my *thinking*. Here are some incorrect thoughts I used to have while searching desperately for the secret ingredient to making my life get better:

- If I could just get my company to grow, and make more money, *then* life would get better.
- If I could just build my own home, in a nice neighborhood, *then* life would be great!
- If I could just break this addiction, *then* I'd finally be happy.
- If I could just get in shape, *then* I'd find what I'm looking for.
- If I could just get "them" to start showing me some respect, *then* I'll have peace.

- If I could just get Jennifer to do "this" or stop "that" *then* all would be well.
- If I could finally just stop sinning, start going to church, and be a "good Christian" so the church-people would like me and approve of me, *then* I'd be good enough for God, *then* life would be so much better!

WRONG, WRONG, WRONG, WRONG, WRONG…Wrong… aaaaaaaand wrong.

Friend, learn from my mistakes. Don't be like me. Although the above list had good intentions to change Old Matt's life for the better, there was still a God-shaped hole in his soul that had to be filled up *first*—that is, before anything else would click into place *just* right! Once *that* relationship is established, then we should have a healthy list to *gracefully* strive for, in order for our lives to get better. And this happens as our minds are renewed by the Holy Spirit, little by little, day by day (see Romans 12:2, Philippians 1:6). As we allow our "do" to match up with the "Who" inside us, life gets good! This is where life starts to not suck any longer.

You are probably thinking, "Okay, so what is it *exactly*? What do I need to do to make my life get better?" The answer is two-fold: 1. RENEW YOUR MIND WITH GOD'S WORD, which I talk about all the time because if you renew your mind with the truth of Jesus' unconditional love for you and others, you will renew who *you* are, which is the customizable part of you—your soul. But let's dive deeper into the second step. Number two lies within the opening verse of this devotional: GLORIFY GOD! Bring attention to Jesus!

Boom! HOW SIMPLE HAS GOD MADE IT?! When the Holy Spirit revealed this to me, my entire life began to change for the better, quickly! I WAS CREATED TO BRING ATTENTION TO GOD! To the Father, the Son, and the Holy Spirit! AND SO WERE YOU!

We were made, molded, and formed in God's mind, to bring attention to something *greater* than ourselves, WHICH IS HIM! We are going to worship some*thing* or some*one*—and sometimes, that is even *ourselves*! This is built in to our human make-up as God's created beings! WE WORSHIP! WE CHEER! WE SING! WE SHOUT! WE MAGNIFY AND *MAKE GREATER*! We can't help it!

You were formed to point to and enjoy something or someone *other* than you. Like breathing, you can't stop this from happening—it happens without you noticing, most of the time.

In order for your life to not suck any longer, you must begin to make God, through *Jesus*, your #1 cheered for Person.

Still don't believe that we worship stuff without noticing? Just look at Sunday afternoons all throughout America during the NFL season. The absolute die-hard passion that these men, women, and children have for their favorite football team is mind-boggling! Some even get in fights over who they are cheering for! THERE IT IS! WORSHIP! It's *in* us!

Another example: You go to your favorite music artist's concert, you're all dressed up and excited, you stand in front of them and sing along! You scream and shout! You *GLORIFY*! And I'm not saying there is anything wrong with cheering for your team or going to a concert—enjoy that stuff. I'm saying keep *everything* in the proper perspective to the "rooting on" of the love of Christ, which should be *much* more than anything else in your life. This is *very* important.

For your life to get better, to begin to feel content in all circumstances, simply begin to understand that your *true* joy, happiness, and fulfillment will only be found in glorifying your Creator! And your Creator walked this planet in the flesh...it's Jesus.

He must be the center! Not going to the gym, not politics, not video games, your phone, social media, not your kids, your spouse, boyfriend, girlfriend, or mistress; not your job, not sex, food, drugs, alcohol, church work, your ministry, sports, or your motorcycle—but *just* JESUS!

Get Him *centered* in your soul, begin to worship Him in *all* things, and acknowledge Him at *all* times—then you got it! And I'm *not* saying become a religious fruit-loop, but simply *think* of Him moment by moment, respect Him, and show Him that you love Him through your words, thoughts, and actions. Let Him live *through* you…*then* He will help you fully enjoy every*one*, and every*thing*, else.

It's like St. Augustine said, approximately 400 years after Jesus was born, "Our hearts are restless until they find rest in you." This is where the non-sucking life begins, through glorifying God. I know that sounds like a Christianese word, but all glorify means is "lift up." It means "bring attention to." Once you begin to do *this*, then and only then, will He fill up your soul with a purpose and a peace unlike you've ever known before!

A prayer for you: *Well good morning Heavenly Father! It's a beautiful morning here in Missouri, crisp and cool. I thank you for that! I thank you for another day alive. You are good. Right now, I lift up all who are reading this, directly to you. For those who are looking everywhere for joy and peace, and their lives are still extremely frustrating, please begin to reveal that a deep relationship with Jesus will give them all they need. After that, He is the one who gives them all they WANT! And in that order! I'm asking for a brand new resolve and desire for each and every person who wants to allow Him to live through them. Show them that in bringing attention to YOU, and in glorifying YOU in every aspect of their lives, that they will finally find meaningful, organic purpose. Strengthen and encourage them, today. In Jesus' name, amen.*

DAY 42

I USED TO HATE CHURCH

*"At that moment (when Jesus died) the
curtain of the temple (which separated
non-priests from God's most holy place)
was torn in two from top to bottom..."*

MATTHEW 27:51 (MY NOTES ADDED)

Have you ever heard the saying, "The veil was torn," but didn't
know what it meant? The above verse explains it. In Jesus' time,
at the temple, where people went to pray to God and make sacrifices,
there was a 3-foot-thick veil which *only* the priests could go past, and
they went back there to present blood offerings to God for the people's sins (see Hebrews 9:7). Gross, I know, but God requires blood to
remove sins (see Hebrews 9:22).

The amazing thing is, when Jesus died on the Cross, that very *moment*
the earth shook and that veil was torn! (See Matthew 27:50,51). Jesus
actually *became* our final blood offering to pay *off* our sins! Once and for
all! (See Hebrews 10:10, John 19:30).

This is why the Bible says in *Hebrews*, AKA, *"Jewish people,"* (the
author is speaking to the Jews who were still bringing blood to the

temple, when it was no longer required), "If we deliberately keep on sinning after we have received the knowledge of the truth (faith in Jesus' blood *only*), no sacrifice (bulls, goats, etc.) for sins is left" (Hebrews 10:26, my notes added).

The author of *Hebrews* wasn't writing to Christians, he was writing to the Jews who kept bringing in the blood of animals to *get* forgiven when God didn't want it any longer! *Jesus'* blood was the *final* sacrifice!

The religious Christians want people to think that verse applies to *believers* in Jesus, and it does not! The author (who was more than likely Paul, but it's not clear), was talking to the Jews who wouldn't fully swallow the work of Jesus' blood *as* the final sacrifice—they were just dabbling with it. They *heard* about Jesus, but were still hedging their bets on the blood of animals.

This is a classic religious manipulation running rampant in our churches. Hebrews 10:26 is *not* applicable to those who have *already* placed their faith in Jesus' blood at the Cross. This incorrect teaching keeps people in fear by setting up unattainable goals of never sinning again. We have flesh! That flesh *will* sin! We have unrenewed mindsets, *with* sinful attitudes. But *sin* is not who we are at our spiritual core–*that* person, is Christ (See Romans 6, Galatians 2:20). The Christian life is not about focusing on sinning less, but instead it's about living *out* Christ who is *in* you. When you do that, *then* you will sin a whole lot less, and you'll do it organically. Because a sin-free person is *who* you really are.

SO PLEASE, STOP TAKING THINGS OUT OF CONTEXT IN THE BIBLE! THE LOST ARE *STAYING* LOST WHEN WE DO THIS! ON TOP OF THAT CHRISTIANS ARE LIVING IN FEAR! JESUS FINISHED EVERYTHING! THERE IS "*NO MORE SACRIFICE LEFT!*" You and I now have *complete* access to God! *And,* our God is *so* loving, He made that access easy!...BELIEVE IN JESUS AS YOUR SAVIOR.

So I had to set that up because I want to point out the fact that we no longer *need* a building to find God, or a middle man to speak to God *for* us. Instead, *we* are now the buildings of God, the temples, and Jesus is our High Priest! And because of *Him*, we can now approach God boldly at any time of the day, at any geographical location, about anything we want or need! (See 1 Corinthians 6:19, Hebrews 4:14-16).

This brings me to the subject of church attendance, which sure, *is* a very good thing, but *only* if it's in the proper place in our hearts. And only if you realize that simply *going* to church doesn't make you in any better standing with God, and *not* going, doesn't makes you any *less than* with Him either. We are justified in full with God by our faith in Jesus, *alone*. Nothing added, nothing taken away. This is called *grace*. (See Ephesians 2:8,9, Romans 1:17).

I used to hate church. I dreaded it. I didn't want to go, and I got nothing out of it. I felt obligated to go to appease others, to make an appearance so other Christians would approve of me, and also, so that I didn't lose my spot in heaven (which, you *can't* lose your adoption into the family of God, see John 3, Ephesians 1,2).

And when I *was* at church, the teaching made me feel like a pile of garbage because I could never live up to the expectations that even the church leaders weren't living up to. It was a charade. Church was simply something to mark off my calendar. *"I went to church. Check. Now I'm back in the black with God. He owes me now."* This was my mindset.

The problem was, my "good enough meter" teetered all the time, it never rested. *If I just do this, or don't do that, THEN I'll find the peace I'm looking for!* Wrong. I soon found out that my religious actions would never bring me peace. And if I didn't get the approval of the pastors or the church people when I did "good stuff," I was defeated in my soul. They rarely approved of me, most of them just walked on by me or gave me a judgmental look, because I was an outsider—not "as good" as they were.

Church was simply a terrible burden in my life which created frustration, fear, and anxiety.

It's no wonder you hear so many stories of people who have fallen off the deep end, but their loved ones will tell you, "I don't know what happened, they grew up in church." Well I *know* what happened because

I was a person who fell off the *deepest* end. IT'S BAD TEACHING. Bad teaching of trying to get people to do what only Jesus can do for them. It's unrealistic, "do better," "be holier," non-gospel. It's, "I gotta add to it to get it!" It's "I gotta try harder to keep it!" It's "I'm only 60% good, 40% bad," CRAP TEACHING!

ONCE (THAT'S <u>ONE TIME</u>) YOU PLACE YOUR FAITH IN JESUS, AND BELIEEEEEEEEEEEEVE HE'S SAVED YOU, YOU ARE 100% GOOD WITH GOD! SPIRITUALLY PERFECT! ENGRAFTED WITH CHRIST! Not because of anything *we* do, don't do, or teeter-totter in doing, but only because of Jesus finishing everything required by God *for* us, at the Cross!

We don't need to die to self, God LIKES yourself! He wants you to be you! YOU AIN'T NO SURPRISE TO HIM! Be you! Enjoy *yourself*! Friend, the greatest, "most perfect" Christian you can think of, hasn't earned a *thing*…it's all been free. The same standard applies to you.

Why? Be. Cause. Of. Jesus…Be. Cause. Of. Jesus. BECAUSE OF JESUS! Say that with me and believe it! "Because of Jesuuuuuuuuuuuuuuuus!"…Now *that's* why it's called *Good News!* That's what the gospel means, good news!

You can't have it both ways. It can't be good news for only a certain amount of "well behaved" people. Churches need to stop teaching that, and instead, *start* teaching that Jesus lived the life *we* couldn't, and now, we *can* enjoy *His* life. They need to begin to teach the truth of the *finished* work of Jesus. They need to begin teaching Christians their *true* identity in Christ.

So what happened to me in regard to my church attendance? Well, I stopped attending the dog-and-pony show at that church. I stopped listening to the lies of the devil as he tortured me with, "You better not be a church hopper!" I stopped feeling guilty about wanting to leave that church, so I did. There are a million church buildings out there, so I found another one to attend. I also forgave that church for hurting me, and I released them from what they owed me, which was grace and unconditional love. Further, I stopped putting my identity in a brick-and-mortar building, and instead, I began to seek Jesus daily on my own, through studying His Word, *myself.*

I also began to read grace-filled Christian books and watch Christ-centered teachings. And lastly, I invited Jesus into *every* part of my life (not just my Sunday mornings) even the parts I was extremely ashamed to bring Him into. By doing so, this has allowed me to form a very deep relationship with Him.

Jesus soon taught me that *I* am the Church—I am—and so are you, if you've placed your faith in Him! Remember, Christ destroyed the need of an actual building to *find* God on the deepest level! Instead, a *better* relationship has come into place through Jesus, a Personal one! (See Ephesians 2:13, Hebrews 8:13).

So today, my friends, know this: You are The Church, once you place your faith in Jesus, and nobody can stop this! When you get this correct mindset established in your soul, not only will you look forward to *going* to church, but you will also find the *right* church because the Holy Spirit will lead you there! And guilt, condemnation, shame, and fear will no longer be a part of your life because you know that Jesus has made *you* a Church! An actual walking, talking, house of Christ! Someone who goes about their lives showing others who Jesus really is!

A prayer for you: *Good morning Heavenly Father! Thank you for this day you've blessed me with! It's Sunday, and I'm pumped about going to church to learn more about you, to praise you with others, and enjoying the corporate feeling of the Holy Spirit! Thank you for leading me to my church! Right now, I lift up all who are reading this, directly to you. For those who have a been hurt so very badly by people IN church, give them peace. Give them a brand new mindset toward church in general. Help them to see that church is good if it's centered on your unconditional love in Christ! Help them to understand that nobody can be perfect in every word or deed, except for Jesus! You chose us humans to run the church buildings, so naturally, there will be huge flaws involved. Give us the grace to cover those flaws with the love and* *forgiveness of Jesus, while at the same time, give us the confidence we need to establish healthy boundaries which those in church must respect. Help us to recognize when someone is trying to manipulate us with guilt or fear, and give us the strength to stand up against it! If there is a religious spirit pestering any of these dear readers, I BIND HIM IN THE NAME OF JESUS! BE GONE! YOU DEMONIC IDIOT! God, begin to make ALL churches what YOU designed them to be, all throughout the world! Which is with Christ as our leader! Which is with Christ as our perfection and identity! I pray for REVELATION in our churches! I pray that you will RAISE UP the Church, which is all of us, so we can begin to change many lives for the better! Amen.*

DAY 43

AM I GOOD ENOUGH FOR GOD'S LOVE?

"But God demonstrates his own love for us in this:
While we were still sinners, Christ died for us."

ROMANS 5:8

It's so easy to become downtrodden and distraught with life. Discouragement knocks at the front door of our souls, every single day. Sometimes with a little peck, and at other times, trying to beat down the door. When this happens, somedays we can question our faith. *"Why am I even a Christian? How can God possibly love me? Am I doing this right?"* The enemy will attempt to push us toward doubt. He'll try to persuade us to repeatedly ask ourselves if God really even loves us.

I recognize him now, but used to, I didn't. From a very young age, this supernatural sissy caused me to doubt God's unconditional love, nearly every single day. But one of the best things I've learned in my walk with Jesus is that He loves us no matter what! That's a "feel good sentence." If you read through it quickly you might not fully believe it. It is hard to believe that Jesus loves us completely—no matter our behaviors or attitudes. He doesn't love us *less* if we fail, or *more* if we "do right."

On one hand, we can be behaving very well morally, ethically, in our relationships, at work, at church, and even in a worldly view. But on the flip-side of the high-ethics "good Christian" coin, you could *not* be doing very well with your choices, and therefore think that God doesn't love you.

You could be depressed, enraged, extremely frustrated with the treatment and decisions of others; you could be ready to give up on living altogether, while making very bad decisions yourself; you could be hanging on by a *single thread* of sanity—*done* with this planet—because nothing good seems to ever happen to you.

These are the very issues which will make you question, not only God's love for you, but what *you* need to do to be sure you *keep* His love. *"WHAT AM I DOING WRONG TO DESERVE THIS?!" "GOD, YOU MUST HATE ME!"* These are lies written on your soul from the pits of hell, and Satan himself is the author.

However, in the good times and the bad, God *still* loves you infinitely! And there is nothing you can do about it! This is your fall back! This is your foundation! *Un*-earnable, *un*-losable, unconditional love from your Creator *through* your faith in Jesus!

The Bible says that "while we were still sinners, Christ died for us" (see Romans 5:8). It doesn't say, "Because we straightened out our lives, did everything right, never missed a church service, never drank, never smoked, never had a dirty thought, did plenty of mission trips, tithed to the penny—and because we never did anything wrong or had tough times—Christ died for us." No. Jesus died for…sinners…created *human* beings. That's me and you *before* we asked Jesus to come into our hearts.

His love for us at the Cross was poured out *freely*, and our sin couldn't stop it—past, present, *and* future. Keep in mind, when Jesus died, *all* of your sins were in the future. You weren't even born yet. This is why *after* you accept Christ as your Savior, one time, you are no longer a sinner. Instead, you are a saint in spirit, and Jesus Himself becomes infused *with* your spirit (Hebrews 10:10, Romans 6:10, 2 Corinthians 1:1, Ephesians 3:16, 1 Corinthians 6:17).

As a Christian, you are a saint who sins sometimes, *because* you still have flesh and your mind is constantly being renewed. But you are *not* a sinner after you invite Jesus into your heart the *first* time. Christ can have nothing to do with sin being in you. It's gone! He cleaned house!

Sure, it's confusing to a lot of people who haven't heard the truth of the gospel, that, even after being saved, we will still sin because of a parasite in our flesh *called* sin, *and* our minds have to be changed by God's Spirit who now *lives* in us. But the actual *good news* of the gospel is *when* our flesh sins *(not if)*, it still can't wear out the blood of Christ! It still can't make Him go away! The Cross actually worked! God's idea of becoming one with us was a *great* idea!

So now, after being saved one time, we are constantly being transformed by the renewing of our minds so that our flesh, and our souls, will begin to match up with our perfect spirits—only, this process will not be complete until we die or Christ returns (see Philippians 1:6).

As Christians, we must never get our *who* mixed up with our *do*. Our *who* is Christ in us; our *do*, is what our flesh still *does* because it's fallen like Adam—not raised yet, like Christ (see Romans 5). So many people fall off course and give up on going deeper into their relationship with God, because they still sin after accepting Christ. The enemy tortures them with doubtful thoughts. "Did it take? Did I *really* get saved? If I *am* saved, then why am I still sinning? I don't even *like* sin! Why is this happening?! What can I do?!"

These are legitimate questions that every believer must address, but it is the *truth* that will set you free from hellish fear, debilitating frustration, and the inner-turmoil that can be caused *by* these questions. Here are the truthful answers:

You didn't *stop* sinning to get saved in the first place. You *believed* you were a sinner, and that you needed Jesus' forgiveness. You repented of your unbelief! You believed in the One who has unconditional love for you *as* the Savior of your sins. Simply put, you believed Jesus forgave you completely, and He actually did. Jesus finished everything *for* you (see John 19:30).

If someone tells you that your sin will un-save you, don't believe it! If someone tells you that you are not good enough for God's love, don't believe it! If you do, then you will go down a path of dead-end religious works of trying, trying, trying, ALWAYS TRYING, to get back *in* to God's good graces, and you never left! He simply wants you to find *rest* in the finished work of Jesus, right now, today. (See Matthew 11:28, Hebrews 4:11).

The truth is, God *never* leaves you, because He is *in* you. The Father won't disown Christ! And Christ, and you, are one! He can't break a promise with Himself because God can't lie! (See 2 Timothy 2:13, Hebrews 7:18, Hebrews 7:22, 24, 25, Hebrews 6:18).

So today, my friends, know this: It is God's unconditional love for us *through* Christ which continually draws us *back* into deep fellowship with Him. We go deeper, because we know He will never leave us, no matter what we do, ever. This amazing grace erases *all* of our eternal sin punishment, *once* and for all! *This* is where you will find your confidence! Which is in His unconditional love! Christ's sacrifice at the Cross allows you to never worry about losing God's love! You *are* good enough! You are! Enjoy it.

A prayer for you: *God, today I want to thank you for waking me up. So many people pass away each day, and I was not one of them. Instead, you chose to keep me here to bring more glory and attention to Jesus, and to enjoy my life! Thank you. Right now, I lift up all who are reading this, directly to you. For those who have been lied to about your love, those who have been taught that it's conditional, or that they have to earn it, or worry about keeping it—help them. Reveal in their hearts today a newfound confidence in how great your love really is for them, in Christ! In His name I pray, amen.*

DAY 44

HOW I BEAT ALCOHOLISM

*"Then you will know the truth and
the truth will set you free."* ~*Jesus*

JOHN 8:32

I'm an alcoholic in recovery. For years I drank WAY too much, WAY too often—*as* a Christian. No, I didn't get "all religious" to try to stop drinking, I've been a Christian since I was a kid. I just didn't start to show Jesus any real respect or love until about 2011, and little by little, by allowing Him to renew my mind, He's made me who I am today.

However, I *was* religious *while* drinking. Heck, I would testify with a beer in my hand and not think there was anything wrong with that. And really, there is nothing wrong with alcohol in itself, even Jesus enjoyed a glass or two of wine. If you look at His first recorded miracle in John 2, that wasn't grape juice. The religious Christians want you to think that. Alcohol *was* fermented in the Bible.

And although there is nothing wrong with alcohol, there *is* something wrong with *me* drinking it. I can't. I don't have an "off button." It's like giving a shark a single, little fishy—that's not gonna work for him—or a bear, one scoop of honey. We want more!

So no, there isn't anything wrong with drinking—IF—AND THIS IS A BIG *IF*—you don't have a problem with it. And if you have to constantly ask yourself, "Do I have a problem?" then more than likely you do.

My wife, for example, can have a little wine or *one* margarita, and be done. She won't even think about it any more. Me?…HA. It's like lighting a powder keg. I want to polish off that bottle of wine, and another! Margaritas? I'll have the entire pitcher, and shots, oh, and some beers too!

Now, I can *try* to fight it, but I'd be fooling myself. I. WANT. MORE. When I controlled my drinking I couldn't enjoy it, and when I enjoyed it I couldn't control it. Once I start, I'm off to the races. I'm either going to drink a ridiculous amount, then binge-eat and pass out, or, be grumpy and extremely agitated if I couldn't get access to more.

I liked to drink because it relaxed me…"Ahhhhhhh…" Nothing quite like that first beer and (or) shot. But then, after relaxed, I'd become overly excited! Then I'd become the smartest man alive with "great business ideas" or I'd become "the most handsome man in the world and every lady wanted me"…*pfft!* What an idiot. I look back now at Old Matt, the man who hadn't yet allowed God to renew his mind, and I want to grab him, smack him, and say, "HEY! DUMMY! STOP IT! YOU ARE SCREWING UP!"

I was only fooling one person, and that was me. Unbeknownst to me at that time in my life, I was being a puppet for the devil. Oblivious. A sheep to the slaughter. Digging my own grave. BLIND AS A BABY BAT.

But us problem drinkers, we drink for one *main* reason only, and if someone says otherwise they are lying to you—stuck in denial—and here it is: WE WANT TO FEEL DIFFERENT. That's it. If we are sad, we want to feel happy. If we are stressed, we want to feel relaxed. If we are uncomfortable, we want to feel comfortable. If we feel like a failure, we want to feel like a winner. If we are bored, we want to feel entertained. Truth be told, if we are *already* extremely excited and happy, we want to feel even *more* excited and happy!

We are not trying to hurt people, we just want to FEEL different. We want to LIKE ourselves, by getting AWAY from WHO we think we really are! People who drink heavily are putting on a facade, as they drink, that's who they WANT to be, but are not.

The great news is this: Jesus teaches you who you really are...sober. And you are VERY special, sober. EVEN MORE SPECIAL, sober. YOU CAN UNLOCK YOUR FULL POTENTIAL, sober. REACH YOUR HIGHEST GOALS, sober. LOVE OTHERS AND YOURSELF ON THE DEEPEST LEVEL YOU'VE EVER KNOWN, sober...And you can finally understand just how AMAZING and dearly loved you are by your Creator, sober!

But this only begins when we finally face the truth about our lives. Truth is good for us. As drinkers, we DON'T like the truth. We don't want to face it. Instead, we want to shove everything down deep, and cover it up with a buzz. We want to act like nothing is wrong *in* us, or *around* us. "I'll just pick up a couple tall-boys after work, no big deal." Or we'll say, "Let's just go have a few"—but "having a few" happens few, often, and in-between. Most of the time we are getting smashed, and in the back of our minds, that's the goal.

So instead of belittling this problem of ours, covering it up, or blowing it off, Jesus says, "Give it to me." HE WANTS IT. He can take what "makes" you want to drink, and use it to mold you into a great person of God, AND, help others with it, AND, bring glory to Him!

The devil wants the opposite to happen. This moronic, stupid liar wants you to think that you don't have a problem and everyone else does—this is how he keeps you in slavery, in BONDAGE. This dirty butt-wipe will tell you, "Oh just have a couple, you've not drank in a few days, you're fine. Relax, enjoy yourself. You deserve it! You don't want people to think you have a drinking problem do you? So drink!"...What a liar!

JESUS TEACHES YOU HOW TO STOMP ON SATAN'S FACE—WITH CONFIDENCE.

For me, even as a successful business owner, I was a closet drunk. I hid it well, or so I thought. One of my many excuses was, "I can do whatever I want! It's legal! BACK OFF! I'm free to drink." However, yeah, I was "free" to drink, but at the same time, I wasn't free NOT to drink.

I would try to cut back, or only drink on a certain day—that never lasted, it's all I thought about! I couldn't *wait* for that drinking day to get here! Or I'd say, "I'm only going to drink on Friday," but then Saturday came, and I had left-over beer, so I *had* to drink that—and if I was barbecuing, I had to drink then too! If I didn't, I just wasn't American!

So after drinking on Friday and Saturday, Sunday would roll around and I was usually too hungover to move. Then I'd binge-eat on Chinese food all day, and burgers—and some ice-cream to boot—why not? Who cares about your diet when you feel like a horse's rear? Because of this bad habit of hangover-binge-eating, I stayed bloated, and I developed a fat face and a beer-gut. I was miserable.

But in order to feel better on Sundays, the food didn't always help, so I'd drink again. *"Two beers, that's it."* Nope. That didn't last long. After those two, I'd loosen up and keep going. So then, when Monday came, I'd think, *"Oh what the heck, I've already drank three days in a row, why not have some drinks after work? This time, I'll just drink it at home. I'm not hurting anyone."*

I WAS A SLAVE! Period. I tried quitting hundreds of times, and *all* of those attempts were short-lived! Eventually I just stopped trying to quit, and said, "I drink. It's just who I am. There is nothing I can do about it." WHAT LIES! Then one day as I was begging God, again, "JUST TAKE THIS AWAY FROM ME WOULD YOU?! PLEASE!" I felt something down deep in my heart, and it said, "You *need* to become uncomfortable, that's the only way."

It finally made sense. I knew that the only way I would not just QUIT drinking, but BEGIN a new life, would be to face whatever feelings I kept drinking away—the very feelings that Jesus wanted me to face, with Him and through Him...I had to...*feel.*

I HAD TO FEEEEEEEEEL!!!! I had to feel my feelings, and present them to God as to how to handle them, without drinking.

Also, I had to face…myself. So I did. AND THIS PART HURT, A LOT. Oh my goodness, looking back and just *thinking* about the pain…It felt like I was being nailed to a cross. I finally KNEW what Jesus felt by *me* going through this—and in return, I was being completely remade in my mindset. I was becoming "New Matt," based on 1 Corinthians 5:17! A person who was an actual "NEW CREATION IN CHRIST"—who *lived* that way! The *old* had gone and the *new* had come!

For so many years I didn't want to allow myself to feel this, or *face* this—but Jesus taught me that I *have* to feel it *and* face it! I have to feel *His* pain, in order to grow towards Him! I had to begin to empathize with my Savior's sacrifice! Because of that sacrifice and my faith in it, the fact was, if I *never* stopped drinking He still loved me unconditionally and I was still saved!

BUT HE HAD SO MUCH MORE IN STORE FOR MY LIFE! A LIFE OF ABUNDANCE, PEACE, AND PURPOSE—NOT SLAVERY!

My friend, in the beginning of your sobriety *try* to focus on the pain that you *must* feel, in order to *stay* sober—and actually *enjoy* it. "Enjoy it?!" Yes. This is the pain of *not* drinking because you know Jesus *in you* doesn't want you to. You are doing this to *show* Him that you care. SURE, THIS HURTS VERY BADLY IN THE BEGINNING—but the pain subsides.

Christ rose from the dead after feeling terrible pain, because He loved us—and so will you. Your crucifixion passes, but glory remains. You must remember that *allowing* the Holy Spirit to renew the mindset of your soul is not all about *nice* feelings or getting our wishes granted. Feelings come and go, and God is not a magic genie. He is a sovereign God who loves us so much He wants us to change how we *think*.

In the beginning, this process of having your mind renewed into Christ's is mostly about *you* feeling the same pain that Jesus felt, which, in turn, also allows you to feel how much He loves you.

And now, since I've not had a drop of alcohol since May 7th, 2014, I feel really good. Actually, that's probably the biggest understatement of the year for me. My God-given ministry gift is writing, but I can't even come up with an adjective to describe *how* I feel. My *spirit* was already saved, but now my *soul* feels reborn. So maybe I feel *remade*? I don't know, you would just have to feel it to understand it, by getting sober yourself—that is, *if* you have a problem.

I HAVE SO MUCH ENERGY! Really, sometimes I don't even know what to do with it. It's *amazing*. I'd *never* want to feel like I used to feel now that I have this new life! THIS IS SO MUCH BETTER!

So if this is you, and you are in the bondage of an addiction, in chains, IN SLAVERY—my friend, I'm here to tell you today that there *is* hope! This hope that I speak of is found in Jesus, who is in you, if you believe He's forgiven you. By getting to know Him, studying Him, bringing your pain and joy to Him—and by PRAISING Him no matter what! This hope is found in allowing Him to live *out* of you—to live *through* you! His characteristics, His confidence, His words, His power, and mostly His love for you and others!

The Bible says in 1 John that "God *is* love," and Jesus personified God, literally. When you get to know Jesus, you get to know your Creator. When you get to know Jesus, you get to see real love in action. And make no mistake, He has a *loving* plan for your life! That plan does *not* include an addiction! But it will take you giving up what you want to keep, even if you don't really want to keep it, but can't get rid of it. Hand it over to Jesus! Just say, "Here, take it. I'm ready to be uncomfortable. I'm ready to feel. I'm ready to face myself with your help, and have my mind renewed. I'm all yours."

And lastly, please know this: You must stop trying to quit. YOU CAN'T QUIT! But, you *can* begin a brand new life in Christ! Quitting requires *your* power, beginning requires God's. You can do this *through* Christ! He will strengthen you! Freedom awaits! Break free!...Begin today.

DAY 45

Do All Things *Really* Work Out For Good?

*"And we know that in all things God works
for the good of those who love him, who
have been called according to his purpose."*

ROMANS 8:28

Romans 8:28, this is perhaps one of the most taken-out-of-context verses in the Bible. When you see it, it's easy to get excited and say, "YEAH! OH YEAH! All things are working together for my good!" We do this all the time, and that's fine.

Besides John 3:16, this may be the most *famous* verse in the Bible. It's also used a lot when trying to find comfort during very difficult times in our lives.

I even find myself quoting this particular verse to people who reach out to me for advice or prayer. Those who are facing heart-wrenching circumstances which seem insurmountable. Those who have been defeated in their souls by years of trouble and heartache, the people who have loved ones who refuse to turn their lives around, or those who are battling a sickness or addiction that is causing fear—I'll quote this verse and say, "Everything is going to be okay. God works all things *together* for our good."

And sure, we *should* be standing on the Word of God to overcome our unfair, grievous situations. However, we must ask ourselves, "Just *how* does everything work out together?"

This is the million dollar question. If this verse is true, and the Bible has zero lies, then why does it not always *feel* like this verse is *really* true? Why does it seem so often as if things are *not* working out together for our good? To answer these questions we must do two things:

1. Define "good"
2. Look to the following verse, Romans 8:29

As a Christian, I *know* that Jesus is good! Sure, there are many other things and people which are good, but *He* is the only one who defines goodness in its purest form. So we must replace the word "good" with "Christ," in our hearts, and apply that to Romans 8:28. Let's try it out, "All things are working together for *Jesus*"...now...isn't this starting to make sense? Somehow, some *way*, your difficult situation, or dealing with this difficult person, is creating something good—FOR JESUS! Either, later on down the road, for humanity as a whole—or *IN* us, right now, for our *own* benefit. And this is happening for who? For Christ!

My friend, if you want to fully enjoy your relationship with Jesus, you must begin to allow Him to renew your mind, and realize this: *This life is not about us.* EVERYTHING is about Him. EVERYTHING. This life we live, it's all about Jesus! We are simply supporting characters! He is the one who wins the Oscar for the leading role. It's our job to make *Him* look good, through us! Our goal should now be to win our *own* Oscar for "Best Christ-Supporting Character."

This doesn't always *feel* good! But, IT'S WORTH IT! OUR SACRIFICIAL LOVE AND RESPECT FOR JESUS DOES NOT GO UNNOTICED! He *sees* us.

Next, let's look at the following verse, Romans 8:29. In order to be able to fully enjoy what 8:28 says, always tag 8:29 on because it explains how all things *are* working together for good:

"For those God foreknew (that's me and you–all of us) he also predestined (yes, God has a predestined perfect plan for your life all laid out–it's up to you to step *into* this plan. How do you step into this plan? Let's finish the verse —>) to be conformed to the likeness of his Son..." That's the plan! TO BECOME LIKE HIS SON! JESUS! This is the "how" everything works together for good! BY CHANGING YOUR LIFE TO LOOK LIKE CHRIST'S!

So today my friends, please know this: Yes, all things *do* really work out for good! And God wants to bless you in an unfathomable way! But His blessings aren't always in the form of easy living, everyone loving and appreciating you, or problem-free circumstances—no, they are usually poured out in much different ways...ways that you may not fully understand, just yet. God's main blessing for your life is to do whatever He has to do to get you to rely on Him for everything *through* Jesus. That's how all things work together for good! By allowing Jesus to live through you with His love, forgiveness, confidence, and unwavering hope, everything is *always* working out for good! In Him, we have a good, good, GOOOOOOOOOD life!

A prayer for you: *Father, today I want to thank you for difficult trials. I know that it is in such times, ALL of my complete concentration is on you. So I'm grateful. Keep working everything out in my life for good! Right now, I lift up all who are reading this, directly to you. For the people who are really struggling to see how anything good can come out of their situation, help them. Through these trials, I ask that you begin to renew their minds and heal their souls. Give them a newfound peace and confidence in your loving grace! It is IN your grace that we find all the comfort and hope we need! And it is through our faith in Jesus that we have access to such amazing grace. Thank you, Lord. Amen.*

DAY 46

How Addictions Destroy Your Children

*"Come to me, all who are weary and
burdened, and I will give you rest." ~Jesus*

Matthew 11:28

There is a mall that my family and I frequently shop at. It's a very nice mall, very big and modern. It even has *two* Starbucks' in it. My wife likes to shop; me, not so much. But I'll still go now and again.

Inside this mall is a nice restaurant. It's not overly-fancy or anything, but you can get a nice meal. They have good steak, seafood, sushi, and oysters. But for me, the best part of this restaurant was the fact that it has a bar, *and* it was connected to the mall. This meant easy, quick access, to load up on booze.

Because of this place, I didn't mind going to the mall with Jennifer and Grace. I'd lie to them and say, "I'm gonna go off and shop on my own for a bit." But instead, I'd go to that bar and pound two or three beers, as well as a few shots, and then scoot back off into the mall as if nothing ever happened.

Eventually, I couldn't hide this from them. So instead of going back out into the mall, after quickly smashing a few, I'd just sit there, watching the tv and drinking, while *they* shopped. I get mad at Old Matt while typing this, but it's true. This watering-trough for a closet alcoholic was *perfect*. I could go to the mall and not have to shop, but instead, I could catch a buzz.

About three years ago, I was sitting there at that bar while my family shopped. Jennifer was so annoyed with my drinking by that time, she just ignored it. Grace, however, didn't. She would say things to me some-times that felt like a bowie knife just got slid into my chest-cavity. Of course, I would simply overlook it, and continue to drink away. But this day, as my slightly-drunk rear sat there, something was *different*.

About five drinks in, Grace walked into that bar, pulled out the stool next to me, and sat on it. She then slowly leaned over, put her head on my lap, scooted her stool closer, and then eventually turned over with her face up towards me—as if laying down on her back. She then put her feet up on the next stool over, and was basically using the bar stools as a bed, and my lap as her pillow.

My dumb, buzzed butt, simply scooted back so that she was comfort-able, and I just kept drinking, ignoring the fact that my daughter was laying in a bar, while I drank in the middle of the day.

Then it happened.

She said, "Daddy?"

I replied, "Yes, baby," and I looked down at her face in my lap.

She locked eyes with me, and was as serious as I've ever seen her before...

"Are you ever gonna stop drinking?"...

...That was it. Tears in my eyes started to uncontrollably well-up, and I quickly looked away, immensely convicted of my alcoholism. I couldn't hardly hold back the flow, so I quickly wiped them away. I couldn't let Grace see that I was upset, and taken off-guard. I composed myself then looked back down at her.

"Yeah, baby. I'm gonna quit. I promise."

"Good. Because I don't like it when you drink, and me and Mommy have to shop by ourselves."

This *very* moment was one of the final nails in the coffin of my drinking days. Shortly after, I killed my dependence on alcohol, threw it in a coffin, and buried it. I *killed* my addiction. DEAD. That is, with the help of Christ in me, I MURDERED IT. And that's what you have to do; take away *its* life, so that you, your kids, and your family, can have *your lives*, back.

So today, my friends, know this: Your kids are watching. They are looking to you for EVERYTHING. They are looking to you for *how* to handle all of their problems, for *how* to treat people, and HOW TO LIVE THEIR LIVES! *You* will be responsible for how they turn out. Begin to allow God to transform *your* life, for *their* benefit. LET HIM MOLD *YOU*. LET HIM FORM *YOU* INTO THE IMAGE OF CHRIST! It may not be drinking that you struggle with, it could be anything. But whatever it is that your kids keep asking you to change...change it. They trust you. Today is YOUR DAY—the day you positively alter the life and future of your children, for the better, forever!

A prayer for you: *Good morning, Lord. THANK YOU for this day! Thank you for my sobriety! Thank you for helping me destroy my addiction on May 8th, 2014! You've proven to me that the Bible is true; that I really CAN do all things through Christ's strength IN me! I NEVER THOUGHT I WOULD QUIT DRINKING! AND NOW LOOK! BOOOOOOOM BABY!!!! Right now, I lift up all who are reading this, directly to you. For those who are deep into an addiction,* *or struggle with a bad, destructive habit—HELP THEM. They've tried a thousand times to quit, AND THEY CAN'T! I couldn't quit either. And you don't want us to so much quit, but instead, to BEGIN! You want us to begin a brand new life WITH you! You want us to be transformed by the renewing of our minds. Teach them HOW to begin doing this! Send new people into their lives! REMOVE the people who you want gone! Let them know that you love them EXACTLY as they are! But also, let them know you have a MUCH better plan for their lives, WITHOUT THIS. Speak to their souls and let them know when they DO break free, you will actually USE their past addictions and struggles FOR GOOD! NONE OF IT GETS WASTED! YOU USE IT! Tell them! Let them know that you'll use this pain for an eternal, GOOD purpose—for THEIR PURPOSE, and testimony! Today is the day they break free! I pray this in Jesus' name! Amen!*

DAY 47

CHRISTIANS ARE DEAD TO LAWS, AND ALIVE IN CHRIST

"Christ is the end of the law so that there may be righteousness to everyone who believes."

ROMANS 10:4

I've been asking God to take me deeper in my relationship with Him, my actual prayer is "Lord, help me to know you on the deepest level possible. I want to go deeper."

That type of prayer used to make me cringe because I knew He was going to pull some*thing* or some*one* out of my hand in order to get me to depend on Him, *only*. But now, He doesn't really do that any more. Lots of difficult lessons have been learned, and now fine-tuning is taking place.

Since I've been asking to know Him deeper, the Holy Spirit has lead me to learn more, and more, and MORE about laws and commandments of the Old Testament; how, after Jesus came and went, the Jews kept trying to add to the gospel to make it suffice (see Galatians 3), and how the early churches couldn't fathom just *how* forgiven and righteous they really were with God, simply through their faith in Jesus (see Romans 1).

Like today's churches, they thought there had to be more to it. "You can't *just* believe in Jesus. No way!" This was their mindset (see Hebrews 10). Honestly, I've wanted to move on to something else I could learn about, including a deeper understanding of Islam, or something else I can incorporate into my ministry and books—something more broad and encouraging—something *practical*.

But no. God keeps telling me to learn about how we *can't* earn anything—and that no law or command can be sprinkled in with the gospel at all (see James 2:10). He's wanting me to know that absolutely *everything* is free because of His grace (see Ephesians 2:8,9). And once we simply *believe* that Jesus has forgiven us, we are not *required* to do anything else to *be* a Christian or to *stay* a Christian (no other hoops to jump through or charade to make, see Romans 10:9).

This has upset a lot of legalistic people. "Matt, you can't tell everyone that all they have to do is believe. EVEN THE DEVIL BELIEVES!"

Yeah, that's true, but the devil isn't asking Jesus to forgive him or come into his heart, we are. Sure, the devil's theology *is* correct, he knows the truth: Jesus is the Son of God—but, he is already damned to hell, we aren't. We still have the option of believing in Him *as our Savior*. Satan has no interest in doing that, even *though* he believes. So we gotta stop using that verse (James 2:19) as our defense against faith alone to achieve salvation—it's out of context and incorrect. It's not applicable to this setting of receiving salvation, at all. Instead, it creates fear for new or weak believers in Christ.

When the gospel is completely undiluted—*naked*—all fear goes away because you realize God's love for you in Christ is perfect! This is why John said there is *no fear* in God's love, because fear has to do with punishment. *That's* the reason why we don't have to be afraid! It's because we are *not* going to be eternally punished anymore *for* our sins! Jesus took them away for good! (See 1 John 4:18, Hebrews 9:28).

My goal is to get people to understand this, both believers *and* nonbelievers. The Christians who don't fully "get" what Jesus has done—those who try to make people afraid—they *can't* create fear in you any longer *once* you have invited Jesus into your heart. The Spirit of Christ *in you* cancels out *all* religious fear!

So if you have any fear about the permanence of your salvation after you've accepted Jesus' forgiveness, that fear is not coming from God, but from the darkest pits of hell—DON'T BELIEVE IT! DON'T BE AFRAID!

His grace, which is now your lifeblood, saves you, empowers you, and supersedes *everything* in your life—even your *future* sins. "Future sins too?" Yes. The Bible says as long as Jesus lives, He is able to save us *completely* because we've become one *with* God *through* Him—and He isn't dying again and again, up in heaven, each time we sin! Instead, Jesus has sat down in a place of rest—and He's not making *anymore* sacrifices *for* our sins (see Hebrews 7:25, 10:12, 10:26).

Christ's eternal saving ability, and our access to it by grace through faith in Him, makes the fear of hell and the fear of losing our salvation, go away *despite* the struggles we have with our *un*-renewed behaviors or attitudes which haven't caught up to the truth of Jesus being *in* us.

Further, in regard to losing our salvation, the gospel makes known how *impossible* it is to lose such redemption once had. Ephesians, chapter 1, states that we've been "adopted into God's own family," and "marked with a seal until the day of redemption."

When you get down to the brass tax, the actual Covenant in itself which saves us is between the Father and Jesus, it has nothing to do with us. We are simply the beneficiaries to that contract, and that contract was finalized with Jesus' perfect blood at the Cross (see Hebrews 8:13, 9:22, John 19:30).

We didn't *create* this Covenant through our behavior, and we don't *sustain* this Covenant through our behavior. Instead, we simply open up our hands and *receive it* by believing in it as true for our sin. This is why you *can't* lose your salvation once had, because if you *could* lose it, then it wasn't really free in the first place. And if you could *forfeit* it, after you first believed you were forgiven, then the Father would be forfeiting His end of the deal with Jesus and breaking His *own* promises of *not* remembering our sins any more—and that, He will never do! (See Hebrews 8:12, 2 Timothy 2:13).

This is why God keeps bringing me back to the very thing which the law-based-teaching preachers, who can't fathom grace *by itself*, keep getting mad at me about: No type of *sin*, Old Covenant commandment-breaking, or law-breaking, causes you to lose your seat in heaven. Jesus is *holding* your seat, He paid a very high price *for* that seat, and He ain't letting anyone else sit *in* that seat! IT'S YOURS! We do NOTHING—in action—to get this! We only *take it* from Jesus by faith and say, "Thank you." After that, we show Him *how* thankful we are by allowing Him to live through us.

So, what I've learned by going deep into the books of *Romans*, *Galatians*, and *Hebrews*, is this: OUR BEHAVIOR DOES NOT SAVE US—or *keep* us saved—in any way, shape, or form. *And* our behavior doesn't make our saving any *more* legit. *Only* believing that Jesus has forgiven us of our sins—past, present, and future does...in full...*once*.

Do you believe that? Do you actually believe you have sin which *needs* to be forgiven? Do you believe Jesus *doesn't*? Do you believe He is the Son of God, who died and rose again? Do you believe He has *forgiven you* of your sin? Yes? GOOD! Then you *are* a Christian! You are going to heaven and nobody can change that! Not even you!

My friend, today I want to encourage you to go deeper into *your* relationship with Jesus by removing any notion of fear. Rather it be the fear of not being good enough or the fear of losing your salvation, go *deeper* and begin to realize the truth: *as* a Christian you *are* good enough and it's *impossible* to lose your salvation! I also want to encourage you to finally accept the fact that you are SPIRITUALLY PERFECT! Why? Because Jesus *lives* in your spirit! Once you realize this amazing truth, everything you do from here on out, you will be doing for one *main* reason, "Because I love God." This is all He truly wants from you!

A prayer for you: *Father, today I want to thank you for the revelation of your amazing grace. A grace so deep and wide, that nothing can* *override it—not even the sin of the whole world. I want to thank you for this grace of the Cross, and the grace of your New Agreement with Christ, which has saved me. THANK you, SO much. Right now, I lift up all who are reading this, directly to you. For those who don't understand they can't be un-saved, or un-born again, please, reveal this to their hearts. Reveal to them that we've been adopted into your Family, and you'll never get rid of us—you love us too much to do so. Let them know that THIS is the truth which will finally set them free! Help them to realize they are exactly like you in spirit—because of Jesus— and let them feel the freedom found in not living by a single law, except one: To love you with everything they are, because they don't have to. In Christ's name I pray, amen.*

DAY 48

HOW MANY TIMES SHOULD I FORGIVE OTHERS?

"Then Peter came to Jesus and asked, 'Lord, how many times shall I forgive my brother or sister (or spouse, child, relative, in-law, family member, neighbor, friend, co-worker) who sins against me? Up to seven times?' Jesus answered, 'I tell you, not seven times, but seventy-seven times' (as in 'infinitely,' like Jesus forgives us)."

MATTHEW 18:21-22, (MY NOTES ADDED)

Forgiving others infinitely doesn't mean you continually overlook or *accept* unacceptable behavior. Religious Christians (those who find their identity in what they "do" and "don't do" *for* God) will try to make you feel guilty when you no longer put up with the abuse or poor treatment of others.

When we *do* constantly put up with NOT NORMAL treatment AS NORMAL, this creates *codependency*. Codependency is when you are *not* okay, unless someone else *is* okay—even if it's at the expense of your well-being. It's when you *can't* be happy, unless you make someone *else* is happy. It's trying to control and change the improper behavior of others, and *your* life can't be complete until *you* control *and* change them.

This terrible mindset must be unlearned, by *learning* your full value in Christ. Codependent behavior is rampant in the church, as well as among Christians who *don't* attend church regularly. The "church law" of *forgiving others until your life is on a near-suicidal level* is a seed planted in the souls of believers. The problem is, this is *not* the gospel, and it causes relationships to be frustrating and out of balance. Soon enough, this seed, when watered with legalism, sprouts up into our lives, *growing* a tree of codependency. The fruit that grows *out* of codependency is fear, anxiety, low self-esteem, guilt, and condemnation, all because, "You're not allowed to stand up to others, just take the abuse, *because* you are a Christian."

However, God does *not* agree with this, and Christ teaches you how to break *free* from codependency by planting *new* seeds and reshaping your soul. Jesus, through the example of His sacrifice, teaches us that we are *so* infinitely loved and valued, that He would die for us! So YES! WE *CAN* establish healthy boundaries which others *must* respect.

As the Holy Spirit guides us into this new strength, little by little, we learn to stop trying to change others, and instead, we allow Jesus to change *us*. We stop getting upset about *people* not changing, and we stop trying to change them. *We* are okay, even if they are *not* okay—and we stop ruining our lives *attempting* to change them. This renewed mindset gives us peace as we let the chips fall where they may, while we set healthy boundaries and enforce them with confidence, respect, and love—both, for ourselves *and* others.

When we factor in the *removal* of codependency from our lives, forgiving others infinitely simply means you forgive repeatedly and unendingly *without* resentment or *fear* in your soul. Forgiving infinitely, like Jesus does, means you always hold out hope that the offender will no longer make the same poor choices which are causing you (and possibly others) so much harm. It doesn't mean you continue to *allow* the harm to happen. That's codependency in the fullest! I know about codependency very well because it has run in my family for generations, and *I* finally broke *free* from it with God's help!

But even *worse*, codependency will cause *dependency* on vices from *outside* ourselves—all because we are ignoring repugnant behavior from others, *or* from ourselves, because we refuse to take a stand. For me, my codependency created dependency on several things: alcohol, porn, sex, video-game binging, earning money, physical fitness, golf, basketball, and much more. Everything was *way* out of balance, and for a time, it was even *religion*. When my codependency would flare up, I would try to douse it out with "being a good Christian" or intentionally overlooking the terrible actions of others. "Covering it with the blood!" "Carrying my cross!" were some of my excuses for not saying, "Hey, this is *not* acceptable. Your choices are effecting my life negatively. This *will* change, or this relationship will not be the same."

Codependency causes you *extreme* frustration and anxiety because you are trying to change how you feel, by ignoring how you *really* feel—all because you *can't* change people, and you don't know what else to do to find peace.

As for religion, me abusing *that* was fair game too. The devil had sold me on the incorrect mindset of, "If I could just be like these church people, *then* I would feel better," all while *still* ignoring the actions of others. Oh, I was *so wrong* in thinking this would "fix" me! My dependency just *switched*, right over into legalism. It jumped to *never* missing a church service, *trying desperately* to get the approval of a pastor, and overwhelming myself (while trying to *force* others) into "religious stuff." In turn, I only compounded my *already* tortured soul! I needed relief, *fast*—on a near-suicidal level.

Codependency + dependency = Miserable life.

Jesus came to set us free from *both*, and to give us an *abundant* life! (See John 10:10).

This abundant life begins by simply making yourself available to God each day. As we do, the Holy Spirit starts to renew our minds, we *then* begin to understand our value! As we start to understand our value, we develop a newfound confidence of *balance* in Him. He teaches us how to forgive infinitely, but at the same time, how to create strong barriers which will keep our souls healthy.

Once you begin to let Him do this, any hint of codependency *or* dependency will fall by the wayside, *organically*. The Holy Spirit teaches us how to forgive those who hurt us repeatedly by making a conscious decision to release them from what they owe us, *before* they hurt us, *infinitely*. But along *with* that, He teaches us how to protect ourselves from harm. He teaches us that just because we are Christians, we do *not* have to allow ourselves to be taken advantage of on a grand scale—Jesus took that brunt *for* us, at the Cross, and *we* are *so* valuable that He actually did!

What happens next is we begin to find a healthy medium as we learn how to treat others as Christ treats us: *expecting change—while always holding out hope*. Forgiving others repeatedly doesn't mean you have to keep allowing yourself to be hurt by them. Forgiveness is instant, but *trust* is earned. This is why you have *got* to stand up to those who hurt you, but do it with love and respect. Remember, confrontations are critical for your spiritual health, yet, they should *always* be carried out with Christ guiding your words and actions.

And if the offender is willing to make changes in their choices and how they treat you, then by all means, move forward and enjoy that relationship. But one last time, I want to repeat: SET. HEALTHY. BOUNDARIES. Step back, pray for them diligently, and *think* of them with goodness and love—and while doing so, enjoy your life.

Yes, enjoy your life! You're allowed to enjoy your life, even in the midst of learning how to forgive others infinitely! While doing *that*, and learning how to understand *your* full value to God—enjoy your life! Jesus gives you this right! You can always, no matter what, ENJOY, YOUR, LIFE!

A prayer for you: *Jesus, today I want to thank you for your complete forgiveness of all my sins. Thank you for removing them as far as* the east is from the west, with your blood. I'm forever grateful! Right now, I lift up all who are reading this, directly to you. First, help them to understand just HOW BIG your forgiveness is for THEM; that they are so special to you, you gave your life to makes sure they were forgiven. After they understand this forgiveness, I ask that you teach them how to give it away, unconditionally. But at the same time, I ask that you give them discernment when it comes to what they should and shouldn't allow from others. GIVE THEM STRENGTH! GIVE THEM GRACE! HELP THEM! Make them bold in your love. In your name I pray, amen.

DAY 49

WHAT SHOULD WE BE TAUGHT IN CHURCH?

"So the law was put in charge to lead us to
Christ that we might be justified by faith.
Now that faith has come, we are no longer under
the supervision of the law. You are all sons (and
daughters) of God through faith in Christ Jesus"

GALATIANS 3:24-26, MY NOTE ADDED

It's Sunday! All throughout the country people will be going to church today! Maybe not so much where I live, because there is ice all over the roads this time of year, unless you are *more* saved than other Christians, you are staying home! And for those of you who didn't catch my humor, I'm joking about being "more saved." You can't be. It's impossible. Either you *are* saved, or you're not. There is no in-between, and there are not different levels of salvation—though some might want you to *think* that.

I recently wrote a Facebook post about my grandma; about how she took on the role of being our caregiver growing up. I told how she lived a life of *extreme* servitude, how she showed unconditional love to everyone, and how she gave all she had to make the lives of *others* better. With it, I posted a nice picture of her smiling warmly.

Grandma didn't do any of these selfless acts to put others in debt to her, but simply because she *exuded* Christ on the deepest level possible. She did what she did, all while pointing to Jesus and telling everyone how much *He* loved them.

Grandma didn't hold her help over their heads while barking at them, "Repent! Sinner!" She didn't use guilt or fear, or tell people they were going to hell if they didn't change their lives. She never told anyone to stop being a backslider because they'll burn in the *hottest* place of hell if they didn't. She never told anyone they were getting what they deserved because of their sin, or that they were justly being punished by God for their poor choices. No way...and why not? Because that's not the truth, and she knew it. Instead, she told everyone about how much God *loves* them and how He has a *good* plan for their lives, if they will just step *into* it.

I didn't expect this to happen, but that post about Grandma went viral. Thousands of people liked it, shared it, and commented on it. One lady even posted under Grandma's picture, "She is the true definition of what a Christian should look like." And I understand what this nice woman is trying to say, but she is wrong.

A Christian is a Christian *at heart*—on the inside, in their spirit—*that's* what makes someone a Christian. There is not a particular look or style on the outside, which achieves a person's membership of Christendom. But instead, it is what their *spiritual* DNA looks like. And the only way we can make our genetic spiritual make-up any different, permanently, is by God's free gift of salvation by grace through faith in what Jesus has done *for* us (see Ephesians 2:8,9).

It doesn't matter what we look like on the *outside*, it matters what we look like on the *inside*. We gotta get things in order here. It's not about our wardrobes or behaviors, but about our love and radiance of Jesus. It is our *new heart* which makes us who we truly are! (See Hebrews 8:10, 2 Corinthians 5:17).

And we get this new heart freely, which makes us a new creation, *freely*.

Just like an oak tree will always be an oak tree, no matter if it is thrown into the river and becomes driftwood, or, if a master wood-worker chisels a beautiful desk out of it—at its *core*, that oak tree will *always* be an oak tree.

Same with us Christians. The difficulties of life, the unfair choices of others which affect us negatively, as well as our *own* poor choices, can beat us up and make us *look* like we *aren't* Christian, but we still are. The word *Christian* is a noun, not a verb. Nothing can change *who* we are in our spirits, *once* we believe in Jesus' blood as the truth for our sin! Not even ourselves! (See Galatians 2:20, 2 Timothy 2:13).

Becoming a Christian is a one-time event. Yes, once. The Cross actually worked! (See Hebrews 10:10, Hebrews 7:24, 25, Romans 6:10, 1 Peter 3:18). The new agreement between the Father and the Son came into effect when Jesus *died* (not when He was born), and you and I are simply the beneficiaries (see Hebrews 8:13). We didn't create this agreement, we can't add to it, and we can't sustain it. Our actions have nothing to do with this contract between the Father and Jesus Christ, instead, we open up our hands and simply *receive* it. This is the *only* way we are saved. This is *how* we become heirs of *Jesus'* inheritance! WOW! (See Romans 8:17, Colossians 1:12, Hebrews 7:18-26).

This will upset those who are constantly pestered by a religious spirit. They'll say "No! There is more to it!" Friend, I'm sorry, but there is not. Jesus finished *everything* (John 19:30), and now, we are *all* equal no matter what, the very *first time* we believed He has forgiven us (see Galatians 3:28).

So just why is it, that us Christians—us *believers* in Christ's forgiveness—see *other* Christians as dirty driftwood? That is, if they don't polish up their lives, or if they aren't doing a bunch of good things? It's because of what we've been taught *in church*. Incorrect teaching.

So many of us can personally testify to this. You walk into church, looking for something to make your life better, but instead you walk *out* feeling judged, holding a new "churchy to-do list" in your heart, thinking, "I gotta do *this* in order to *be* better." You were looking for a new sense of peace, but instead, you get a handed a behavioral-improvement program syllabus. "You gotta become a member!" "You gotta PROVE you belong through a LIFESTYLE change and REPENTANCE!"

Do this! Don't do that! Stay away from THEM. Judge non-church members rightly! straighten up! Die daily! You're a dirty sinner! God isn't here to help you achieve your dreams! Confess every sin, or you ain't forgiven of ALL them—and do this every day! Be godly! Be HOLY!

We get told, "The wicked are taking over the world and we gotta TAKE IT BACK! We gotta make them SEE how God ain't putting up with this sin any longer!" "DO MORE! LIVE RIGHT! REPENT! Make the WORLD repent!"

You walk out of church thinking, *"MAN! I feel terrible! This planet is going to hell in a hand-basket! I don't stand a chance!"* Or worse, you begin to think that you *are* better than the world! Some Christians think that if you don't walk out of the church doors feeling beat to crap, it wasn't a good sermon. *Some* even believe if the pastor *doesn't* point out how bad *everyone* is—not just Christians—and what all *we* gotta do to make those dirty sinners, ear-ticklers, and rotten people, "REPENT OF *THEIR* SINS!"—then they just can't enjoy their fried chicken afterwards.

It's disgusting. We gotta flip the script. We gotta refocus our teachings. Overall, *what* we are being taught in church, has to change. We gotta start making God look good, loving, encouraging, and with His arms open wide for *everyone* who will place their faith in Jesus as their Savior.

The religious Christians will say, "Yeah, YOU'RE RIGHT! But they gotta REPENT! Their faith ain't *real* without TRUE repentance!" Really? What is your definition of true repentance? Being like you? Nobody wants that. That's why so many people won't *go* to church, and why when they *leave* their church, they don't come back. The love of Christ was not shown—instead, religion was.

There are people who will actually go to hell because they look at someone who barks out this type of teaching (turning repentance of incorrect attitudes and actions into a *law*) and they will not even give

Jesus a *chance* because they don't want anything to do with what that legalistic person has got. They know they can't be perfect, and after experiencing this type of teaching, they think they can't be *transparent* either, about their struggles in life—so they won't even try. It's sad.

The false-advertising of Jesus' "conditional love" is ruining many lives, as well as many *after*-lives. Religious Christians are setting up a goal for others to strive for, which *they* aren't even achieving themselves. And if they think they actually *are*, that their "level" of repentance has tipped the scales of God's judgment and favor over in their direction… then…this is sad to say, but they don't really even know *Jesus*, themselves. That is, if they honestly believe their repentance of wrong thinking and actions has earned them *anything*, including salvation. All that is required to be saved, to become a Christian, to have our DNA *swapped* with Jesus, is repentance of….drumroll…….*Un-belief!* We have to stop NOT believing that Jesus has saved us completely. (See Romans 10:9, John 6:29).

I can already hear the angry rebuttal now, "REALLY MATT?! You better be scared of hell, yourself! You are lying to all these people! You are giving them a license to sin! WE GOTTA REPENT OF *ALL* OUR SINS! EVERY DAY!"

Well, I can say this: I'm not afraid. You can't scare me. I know who I am, and I know what Jesus has done for me. I don't have to be afraid, because fear has to do with punishment. And because of what Jesus has done for me, I know that I *won't* be punished, any longer (see 1 John 4:18).

Friend, people are sinning just fine with*out* a license–you, me, everyone. It is when we understand the sinless Spirit *in* us, Christ Himself, that we sin a whole lot less, and for the right reasons. And if you honestly think this way—that you must keep track of your repentance level—you, yourself, are in turmoil, or absolute naiveté. I know because I've been there; thinking I could possibly "repent" of every single sin—even the sins of omission—always trying to keep track of *each* sin, so I could be *sure* to repent of it, and then being anxious and petrified of the punishment God would send my way if I *didn't* repent of each and every one! I repented until my repenter was broken! This was all I focused on—not Jesus, but repentance of my mistakes.

And then I tried to force *other* people to repent like me—and nearly ruined my life trying. I became self-righteous, frustrated, and furious.

Further, because of the incorrect teaching of, "CHANGE! OR ELSE YOU'RE DISQUALIFIED!" the devil had me convinced God wouldn't take care of me, or answer my prayers. I was constantly flinching. Unless my life *immediately* changed, in every single way; and unless my "lack of sin" and so-called "good works" far outweighed my "small" Christian faults, I wasn't *really* saved.

Lies. All lies. Satan wanted me to think that I had to *earn* God's love, and worse, that I had to work to *keep* His love, and *make* others do the same. All that is required to be saved from hell, to become a child of God, to not have to abide by any law of the Old Testament or any modern-day church law, is to repent of my non-belief in Jesus *as* my "good enough." I didn't get this teaching in church for a long time. Instead, I ended up being taught this by the Holy Spirit as I sought Him out each and every *day*—not by being spoon-fed lies, *weekly*.

Before I had this supernatural epiphany, my life was absolutely *miserable* as a Christian. I kept *trying hard* to quit drinking, and failed. I kept *trying hard* to stop having such a bad temper, and failed. I kept *trying hard* to quit flirting with other women who were not my wife, and failed. I kept *trying hard* to put down the video game controller and spend time with my kids, and failed. I kept *trying hard* to watch every single word I said because my mouth was so foul....and failed.

I kept trying to be good enough, I kept trying to "LIVE RIGHT!" as the church people yelled at me each week...and failed. Failed. Failed. Failed...I kept failing because I was focused on the *wrong thing*—myself. I needed to stop focusing on *my* faults, and begin focusing on my *perfection*, which was Christ *in* me. I needed to start focusing on my *Who*, and stop focusing on my *do*–because it's *done*. (See John 19:30).

This is why I left the church I was at and found another, and why many, *many* more people are leaving their churches each week as well. They can't live up to the incorrect teaching.

This is also why so many Christians live double-lives. Rather than be transparent about their struggles, they hide them, or keep battling them privately because they know if they bring them out into the open, they will be shamed. Jesus, on the other hand, wants us to relax in *His* righteousness—not our own. (See Philippians 4:13, James 5:16, Matthew 11:28,29).

When we are focused on the truth of the *gospel*, we don't have *anything* to be ashamed of. *This* is the authenticity of Christianity that will finally set you free! Realizing that *no* amount of behavior/attitude change (definition of religious Christian repentance), will make you right with God—*only* your relationship with Jesus will. And no amount of water (physical baptism) can wash away your sins.

True repentance is understanding who God has freely made you, in *spirit*. *True* repentance is understanding you've been seated in heavenly places with Christ! (See Ephesians 2:6). The supernatural locomotive pulling *every other cart* of Christianity behind it, is *Belief In Jesus*. This is the horse in front of the cart. Behavior and thinking repentance, water baptism, and good works, are all towed behind. Those things are not the *how* we are saved, but the *because* we are saved.

True repentance is finally understanding that you are *not* condemned any longer! (See Romans 8:1). It's finally realizing the truth that you *are* a child of God, saved by grace through faith! (See Galatians 3:26, Ephesians 2:8,9).

So yes, we repent, we change *everything* because we don't *have* to, and, because we know that we can't make Jesus leave us alone no *matter* our behavior. We repent, we change, because we love Jesus. Everything we *now* do, is based on our love for Him. Nothing more, nothing less.

This is why Jesus said, "If you love me, you'll keep my commands" (John 14:15). This is also why Jesus said to Peter *three* times, "Peter, do you love me?" "Peter, do you love me?" "Peter, do you love me?" and each time Peter said, "You know I do!" (See John 21).

It's not about a *have to* anymore, it's about a *want to*. It's about a loving relationship. This is what we need to learn in church, which is *Who* we really are at our core. We need to be told how *good* we are because of Jesus in us! We need to show others a relaxing relationship, not more rules or a strenuous job-criteria. And more than anything we need to begin to show the lost who Jesus really is, how we've not earned a thing, that it's all been free from the beginning of our faith in Him—and that *they* can have Him too, for free, as well.

A prayer for you: *Heavenly Father, thank you. Thank you for making me just like Jesus in spirit, perfect in your eyes. Now, give me the strength to gracefully live Him out, through my flesh and soul. Thank you for loving me so much that you would give me access to you for free, by my simple faith in Him! You are such a good God! I love you! Right now, I lift up all who are reading this, directly to you. For those who have been beat into the ground by incorrect church teaching, help them to realize who they truly are in Christ. Begin to renew their minds by them understanding your unconditional love for them, through Jesus. And for those who might be on the opposite end of that spectrum, those who have strived so hard to be good, that now, they've become self-righteous, bitter, cold, and extremely judgmental towards everyone who isn't exactly like them—renew their minds as well. Give them rest. Give them peace. In Jesus' name, I bring all of this to you, amen.*

DAY 50

HOW TO DEFEAT THE DEVIL

"The thief comes only to steal and kill and destroy; I have come that they may have life, and have it to the full." ~Jesus

JOHN 10:10

Right before Jesus tells us that He came to earth so we can enjoy life to the fullest, He clearly warns us of an enemy—a *thief*—the devil. If you are a Christian and you don't take the devil's work seriously, or you ignore him, you will eventually become bamboozled, disoriented, looking around wondering, *"What just happened?"* and, *"Why things are falling apart? I don't understand?"*

You must begin to recognize your enemy! He is highly organized and very intelligent! He is like a mad scientist, formulating the best temptations and troubles to trip you up. He holds board meetings with his demons to strategize your most painful demise. He has studied and memorized the Bible—verbatim—and his goal is to take Scripture out of context in order to make you hate God, ignore Him, or to be petrified of Him. Satan tries to trick you into making dumb choices that will destroy you *based* on God's Word being twisted! He even tried doing this to Jesus! (See Luke 4:1-13).

RECOGNIZE YOUR ENEMY! HE IS HERE TO RUIN YOUR LIFE! HE *HATES* YOU WITH EVERYTHING HE IS! HE WANTS YOUR SOUL IN HELL! Jesus said that Satan is the *father of lies*, and that he doesn't even have the *ability* to tell the truth! (See John 8:44). Jesus also said the devil only has *three* main objectives for his disgusting existence: STEAL. KILL. DESTROY (see John 10:10). Spiritually, he is always hard at work—mostly in our *minds*. This is where the battle rages and where we must grow each day, becoming stronger and stronger in Christ as time goes by (see Romans 12:2, Philippians 1:6).

But we are *not* powerless! We have weapons! Weapons which are not carnal, but *spiritual* (see 2 Corinthians 10:4,5). From the moment we place our faith in Jesus we are fully equipped with every weapon we need *because* He then lives *in* us! Now, we just have to allow the Holy Spirit to teach us how to let Him live *out* of us. This takes time, but it *is* possible as we allow the Holy Spirit to guide our actions and attitudes. And when we begin to *do* this, the enemy stands no chance! He becomes an ant, Christ in us becomes the boot.

The Apostle John, goes so far as to call us *overcomers* because he said, "He who is *in* us, is greater than he (Satan) who is in this world!" (See 1 John 4:4). The Apostle Paul, builds on this by saying, "put on the full armor of God, so that we can take a stand against the devil's evil schemes...(we are) strong in the Lord and in *his* mighty power!" (See Ephesians 6:10,11 emphasis added). We have nothing to be afraid of, ever! That's why Jesus said this *all* the time! Christ *in us* gives us the authority to *stomp* on Satan's head—spiritually! (See Luke 10:19).

So just *how* do we do this? John tells us: "through the blood of Jesus and by our testimonies" (see Revelation 12:11). As believers, Christ's blood has "sealed us up in heavenly places until the Day of Redemption" (see Ephesians 2:6, 4:30), there's step one. So what's next? Our *testimonies*! We gotta tell people what Jesus has freely done for us!

Once we begin to use our testimonies, so that we are relatable, we move *forward* by overcoming evil *with* good! (See Romans 12:21). We gotta do *good* things! (See Ephesians 2:10). The more evil that hits us, the more *good* we should be doing! THIS IS HOW WE FIGHT BACK!

But most of all, in order to defeat the enemy and allow Christ to live through us in His most *pure* form, we gotta love people. Paul said that without love, his words and actions mean nothing (see 1 Corinthians 13). We *must* love. We must. We must love God, people, and ourselves. They all link together, and the love of *Jesus* should be the bond.

So today, my friends, know this: The devil is a sissy. Do *not* be afraid of him! Instead, run at him like David did Goliath! Use the Word of God, praise, thankfulness, and prayer, as the rocks in your slingshot! Don't cower *away* from hell, but instead, *attack* hell—not people, not sin—but hell. Let Jesus live through you *gracefully* and you'll accomplish this feat *organically*. You see, once Jesus is sealed up inside your heart, by grace through faith (see Ephesians 2:8,9) the devil and his demons can't get in there. Once Jesus lives in you, Satan becomes like the Wizard of Oz, a weak old man behind a curtain, making loud noises and blowing smoke...harmless. Sure, the devil and his demons can *try* to poke at you, prod, scream and shout, but CHRIST IN YOU is *not* sharing your heart—He *finished* you at the Cross, you accepted Him, and now He is staying forever. So *don't* be afraid. (See John 19:30, 2 Timothy 1:7, 2:13, Hebrews 7:25).

A prayer for you: *God, I want to thank you for making your home in me. I know that because you are always there inside my heart, I am strong. No matter what or who I face, I have all the power, weapons, and armor that I need to protect myself and demolish every stronghold—which is you IN me. I'm never without JUST the right amount of strength needed to make it through anything. You always give me grace, upon grace, upon grace! And it is your grace which allows me to do ALL THINGS THROUGH CHRIST—including overpowering the enemy and leaving him discouraged each day. HE IS NOTHING. I AM EVERYTHING—all because of your Holy Spirit in me! Right now, I ask that you infuse your graceful power into these dear readers.*

For those who can't fathom this, reveal it! For those who doubt this, increase their faith! And for those who are afraid, give them courage to simply take a step forward, and then another, and then...another. You love us! And we are so grateful for the abundant life you've given us, through Jesus. Amen.

Day 51

How Is Your Outflow?

*"Each of you should give what you have decided
in your heart to give, not reluctantly or under
compulsion, for God loves a cheerful giver."*

2 Corinthians 9:7

Are you a giver? Let me tell you a story about someone who is. My older brother, Luke, is a barber, a very popular one. People flock to his barbershop to get a great haircut. He takes his time, as if he is an artist painting a picture that everyone will see. People like Luke—a lot. He is very likable.

But being an extremely talented barber isn't Luke's best feature. Luke's best trait is that he is a "giver of his company." What I mean by that is people will *also* flock to his home—not only the barbershop—just to hang out with him and his family. They have that old-school, busy house, food cooking, kids playing, chill, wholesome atmosphere.

Someone is always joking, the kids are chasing the dog, a video-game challenge is going on—*something*, at all times, is happening. And the backbone of this family is Luke and Paula's *giving*. Giving of what? An open, welcoming home, to anyone.

There is something comforting about going to Luke and Paula's house; being with them and the girls makes you feel like family, even if you're not. They have four beautiful little girls (and they wanted more, believe that?). Emma, Sophie, Bella, and Layla are always smiling, running around playing, hanging on you, asking for a bite of your food, and just being good kids.

Luke is a *giver* of his space—his home. I couldn't say I'd be able to do it on the level that Luke does. He is always taking someone in who doesn't have a place to stay, when everyone else rejects them. When people are having a hard time in life and they just want a place to go and sit, to be around others for no particular reason, they go to Luke and Paula's house.

Someone is always there, and Luke is always sitting right there with them, giving his company, time, home, and space. He gives. The Bible says that *God loves a cheerful giver* (see 2 Corinthians 9:7). What most people don't understand is that this does *not* always have to be money.

Being a barber, Luke is not rich. And he has a large family so he has to pay close attention to the amount of money he spends. He might not be able to fund an orphanage overseas, or financially support a new addition of a church—but he gives what he *has*—his home, his company, his family, his time.

This is what *he* gives. We all give differently. It could be your ear, your FaceTime, your phone call, or simply your presence. Giving is handing over *your* time, *your* energy, *your* talents, *your* resources, and your prayers. We *give* forgiveness, gratitude, honor, and love.

And when we give, we can tell we are doing it right, because there is a steady *outflow* from our lives into others'. In Israel, there is a place called the Dead Sea. It is a giant salty lake that has no life in it, no fish or creatures; matter of fact, it is ten times saltier than the ocean. Why is this? It's because it has no *outflow*. It takes water in constantly, and none ever goes out. It doesn't *give* anything back, so it is dead.

Ask yourself today: *"How is my outflow? Am I taking so much in that I've become salty? So salty, there is no life in the waters of my soul?"*

Now, I'm sure that's not the case with you, but some people actually *are* like that. WE *MUST* GIVE! WE MUST! And we must give out of the goodness of our hearts, which is *where* Jesus lives! God is a giver, and His home is inside us, so *we* should be givers too (see John 3:16, 2 Corinthians 5:21). And always remember that we don't give to *get*, we give because...we *love*. That's why God gives. Luke and his family *love* people. They are grace-filled, non-judgmental Christians and everyone is welcome in their home at all times. That's outflow. That creates *life*.

So today, my friends, know this: Your Creator is the Ultimate Giver! And He's already inside you once you place your faith in Jesus as your Savior! He loves you so much, that He *gave* you Jesus! Let's all evaluate our giving today, and ask God, "Will you show me how to give like you?" Make no mistake, He will!

A prayer for you: *Heavenly Father, today I'm grateful for how giving you are to me because you love me. Thank you for Jesus, thank you for your Holy Spirit, thank you for my family, my home, my job, my sobriety, my ministry, and my good health—just to name a few things to be thankful for. THANK YOU, so much! Right now, I lift up all who are reading this, directly to you. For those who are NOT grateful, but they WANT to be, help them. Begin to reveal in their hearts, through your Holy Spirit, the blessings you've ALREADY given them. Teach them how to have a grateful and GIVING attitude. Help them begin to understand that all they have in life is because of you giving it, INCLUDING their life. And teach us ALL how to give, myself included, like you do. Thank you, thank you, thank you—we are grateful, and we love you. Amen.*

DAY 52

How To Break Free From Self-Made Slavery

"So if the Son sets you free, you will be free indeed." ~Jesus

JOHN 8:36

W hat does it really mean to be a slave? Does it mean you're bound up in shackles? Does it mean you are being *forced* to work, or something else you don't want to do, for free?…What *is* slavery?

Jesus defined what true slavery is: *self-made* slavery. He said, "You're really only a slave if you are a slave to sin" (see John 8:34). What I didn't understand for so long was how could *sin* make *me* a slave? After all, I'm in control of my own attitudes and actions, right? And further, the Bible says that I'm dead to sin and alive in Christ (see Romans 6:11).

So if I *do* sin, *because* I'm a new creation *in* Christ (at my spiritual core, I'm Jesus is there) then it's not really even *me* who sins (because Jesus *can't* sin), but instead, it's sin itself *in* me, as a parasite, a foreign object (see 2 Corinthians 5:17, 5:21, Romans 7:17).

Yes, I know this is difficult to grasp, but *this* is the truth of the gospel which sets us free, which is…*we've* had a supernatural DNA swap with Christ! This is *hard* teaching to understand! And it was *Paul* who began to teach this way. The self-proclaimed, *best* former legalist ever (see Philippians 3:4-6), Paul said sin has *no* control over who we really are, as Christians! How is that even possible?! This is why Peter said, "Paul's letters contain some things that are hard to understand," but he goes on to call Paul "a dear brother with the wisdom that God gave him" (see 2 Peter 3:15,16).

So, if sin *in* me is simply a leech, and I can't rid my body *of* sin on this side of heaven, even *as* a Christian, what am I to do? Paul answers that exact question right after he calls sin a foreign object in his own body: "Thanks be to God, who delivers me through Jesus Christ our Lord!" (Romans 7:25). *Jesus* is who sets us free *from* the slavery of sin! Not us! Instead, we die *in spirit*, by grace through faith—once—and we become alive *with* Christ, actually resurrected in *His* spirit (see Romans 6:3,4, Galatians 2:20, Hebrews 10:10). So now, as believers in this, we are *all* holy saints who "sin sometimes," but make no mistake, sin does *not* define us in any way!

Knowing this truth about our spiritual identity is crucial because sin is still a part of our lives as human beings—as *flesh*. So what do we do when sin *does* peak out its ugly head? We *recognize* it, and *turn* from it. This is called "repentance." Repentance of attitudes and actions that don't match up with the character of the Holy Spirit *allows* Christ to live through us—but this is *not* what keeps Him *in* us. What keeps Him in us, is our one-time repentance of unbelief in His forgiveness *of* our sin.

So the longer we take to repent of sin—*not unbelief*—the longer we will be a slave to it. This does not mean you become *un*-saved until you turn from a particular sin. If that were the case, we'd all be in trouble because Christians sin, a lot.

So the question is, "How do we break free?!"…Jesus tells us! One of the best things about Jesus is that when He tells us what's wrong with us, He doesn't just leave us there—He wants to help us learn and grow, in Him. As He gently corrects us, He always guides us in the right direction, *away* from sin, so that our actions and attitudes will begin to match up with God's plan for our lives, as well as *Who* is living in us.

His answer to help us break free from the self-made slavery of sin, is one word: *Grace*. All of *your* power to overcome sin comes from *His* grace. Most of the time, when we can't break free from a particular sin in which struggle with severely, it's because we are trying *too hard* to stop. What we need to do is *stop* trying to stop, and rest in His grace. Sure, it sounds counter-productive, but when *we* stop trying, and instead, we begin to rely on *His* grace, miracles can happen! My sobriety is proof of this! It wasn't until I stopped trying to quit, that I actually did! And that's because instead of focusing on quitting so much, I began focusing on *beginning* a new life based on showing Jesus that I actually loved Him—*because* of His grace.

When we begin to base all of our thoughts, words, and actions *on* Him; when we run everything *by* Him first, to make sure it's truthful *according* to Him—even if it hurts—*then* we can break free from our self-made sin slavery *by* His grace!

His grace is what gives us the ability to break free from addictions, fear, codependency, guilt, loneliness, anguish, legalism, hate, criticism, unforgiveness, bitterness, and everything else that does not match up with Jesus Christ, who is in you.

So today, my friends, let me ask you something: Are you ready to break free? Jesus will *personally* set you free from sin and break your chains! Ask Him to! Allow Him to live *through* you, and *He* will make you a very free person, today!

A prayer for you: *Father, thank you for making me spiritually perfect like you. Through my faith in Jesus' sacrifice for me, I know this is what I am, at my spiritual core—perfect. Thank you for killing off my sinful spirit with Jesus, and raising me to eternal life with Him as well. Your Word says in Romans 6, that I have been set free from sin and I have become a slave to righteousness. Thank you for this gift! I AM a slave to righteousness! Shackled forever! Since I am like you in spirit, please use my body as a tool for YOUR good work, and reshape* *my soul—my mind, my will, and my emotions—as I get to know you deeper and deeper each day. The sin that is in me, help me to chain it up and starve it, as I continue to water my soul with all things Jesus. Right now, I lift up all who are reading this, directly to you. For those who are stuck in a particular sin pattern, drench them with your grace. It could be an addiction, dishonesty, jealousy, pride, or an incorrect attitude of being extremely judgmental and hyper-critical—any sin struggle— help them. Let them come to understand just how much power is really in them, because of your grace! In Jesus' name, amen.*

DAY 53

WHY YOU SHOULDN'T BE AFRAID OF GOD

*"The fear of the Lord is the beginning (not
the middle, or the end) of wisdom, and knowledge
of the Holy One (Jesus) is understanding."*

PROVERBS 9:10 (MY NOTES ADDED)

The Bible says that God has not given us a spirit of fear, but of power, love, and a sound mind (2 Timothy 1:7)—and that *Spirit*, which He has given us, is Christ Himself *in* our bodies (see 1 Corinthians 3:16). As Christians, Jesus is infused with our spirits, once we believe He has forgiven us of our sins (see Romans 6). The devil, however, has been using the incorrect notion of, "Be very afraid of God," to torment Christians for centuries; and he does this *in our minds.* He tries to get us to believe God is not happy with us, or that He is disappointed in us, or that He doesn't *really* love us—as if His love is conditional and based on our lack of bad behavior combined with our overabundance of good works.

Satan wants us to think we must *do* more, and *keep* doing more, in order to make sure God doesn't stay mad at us. Friend, God is *not* mad at you. You are no surprise to Him! He knew what He was getting when He decided to create you, and He has a great plan for your life! But the devil's goal is to attempt to keep you fearful and frustrated by constantly striving to achieve more good works, and produce more good behavior, as if you are making "deposits" into God's bank account—and in the back of your mind, the enemy wants you to believe you can one day cash out.

To counteract this demonic cycle of lies, all we need to do is go to God's Word and see what He says about His love for us. HIS LOVE IS GOOD! It's unlike anything we can imagine in our finite brains! Is His love based on anything *we* do? Obviously it's not, because the Bible says, "while we were still sinners, Christ died for us," and that, "this is how He *demonstrated* His love" (see Romans 5:8). So if He loved me before I even placed my faith in Jesus, what makes me think that anything I do, or don't do, afterwards, would make Him love me more?! He loves us all equally—believer or not—He just wants us to be *forgiven*. That, we must choose.

Since we are talking about *not* being afraid of God, what does love have to do with that? John, the self-proclaimed, "disciple whom Jesus loved" (see John 13:23), asserts, "God's love for us is *perfect*," that, "there is *no fear in His love*," and, His "perfect love *casts out all fear* because fear has to do with punishment" (see 1 John 4). John's *last* statement, "fear has to do with punishment," ties this all together!

As a Christian, because of our faith in Jesus as our Savior, we are no longer going to be eternally punished by God, no matter what we do or don't do (see Romans 3:21-31). The devil, also known as "the accuser," (see Revelation 12:10), doesn't want you to believe this amazing truth. He knows if he can get you to become petrified of God, even as a believer, (and he does this by accusing you in your mind, all day long, of lies), he will then be able to accomplish one of two things in your life:

1. **Because you are so afraid of God, you'll work *harder* and *harder* to do religious stuff and "behave," in order to make sure God isn't mad at you.** You will constantly be trying to tip the scale over into your favor through church works, begging for forgiveness, trying to keep track of all your sins so you can be

sure to ask for forgiveness of each one, and repent—*and*, you'll constantly be judging yourself on how well you're doing at this (and you'll also keep track of how well *others* are doing, compared to you). But deep down, you know that nothing you're doing—or not doing—can possibly make God happy. This fear of God is based on what *you* do, not on what Jesus has done *for* you.

2. **Because you are so afraid of God, you'll begin to ignore Him, and eventually you'll give up on Him altogether because you've tried so hard to "be good," and you never seem to be able to pull it off.** Plus, the hyper-critical Christians always point out what all is wrong with you, rather than *Who* is right *in* you. And instead of bringing their incorrect opinion of you to God, so you can get *His* opinion, you just believe them. You can never live up to your *own* expectations, or theirs. Deep down, you know that nothing you're doing—or not doing—can possibly make God happy. This fear of God is based on what *you* do, not on what Jesus has done *for* you.

Both ways of fear eventually create depression, anxiety, and then lastly, *anger*. For #1, anger towards those who aren't "good like you." For #2, anger towards those who "think they're *holier* than you."

There is a better way! A way of living a *fearless* life! A life based on courage and confidence in knowing who you really are at your spiritual core! Jesus! This is why Jesus said *He* is the way! (See John 14:6). This courage and confidence comes from Christ *in* us, coming *out* of us, strengthening us *spiritually*! (See Philippians 4:13).

What happens after we have this supernatural epiphany is this: we no longer focus on what *we do* to get right and stay right with God, because we know that we *are* right, by grace through *simple faith* in Jesus as the truth! (See Ephesians 2:8,9). After this revelation is set in our souls—GOD'S PERFECT LOVE FOR US IN CHRIST—we become BOLD Christians because we understand that everything we are *is* Christ! OH MY GOSH THIS IS GRRRRRRREAT NEWS!!!

This new bravery sky-rockets our good works, correct attitudes, and right behaviors, ALL BECAUSE WE AREN'T AFRAID OF HIM! These actions and mindsets *then become* authentic in His grace alone! If you really think about it, what kind of father wants their kids to be afraid of him? Not a good one! And *our* God, is a good, good Father!

So today, my friends know this: If you are looking for rest from fear, please begin to recognize that Jesus *is* your rest. It was Jesus who satisfied the wrath of the Father, once and for all, at the Cross! (See Hebrews 10:10). And now, because of your faith in Him, *He* is your fearless life! *HE* IS! Christ *in* you! Jesus finished everything required by God *for* you, for free! Enjoy it, live *Him* out, and don't be afraid! (See John 19:30, 1 Peter 2:24, 2 Corinthians 5:21, Galatians 3:13, Hebrews 4:11).

A prayer for you: *Heavenly Father, thank you for being a good dad. Thank you for loving me, disciplining me, guiding me, protecting me, and for showing me that I don't ever have to be afraid of you. I'm so grateful for you being my dad! Help me to be a good father, just like you. Right now, I lift up all who are reading this, directly to you. For those who have been lied to, and taught wrongly about you; for those who think they must constantly hold their heads low, be meek, or think twice about asking you for anything—REJUVENATE THEM WITH YOUR LOVE! Make them BRAVE, make them CONFIDENT, show them they can approach you BOLDLY, because of Jesus! Make them CARING LIKE YOU! Help them to understand just how WIDE and DEEP is your graceful, unconditional love! MAKE THEM NOT AFRAID ANY LONGER, BUT INSTEAD, GIVE THEM YOUR GRACEFUL STRENGTH TO EXUDE JESUS CHRIST! If you can do this for me, you can do this for anyone. Help them. Please. Help them to change the world with this love. In Jesus' name, amen.*

DAY 54

How Do I Control My Mouth?

"The tongue of the wise brings healing."

PROVERBS 12:18

Have you allowed the Holy Spirit to teach you how to control your mouth? It took me *forever* to learn how to do this; and I *couldn't* do it, on my own. It wasn't until I came to know Christ closely that He taught me just how extremely important my words actually were. Before that, I didn't really care what I said or how I said it—or to *whom* I said it to.

For years, I was a Christian who couldn't give a rip about my words. I'd be the first to slam someone on social media, or in real life, completely dishonoring them. I'd be quick to voice something negative about another individual, send a nasty text, or jump in on a conversation where someone was getting verbally destroyed; it didn't matter if I liked them or not. Plus, I always added my own fuel to the fire of the gossip—gossiping was almost a hobby for me.

I WAS A CHRISTIAN WHO COULDN'T CARE LESS ABOUT WHAT I SAID. PERIOD. I HAD *NO* HOLY SPIRIT FILTER. My mind hadn't yet been *renewed*.

I'd slander others on a whim, it didn't matter if they were standing in the room next to me, or *in* the other room; then I'd get mad at *them* if they took offense to my so-called joking, "Oh you're just being a baby." I'd poke fun at people with no regard for their feelings, and then I'd resent them for being so "sensitive." I think back now, on some of the stuff I said to people—my wife, kids, friends, employees, and even some of my enemies—and I cringe. If I'm not careful, I can allow the enemy to make me think that's who I still am, but I'm not. 2 Corinthians 5:17 says otherwise, that I'm a *new* creation in Christ!

Although I'll let one slip out now and again, and I don't like it, back *then* I'd curse left and right as if I just got out of military training—and I wouldn't even think twice about it. "Don't you *dare* judge me!" was how I responded when I got called out on just *how* foul my language was.

I WAS A SLAVE TO MY MOUTH—my *flesh*. And my *soul*—my mind, my *words*, and my emotions—hadn't yet caught up with Christ who was *in* me. Oh, and if you wanted to get into an argument with me?...Brace yourself...I was one of the best when it came to insults and verbalizing "what all is wrong with YOU!"

My problem was, as a Christian—*a person who Christ Himself indwelled*—I would *not* allow Him to control my mouth. He was there, infused with *my* spirit (see Romans 6, Galatians 2:20), but I had Him gagged by my own free will. He was in me, but I wouldn't allow Him to exude any self-control *out* of me. Although, that *is* a fruit of the Spirit—*self-control* (see Galatians 5:22, 23)—something which should grow *from* me, organically, *without* effort, as a Christian.

Still yet, I refused to listen to Him which resulted in my mouth controlling *me*, which constantly caused severe trouble in my life. This is why the Bible says, "The power of life and death is in the tongue" (see Proverbs 18:21). James, the half-brother of Jesus, even makes the claim that our tongues are like small sparks which can set an entire forest ablaze (see James 3:5).

I kept hearing in my spirit, "Matt, watch what you say." "*Maaaaatt*, do NOT say that." "Matthew, don't send that text." "Matt! Please, *don't* post that!" Even now, I still hear these things, and when I do, I try my best listen and obey, and I use God's grace to give me the strength to pull it off. Sure, I fail sometimes, but my goodness, I'm so much better than I used to be!

The main reason why I didn't control my mouth was because I had no respect for Jesus, *because* I still didn't know Him very well. He had saved me from hell, and that was about it. So how could I possibly let Him live through me if I wasn't deeply acquainted with Him? I couldn't. I needed to get to know Him, and to this very day I'm still doing that.

Thankfully, God has promised me that this process of getting to know Him will not end until I shed this body-shell (see Philippians 1:6). So I'm always confident in the fact that Jesus is constantly taking me up to new levels of intimacy and knowledge of Him—but today, right now, this *very* moment—I have all the knowledge I need to accomplish what He wants me to accomplish, *today*. This is why the Bible says God takes us from glory to glory as we learn more about His will, which is Jesus Christ in us, living out of us (see 2 Corinthians 3:18).

I realized as a teenager that God had given me a gift of creativity with my words, and for most of my life I wasn't using my words for Him. Unbeknownst to me, because I *didn't* know Jesus deeply, I was using my words for the devil's benefit. I had tons of self-made excuses as to why I said the things I said, and I had many people and situations to blame for why *my* mouth was out of control. God wanted to change that.

How?

Simple: By *me* getting to know *Jesus*, personally, *daily*.

If you're ever going to learn how to control your mouth, you *have* to allow Jesus to live through you, it's the only way. If you try to pull this off any *other* way, you will be putting too much pressure on yourself. And the only way you can let Jesus live through you without effort, is you *have* to understand Jesus' personality and how *He* spoke. You can't just guess or fly by the seat of your pants when it comes to knowing your Creator's nature, temperament, and disposition. Your *deep* relationship with Jesus Christ—actually having a "meeting of the minds" with Him—*knowing* Him on an intimate level, has to be *purposeful.*

His Holy Spirit in *your* body reshapes this part of you—the customizable part, your soul—*as* you get to know Him and start to *show* Him that you love Him. Spiritually, He educates you on how to use your words for love, not for hate; for healing, not retaliation; for peacemaking, not for trouble-making. Christ *in you* teaches you self-control…SELF…control, in all things, this includes your words.

So today, my friends, don't be like I used to be, don't take so long to get to know Jesus. If you want your life to get better, begin to allow Him to teach you to be conscious of what comes out of your mouth, at all times. Sure, at first it will be like trying to cage a wild animal, but as time goes on, Christ's love in you will tame it! Give it time! Give it *His* truth! Eventually you'll see that God gave you your mouth for a wonderful purpose, which is to help change the world for the better—for Jesus! Begin today!

A prayer for you: *Heavenly Father, thank you for helping me get my words under control. You and I both know how OUT of control my words were. Wow, when I think about how I used to speak on a regular basis, all I can do is say THANK YOU. Thank you for protecting me, correcting me, seeing Christ in me, AND my potential at that time. Thank you, thank you, thank you, for your mercy and grace. Please keep helping me, as I've not yet made it to completion. I need you. Right now, I lift up all who are reading this, directly to you. For those who feel as if they are under the control of their mouths, rather than the other way around, HELP THEM. In the name of Jesus, I ask that you begin to draw them near to your Word, and all things Jesus. Help them to understand your unconditional love for them, and others—despite their mouths. Bring new people into their lives who will help them achieve this task, and REMOVE the people who contribute to the opposite. And* *for the people and situations that you allow to stay—in order to mold them—give them your grace on deep levels to grow in your love, patience, and self-control. Help them to begin to exude ALL THINGS JESUS, who is in them, each and every time they open up their mouths, or type out words. Give them the extra grace they need WHEN it's needed! They can do this! Christ inside them will STRENGTHEN THEM! Amen.*

DAY 55

HOW TO OVERCOME THE ATTACKS OF CHRISTIANS

*"For through the law I died to the
law so that I might live for God."*

GALATIANS 2:19

The gospel literally means, "good news." It is meant to free us from *all* our bondages. Rather it be an addiction, constant fear and anxiety, codependency, greed, or never-ending religious works attempting to achieve status with God—the *good* news about what Jesus has done for you is meant to give you rest (see Matthew 11:28), not create more rules to follow.

However, after you accept this gift from God, some Christians will want you to *stay* in a state of panic—as if you can lose what God has already freely given to you. If you want to be attacked by this quasi-type of Christian, simply begin telling *other* Christians that they are *completely* forgiven once they place their faith in Jesus.

There are certain people who actually think they've done something, or that they are *doing* something, to stay in good standing with God—as if they are sustaining their salvation through *their* actions. They say things like, "You are wrong! There is more you gotta do than simply place your faith in Jesus! You can't *just* believe that Jesus has forgiven you! God throws backsliders in the deepest parts of hell! You gotta live it *out*, just *right*, or it's not real!" They want you to be like them, and *nobody* wants to be like them *except* for other Christians who like to have their ears tickled as the preacher strokes their self-righteous egos.

These graceless Christians are still *very* lost, themselves, because hey don't understand what Jesus has *really* done for them. The very same unconditional grace which they are against, they too, will be in desperate need of when they stand before God.

I get a lot of positive feedback from people who follow my ministry and read my books. It feels really good to hear what Christ is doing in the lives of those who realize just how valuable they are to Him! When they finally get to the point of...relaxing in His grace... (see Hebrews 4:11).

The good feedback far outweighs the bad, and the bad feedback usually comes from those who attempt make Jesus' finalized work at the Cross conditional—as if you have to be in a special club to access it. For them, when I emphasize just *how* forgiven we truly are, it's like lighting a powder-keg.

They become infuriated because they find their *true* identity in themselves—not in Christ. They honestly believe that what they do *completes* what He's done—as if He couldn't *possibly* do it without them. It's sad. And right after they flip their lid, or become condescending, they usually begin to take Bible verses out of context in an effort to try to create fear. That, or to prove their *own* self-righteousness, because their legalism "matches up" with God's Word.

But deep down, even *they* know they aren't doing it all perfectly, and they know they can't. This is why they get so aggressive. They are trying to prove to the world they are good, when all they really need to do is point to Jesus as being good *in them*. They ferociously want to convince others that they've done something, or are *doing* something *themselves* to achieve holiness, but their *spirit* is telling them, "It's a big lie." I understand this, because I used to *do* this.

Until you try to earn–or worse, *sustain* your salvation—through attempting to be 100% perfect in word, thought, and deed, you'll never fully understand that you *can't*. To get to this point, all you have to do is burn yourself out. The sooner you fall over in exhaustion, the better. Only then can Christ pick you up, nurse you back to health *His* way, and then fully work *through* you, in partnership…in an actual *relationship*.

But you gotta give up! You gotta realize that its all been free for you from the very beginning of your belief in Him! As for now, I'm willing to be misunderstood by a few people in order to help many, *many* more people, understand God's love for them in Christ—which *is* 100% unconditional, *un*earnable, and once had, *un*losable. This is called *grace*. If you can't grasp grace, then you can't grasp what Jesus has really done for you.

So today, my friends, know this: Even if certain Christians reject you, Jesus will *never* reject you! He has become one with your spirit! The first time you invited Him into your heart and believed He saved you from all your sins, He actually did! Even your future sins! So stop worrying about those too! Keep in mind, when Jesus died, *all* of your sins were in the future! So for the Christians who attack you because you stand on such a bold claim, what should *you* do about it?!…Love them. *Think* of them with the same love that Jesus thinks of *you* with. If you will do this, you will be positively altering the course of humanity forever, with *your* love. So love them! Love them, love them, love them.

A prayer for you: *God, today I want to thank you for the revelation of your great love for me, which is found in Jesus. Thank you for teaching me that I've done nothing to get right with you, but Christ in me, is all the rightness I'll ever need! Thank you for letting me know HE'S DONE EVERYTHING, FOR ME. Thank you for showing me that all I gotta do each day, is wake up, and let Him live THROUGH me— that's it! Thank you for removing the legalistic mindset I had for far too long—a mindset of doing more and behaving differently to make sure you still loved me. It's very freeing. Right now, I lift up all who* *are reading this, directly to you. For those who have been badly hurt by other Christians who don't understand your grace, heal their souls. Let them know that was NOT you, but the people incorrectly attempting to represent you. And for the ones DOING the rejecting, please, give them a supernatural epiphany of just how great your love is for them—and then teach them how to give it away to everyone. In Christ's name I pray these things, amen.*

DAY 56

How To Do Your Best For God

"Therefore, since we have been justified through faith,
we have peace with God through our Lord Jesus Christ"

ROMANS 5:1

D o you ever have those days where you feel like you're not good enough? You can't quite put your finger on it, but there is a presence of lack, dread, and weakness—even as a Christian?

You are not alone! Those days try to sneak up on me as well. And to be honest with you, it's not a "day" that is sneaking up on us, but our enemy. He wants you to believe that no matter *what* you do, it's never good enough. The devil torments Christians each day, not just unbelievers. How? Through legalism. Through our mindset of, "I gotta do more! If I don't, God won't love me! I won't be good enough!"

Let me tell you a secret: You *are* good enough, because of your faith in Jesus as your Savior, right now, this very second—and nothing can change this. Because of this fact, even if you *never* do another thing for God, you are good! I need to repeat that because just *because* you read it, that doesn't mean you believe it—it's hard to believe!

So let's say it again, and I want you to consciously do your best to believe it as the truth, because it is: *"Even if I never do another thing for God, I'm good!"* And I need to reiterate, that is, if you've placed your faith in Jesus.

You see, as humans, we are all "works based" in our thinking. If we do *this*, we get *that*. However, it doesn't work like that with our Creator, He's different. It's *so* hard for us to grasp that everything we have from God is *all free* by grace through faith in what *Jesus* has already accomplished *for* us (See Ephesians 2). So let's say it again, and this time, exhale. Allow yourself to deflate a little. Here we go:

"Even if I never do another thing for God, I'm good."

Again.

"EVEN IF I NEVER DO ANOTHER THING FOR GOD, I'M GOOD."

If you have a religious spirit that normally pesters you, it's probably going bat-crap crazy at this point. But let's do it one more time just to tick him off...

"EVEN IF I NEVER DO ANOTHER THING FOR GOD, I'M GOOOOOOOOOOD! I HAVEN'T EARNED ANYTHING AND ALL I HAVE HAS BEEN GIVEN TO ME FOR FREE! THANK YOU, JESUS!!! WHAT A WONDERFUL GIFT!!!!"

My friend, this is the truth. And it is this *truth* about your true identity in Christ's work alone, that gives you the freedom you are so desperately looking for (see John 8:32). Once you get this down pat, deep in your soul, all of the pressure gets taken off of *you* and placed on *Jesus*—where it belongs.

Once you realize you've been freely justified, and all you have is free, you'll always *want* to do your very best!

You'll always *want* to do as much as you possibly can! You will *strive*—as you *rest in grace*—for more and more and MORE! You'll finally begin to do the best you can, *because* you are already the best you possibly *can* be!

C'MON SOMEBODY! This is some back-flippin', knee-slappin', brother-huggin' sweet news! That's why it's called THE GOOD NEWS! That's what "the gospel" means! GOOD! NEWS!!! AHHHHHHHHH!!!! I could get up right now and run a circle around my house!

SO! *Because* of this great news, YOU'LL DO SO MUCH MORE WITH YOUR LIFE *FOR* GOD. Why? Because you don't have to! This is called a relationship—NOT RELIGION. This is what God is longing for from you. He wants you to *want* to do stuff for Him, because you love Him—because He loves *you* unconditionally through Christ.

Here are five things that will help you *do* your very best—because you *are* the very best, inside:

1. **ASK GOD TO USE YOU.** This is a very important step to unlocking your God-given destiny. There are many Christians who go to their graves with unfinished work for God here on earth. Don't be that person! Simply say, "God, use me, no matter what. I'm ready." And then prepare yourself, because He will!

2. **STUDY JESUS, HARD.** Friend, you will never be able to exude Christ's character if you are simply living off of second-hand faith for an hour each week—or less. You must get to know Him for yourself! I fell into this trap—the trap of believing others, blindly—and for years I had the wrong impression of Jesus. Because of incorrect teaching, I thought I had to shape up before I could enter into a deep relationship with Him—WRONG. So study Him for yourself, daily! He's given you all the material you need to understand His personality. Ask Him to reveal Himself

to you through His Word and grace-filled teachings, and He will. What you'll soon find out is that He is nothing like you thought—that is, when you hated Him, ignored Him, or, were afraid of Him.

3. **BEWARE OF THE RELIGIOUS CHRISTIANS.** There's not many other things that can zap your confidence in who you are in Christ, quite like the religious Christians. They are cold, harsh, and they have a condition-based love. They are sin-focused, and not grace-centered. They categorize sins from "bad to worse," while completely ignoring that they too, have sin in their own lives which they belittle. They will try to convince you that you're not as good as them; and that their church work, church attendance, and Scripture memorization has earned them more favor with God than you. They will want you to fall in line behind them, and if you don't, you're not really saved. They are meaner than most non-believers and they will try to make you feel like a beat dog. IGNORE THIS. Have your mind made up ahead of time to ask God to bless these arrogant types of Christians, genuinely. Force yourself through God's grace to *think* of them with love. If you don't, you'll hate them and the devil will have his way with your joy, confidence, and peace. Remember: They've not earned ANYTHING. *You* are on the same level as them, if they believe in Jesus too. So pause, pray, and *then* proceed when you face these types. AND LOOK THEM IN THE EYE. Christ lives in you, and they need to see Him.

4. **REMEMBER THAT THE GRACE OF THE CROSS TRUMPS ALL.** Lots of religious Christians, as well as unbelievers, will want to point to "works" as the measuring stick of sainthood. The religious Christians will even throw in one of the most taken-out-of-context verses, "Faith without works is dead" (James 2:17), to throw you off course. James however, was speaking to people who already believed! Actual *believers* were being

told, "Do something, do ANYTHING! Revive your faith by taking *action!*" (Kinda like I'm doing in this devotional). He wasn't saying work to *be* saved—that would remove grace completely. So always keep in the forefront of your mind that God's gift of free forgiveness by grace through Jesus' blood sacrifice supersedes *everything* in the Bible. "But Matt, what about—" Nope. Everything. The Cross was was the final piece that *gave* us peace, with God. Enjoy it!

5. **BE AWARE OF THE SPIRITUAL WORLD.** In order to do your best for God, I need you to realize that *you* are a spirit—not just a body. This is why Paul said for us to, "Fix our minds on things above, not on earthly things" (Colossians 3:2); which simply means *be aware of your spiritual surroundings.* At all times, since the creation of this universe, a war has been raging in the spiritual realm between heaven and hell, and *we* are in the middle of it. God wants your soul in heaven, and Satan wants your soul in hell. "Our struggle is not against flesh and blood, but against spirits..." (see Ephesians 6:12). Evil spirits from hell (and no other place) influence *people* in their minds. The devil and his little marching morons are always trying to not *just* influence us, but also, discourage us! They are as real as gravity! It is their *purpose* to try to make you hate others, refuse to forgive, hold grudges, be ultra-critical, be envious, hate your neighbor, gossip about people, be addicted, constantly be lustful, and many other diabolical things. So pay attention and recognize you are at war, spiritually! BUT—Christ is *in* you, so you never have to be afraid! He is always strengthening you and protecting you! Most of the time, He's strangling out a demon, or a sickness, or even when *death* is trying to get at you, He's stopping it—and you don't even realize it.

Of course, there are many more things that God will teach you through the Holy Spirit—techniques and methods which will help you do your best each and every day! But mostly, if you'll just remember that because of Jesus, you are *already* the best you possibly *can* be, in turn, you'll begin to do great and mighty things *through* Him!

A prayer for you: *Heavenly Father, thank you for this day! Thank you for waking me up, and for the air in my lungs. Thank you for my life! What a gift it is to be able to live through you again today! Right now, I lift up all who are reading this, directly to you. For those who have been beat down by religious works or the guilt from complacency, HELP THEM BEGIN TO EXUDE YOUR STRENGTH! Begin to teach them who they really are in Christ! I rebuke any religious spirit that is tormenting them, BE GONE, YOU IDIOT! YOU HAVE NO POWER! IN THE NAME OF JESUS, FILL THEM UP WITH YOUR CONFIDENCE! You created us to BE confident, in you, so show us how! And please, lead us, guide us, and protect us along the way. Help us to do our best each day as we already know that we ARE the best, in Christ. Amen!*

DAY 57

DO YOU *WANT* JESUS TO HELP YOU?

"What do you want me to do for you?"

LUKE 18:41

There is a story in the Bible about a blind beggar receiving his sight (Luke 18:35-42). Jesus was walking by, on His way to Jericho, and the blind man heard the crowd around him begin to bustle. He perked up and asked what was going on, and they told him, "Jesus of Nazareth is passing by" (Luke 18:37).

He immediately called out, "Jesus, Son of David, have mercy on me!" (Luke 18:38) Side note* He called him "Son of David" because Joseph, Jesus' earthly father, was a descendant of King David.

When he yelled out at Jesus, the people standing around this blind beggar, immediately shooshed him—but he was *not* going to be quiet. He had heard that Jesus was performing many miracles, and now was the opportunity to get his!

So he got LOUDER! "Jesus! Have mercy on me!" (Luke 18:39).

...Jesus stops...

...He looks over, and says, "Bring him to me."

I could stop writing right now, and a point could be made that this man *refused* to let Jesus pass him by, even in his turmoil! And *that* level of faith impressed Jesus so much, that He stopped in His tracks to help him. However, that is not my point...

So the people standing around this blind man help him up, take him by the hand, and slowly walk him over to Jesus. Notice what Jesus says next, right after the blind man is standing in front of Him. He doesn't just quickly touch him, and heal him (He could have done that from afar), but instead, He asks the beggar a question He already knew the answer to:

"What do you want me to do for you?" (Luke 18:41).

Jesus wanted to hear it from *him*, so that the man could hear *himself*.

What most people don't understand is that Jesus was not an enabler, He wasn't going around healing and helping those who didn't *want* His help. Instead, He helped everyone who *came* to Him, those who *asked* Him for help.

Whoever needed help from Jesus, either them, *or* their loved ones, had to first *want* His help, and second, go ask Him for it. The great news is, He was always willing to give help to those who wanted it! *And* He gave His help away for free, through simply *believing* and *asking*.

So the blind man said, "Lord, I want to see" (Luke 18:41). He wanted it! He wanted a new life! He wanted *change* in his life! So he reached out to Jesus as He was walking by and in essence, said:

"I'M DONE BEGGING! I'M DONE DEPENDING ON OTHERS FOR EVERYTHING! I'M DONE LIVING IN DARKNESS EVERY DAY OF MY LIFE! JESUS, HELP ME! CHANGE ME! HEAL ME! I KNOW YOU CAN DO IT!"

So Jesus said to him, "Receive your sight; your faith has healed you." Immediately he received his sight and followed Jesus, praising God. When all the people saw it, they also praised God (Luke 18:42,43).

…How amazing.

And notice in that last verse, once Jesus *does* change your life, you simply cannot *help* but follow Him, praise Him, and show the world all He's done for you!

A prayer for you: *Heavenly Father I want to thank you for giving us the ability to make our own choices. It is in our free will that we can decide what we want to do with our lives. Thank you for sending Jesus here to show us the things we should choose. Give us the spiritual guidance we need today, and every day, to let Jesus live through us! We're ready, Lord! Use us, mold us, guide us, teach us! WE ARE READY FOR A CHANGE! In Jesus' name, amen.*

DAY 58

How To Break Free From Church Laws

*"A man is not justified by observing
the law, but by faith in Jesus Christ."*

GALATIANS 2:16

"Backslider! There is no hotter place in hell than for a person like you!"

"You have a rebellious spirit! God will rightly punish you!"

"You *refuse* to give your tithe?! How DARE you steal from God! You will MISS your blessing!"

"REPENT! GET BAPTIZED! IF YOU DON'T, YOU ARE GOING TO HELL, SINNER!"

...Have you ever been preached to like that? Maybe the man or woman preaching can't stand still, they run around all over the place, yelling at you like you're a dog? As if you are going to fall in line if they get louder...and LOUDER?

Or maybe, it's the opposite. It's calm and quiet. You sit, stand up, sit, stand up, and you feel like a robot? There is no real relationship with Jesus, just showing up to be sure you keep your spot in heaven? A steady diet of bodily movements, robes, and the placing-on-a-pedestal, a particular human? As if they are "holier" than you? Maybe you've even experienced a church law which forces you to see a particular leader as *higher* than the regular parishioners and members—even higher than *you.*

Or maybe you've felt the extremely frustrating and impossible church law of, "Confess every single sin, or else you're not forgiven of it." You might have to confess to a man in a box, or in front of a congregation. "You gotta be *quick* to repent!" "You *must* confess!" And if you don't, "God is gonna get 'cha!"

You may have also experienced being told you need *water* to wash away your sins, when you know deep in your heart, *no* amount of water in the entire universe can achieve this church law. Or *maybe,* you've been told you gotta spout out a bunch of non-English gibberish in order to "get more of God," yet, you can't seem to do such a weird thing, *organically,* so you are frustrated and scared that you don't have God's Spirit in you. "What am I doing *wrong,* God?! WHY WON'T YOU LOVE ME TOO?!"

Because you don't want to *force* some strange words out of your mouth, or because you can't decipher what they are saying when someone *does* this, you feel as if God doesn't love you as much as He does them. When they shout out crazy stuff in the middle of service, or they wiggle around on the ground in convulsions, you think to yourself, "Does God's grace not apply to me because I'm not doing that stuff?"

Friend, this is *not* the gospel. The gospel brings *peace,* it's orderly, and it's not exclusive to certain legalistic actions or wonky rituals. The gospel brings love, joy, patience, kindness, and gentleness. God's love found in the gospel, keeps no records of your wrongs, it does not dishonor you, it isn't angry, it rejoices in the truth of Jesus' finished work at the Cross, it always protects you, always trusts you, and always has a hope and a plan for your future. And God's love for you has something which a lot of preachers need to get ahold of, *self-control* (see Galatians 5:22, 23, 1 Corinthians 13, Jeremiah 29:11).

Sure, I'm all for getting excited about God, and I also think the pageantry of some churches is absolutely beautiful, but when you are trying to create fear, guilt, or condemnation—or, placing too much emphasis on a building, denomination, or human person (in order to get people to grow in Christ) *that* is just plain wrong. Jesus was never out of control, so we shouldn't be either (even when He did get angry in Matthew 15 and Matthew 21, He kept His scruples—in His anger, He did not sin). Further, Jesus never put any building, activity, or *person* on a pedestal, so neither should we.

These issues are called *church laws*. Church laws are man-made rules that go against the finished, graceful work of the gospel—a work that Jesus completed for us in full. Church laws create stress, confusion, and division. They make Christians strive to no end, *attempting* to achieve a higher level of status with God and man. Church laws put people on a hamster-wheel that creates fear and Christian classes, in turn, ruining *many* lives.

Church laws were an early distraction the apostles faced after Jesus ascended, and they continue on today. As a matter of fact, it was church laws–old *Jewish* religious traditions—which caused Paul and Peter to get into it! The Apostle Paul said in Galatians 2:11, "When Peter came to Antioch, I opposed him to his face, because he was clearly in the wrong" (Galatians 2:11). What was Peter wrong about?

Paul had heard that Peter was allowing some Jewish laws to sneak in *with* the gospel, namely, circumcision. So Paul said, "For in Christ Jesus neither circumcision nor uncircumcision has any value. The only thing that counts is faith expressing itself through love" (Galatians 5:6).

And isn't that just like us? We get saved, and then we think if we do "this" or "that," our saving is even *better?* We create "Christian status departments" and hierarchies, naming some "First Class," "Second Class," "Holier," and "*not* as holy." THIS IS WRONG! Paul flew off the handle with Peter to get his point across–that it is JESUS PLUS NOTHING!

He stood up and publicly corrected Peter: "How is it that you force Gentiles to follow Jewish customs?" (See Galatians 2:14). I'd personally bet a day's wages that nearly all of the people reading this devotional are Gentiles! You and me! We are *not* Jewish! Anyone who is a non-Jew *is* a Gentile—we weren't even *invited* to follow any Old Testament laws— only the blood of Jesus brought us in.

Paul continued, "a man is *not* justified by observing the law, *but by faith in Jesus Christ*. For through the law *I died to the law* so that I might live for God" (Galatians 2:16,19).

DO YOU SEE THAT?! The law isn't dead, but as Christians we are dead *to* the law and alive in Christ! Church laws included! THERE IS NO DIFFERENCE! What makes us think that giving a certain percentage of our money to a church organization is *not* a law? Or that we won't "receive our blessing," if we don't give an *offering* "on top of" the tithe?!

WE MUST STOP LEGISLATING GRACE! I'm all for giving, but there is *no* directive in *any* New Testament epistle which states we must reconcile our bank accounts with a church building to the tune of ten percent—not *one* book after the Cross states this. The tithe is a church law. We must *stop* mixing in church laws with the gospel, just like the Jews had to stop mixing in the Mosaic Law as well!

I know this may be heavy for some of you because of what you've been taught, so please allow me to break down "law" for you. This is crucial if you want to escape any religious bondage holding you back from enjoying your life with Christ to the fullest: A law is any act *we* perform to gain a better status with God or man—or to achieve salvation—or to be sure we *keep* our salvation.

Religious Christians get *furious* when you speak against their church laws. "I'll pray for you! You'll need it!" they'll say, when you simply ask them a question…"Why?"

It's in our human flesh's nature to want to make what we already have *better*. But when it comes to the finished work of the gospel, of JESUS ONLY, we can't! No amount of "sprinkling in" of *anything* can add to what Jesus already finished. This includes church activities, church attendance, church volunteering, donations, mission trips, Bible reading, attending Bible college/seminary, tithing, giving away our stuff to look more holy, water baptism, repentance of incorrect behaviors and attitudes, pastoral actives, pastoral approval—you name it—NOTHING can earn you more prestige than you already *have* after you *first* come to faith in Jesus! (See Hebrews 10:10, Romans 6:10, John 19:30).

Let's talk tithing again for a moment. There is not one verse in the New Testament which says we must give a certain amount money or goods to God or a church. Jesus does *refer* to tithing in Matthew 23, but when He did so He was pointing out the hypocritical greed and nasty hearts of the Pharisees; those who looked to their tithing as righteousness. Jesus scolds them about how wrong they are, saying they should have been practicing "justice, mercy, and faithfulness" (see Matthew 23:23).

After the Cross, the apostles tell us to *not* give under compulsion or pressure, but instead to give out of the abundance of our hearts because God loves a *cheerful* giver—not a *lawful* giver (see 2 Corinthians 9:7). A lawful giver is someone who does math to give to God, thinking that math percentage earns them kudos with our Creator—as if God is a "heavenly waiter" wanting His tips to be "just right," so that we can get a nod of favor. It doesn't work that way as New Covenant believers. JUST, GIVE—because you don't HAVE TO.

If you want to give ten percent, give it. If you want to give three percent, or thirty-three percent—give it away! God is not looking at your ratio of giving, He's looking at your heart. IS JESUS THERE? Yes?... THAT'S ENOUGH FOR HIM!

When it comes to your giving, God isn't needy or expecting anything. And don't believe the lie that your money is on loan from God, as if He expects it back. HE'S DOESN'T. He doesn't expect *anything* from you. Expectation is not what any good relationship is built on. God isn't disappointed in your giving, or overly-impressed by your giving; instead, He just smiles, loves you, and says, "I've got plenty for everyone."

This church law of tithing creates fear, or worse in my opinion, smug self-righteousness. Friend, we don't give to get, we give because God is a giver and He lives in us! We are all even-Steven because of our faith in what JESUS has given for us—His blood. Without this truth, the grace of God is nullified, and *instead* of grace, we get "earned rewards." We are then right back to the old way of doing things, B.C.

A religious Christian might attempt to pull grace away by rebutting, "So Matt, are you saying we don't have to do anything? That we can just live however we want?" WELL NO! Why *would* you?! Why would you want to take the face of Christ, and SLAP IT?! He *lives* in you!

What you must begin to do is form a loving relationship with the One who is infused with your spirit. Are you perfect in your relationships with *people?* No. So don't expect to be perfect in your relationship with God. You don't have that ability, just yet, and He knows that. This is why He sent Jesus here, to do what you *can't* do.

Only in heaven will you take on absolute perfection in word, thought, and deed, because you will shed your flesh and your mind renewal will be completed—you will finally be one with God, perfectly.

So for now, do your best to show Him how much you care. But be sure to realize there is nothing you can do to make Him love you more, or leave you! The truth of the gospel is this: YOU ARE *JUST* LIKE JESUS, IN YOUR SPIRIT, ONCE YOU BELIEVE HE'S FORGIVEN YOU! GOD, THE FATHER, SEES YOUR FAITH IN JESUS' BLOOD!

THE FATHER CAN'T, AND WON'T, BREAK THIS COVENANT WITH CHRIST! The Messiah is *in your body*! How? By grace through faith! By a *new* agreement between the Father and Son— we are simply the ones who benefit from this bloody contract! We don't create it, add to it, or sustain it! We open up our hearts and *receive* it! We are FOOLS to think we can possibly do ANYTHING to get on God's good side! HE IS GOD! The only thing that makes us good is God *in* us—Jesus Christ! (See Hebrews 7:18-25, Hebrews 8:13, Ephesians 2:8,9, Galatians 3:1).

So what good is law? Lots of good, for unbelievers. It reveals the character of our Creator, and shows you what you *can't* do on your own. It points out all of the dirt on your face, and then it does nothing to remove it. Only Jesus can do this. Only your faith in Him as your Savior can, and will, do this completely—once—as in, *one time.* (see Hebrews 7:25, Hebrews 10:10, Romans 6:10, 1 Peter 3:18).

The law only applies to non-believers in Christ. Jesus took on the impossible-to-complete laws of God on *your* behalf, because you never could. That's how much He loves you. He became His own creation to *save* you. Your job now, is to allow Him to live *through* you, while relaxing, with grace…How amazing…How *freeing* (see Hebrews 4:11, John 6:29, 8:32).

This is why Paul said to the Romans, "It is the goodness of God which will lead you to change your life" (see Romans 2:4)—not more laws. When you finally realize that you are completely forgiven, forever, no matter what you do in your flesh or mind, your entire view of life becomes different. You begin to organically grow spiritual fruit for all to enjoy, including yourself! (See Galatians 5:22,23).

Paul was correcting Peter in his letter to the Galatians because Peter was attempting to add to Jesus' finished work through circumcision, so he said, "I have been crucified with Christ and I no longer live, but Christ lives in me. The life I live in the body, I live by faith in the Son of God, who loved me and gave himself for me" (Galatians 2:20).

Do you see that? We've been spiritually crucified with Him, and now we are vessels, actual *temples* of God. This is the gospel, the truth that will set you free from *any* religious church law prison. Church is good, sure; that is, the building we gather at, *if* the graceful good news of the finished gospel is being preached—*if* a sense of ease and relaxation in Jesus' completed work is present. If not, don't go there. Find another one, or start one yourself.

There are no church laws that will make you look any better to God—instead, Christ in you makes you look perfect in spirit! And that's what counts! This is the free grace of God, which is what we all truly need. A grace that Paul describes: "I do not set aside the grace of God, *for if righteousness could be gained through the law,* Christ died for nothing!" (Galatians 2:21, my emphasis added).

So today, my friends, know this: Christ didn't die for nothing, He died for *you*. And if you believe that He died on the Cross for your sins, and that He was raised from the dead—you are 100% acceptable to your Creator for eternity. When you finally realize that God loves you *so* much, He would actually come down and pay off your law-debt with Him, freely…everything changes. You finally understand why the gospel means "good news." Because that's what it is!

A prayer for you: *Heavenly Father, today I want to thank you for your grace! When I think about how kind you are—SO KIND that you would allow me to have access to your presence through UNEARNED salvation—I get excited! I feel so free! Thank you! Right now, I lift up all who are reading this, directly to you. For those who have misunderstood what it is that you truly require, as if there is more to do than simply believe Jesus has forgiven them, help them. Show them that it is by grace through faith we become one with you, THROUGH Jesus. GIVE THEM A BRAND NEW OUTLOOK AND A BRAND NEW CONFIDENCE IN THEIR RELATIONSHIP WITH YOU! Let them know that there are no special tricks or church laws required for proof. We just believe in you and receive you, in full. And one last thing, I rebuke any legalistic, religious spirit from anyone reading this, in the name of Jesus set them free! Amen.*

DAY 59

WHAT'S SO GOOD ABOUT GOOD FRIDAY?

"For God made Christ, who never sinned,
to be the offering for our sin, so that we could
be made right with God through Christ."

2 CORINTHIANS 5:21

Today is Good Friday! But *why* is Good Friday *good*? If we look back on that particular day, approximately 2,000 years ago, and think about the excruciating pain that Jesus went through, it doesn't sound so good to me. And by the way, the word "excruciating" was derived from the word "crucify," explaining how it *felt*.

Plainly stated, Good Friday was *not* good for Jesus—it was the toughest decision He ever had to make (see Luke 22:41-44)...instead, it was good for *us*.

So, what's the deal with Jesus having to die? Why couldn't God have made it any other way?...The most intelligent answer I can come up with is this: *I don't know. He's God, I'm not.* I'm simply one of His many creations. But I *do* know He was mad about sin, and the world's sins were left *un*-punished *until* Jesus' blood was shed (see Romans 3:25,26).

What is strange to us is that *when* God was mad about sin, He required *blood* (see Hebrews 9:22). He doesn't require "confession" or "repentance of behaviors/attitudes"—those are carts after the horse. Instead, He is, for lack of a better term, *bloodthirsty*. This is why the actual *New* Covenant doesn't begin when Jesus was born, but *after* His Spirit left His body (see John 19:30, Hebrews 8:13).

Before the event on Good Friday, God required blood for sins, now He doesn't (see Hebrews 10:26). This is the reason why, once a year, on the Day of Atonement, the Jews would sacrifice the blood of their very *best* animals to *cover up* their sins—not take their sins *away*, or make them *unpunished* or completely forgiven—but to simply cover them up for one more year, until the *next* Day of Atonement (see Hebrews 10:4).

But when Jesus came along, and shed *His* perfect blood, He actually *took away* our sin, for good! He never sinned, so His *human* blood was perfect! This is why Jesus didn't simply *cover* our sins, but He banished them into oblivion! (See John 1:29, 1 John 3:5, Psalm 103:12, Isaiah 53).

And *after* Jesus did what He did, and once *we* place our *faith* in that event for our *own* sin, God doesn't even *remember* our sins any longer! (See Hebrews 8:12, Romans 10:9, Ephesians 2:8,9). We become new Creations *in* Christ, actually placed "inside of" *spiritually*, "baptized into" Him—not through water, but through faith. Water baptism is simply a celebration *of* your spiritual birthday (see 2 Corinthians 5:17, see Romans 6, Galatians 2:20, 1 Corinthians 1:17).

So why did Jesus have to die? Because of sin. The Bible says that the wages of sin is *death* (see Romans 6:23). And you might say, "But Matt, He didn't sin! That's doesn't seem like a very loving God to me!"...Oh, but my friend, He *is*...

He loves us *so* much that He *gave* us a way to become *just* like Him... the sacrifice of His very own Son. Jesus is a gift *to* us, *from* the Father (see John 3:16, Romans 6:23). Sure, Christ was a man, and He had to make His very own choice of laying down His perfect life...but He *willingly* did so, to make a *way* for us to be spiritually spotless, just like Him. Those nails didn't keep Him on that Cross, HE IS GOD, NOTHING CAN

STOP HIM. Instead, His *love* for you did. He thought of *you* on this very day, as He hung there in pain, personally paying off your sin-debt punishment with the Father, forever.

He did this for you.

So today, my friends, know this: This is *your* Good Friday. Jesus was focused on the upcoming Sunday, but *today* was *not* good for Him. As He fulfilled the prophecy of becoming our Messiah, Christ was publicly ridiculed, beaten to a bloody pulp, forced to carry His own cross, and then *hammered* into it with huge nails. I BELIEVE THIS AS TRUE, DON'T YOU? I'm *choosing* to thank Him and *choosing* to believe, on this Good Friday. What about you? It's your choice. God loves you so much, He'll never force you to believe. Today can be *your* Good Friday as well! Simply tell Jesus, "Thank you, I believe." That's all you gotta do, and you will *instantly* become *just* like Him, in spirit.

A prayer for the day: *Heavenly Father, thank you. I believe. Oh my goodness, THANK YOU! Thank you SO MUCH for giving me Jesus! I know it wasn't easy to allow Him to take on the sin of the world, including mine, but I'm forever grateful! Thank you for the life you've given me IN HIM! I'm all yours, Lord. Continue to use me however you see fit. Continue to live through me, and take me into even GREATER knowledge of your grace. Guide me, protect me, give me wisdom, and help me to live this life THROUGH you! I love you SO MUCH! THANK YOU. THANK YOU. THANK YOU. And thank you. Thank you, Jesus, for your blood on the Cross, and what you did for me that day. Amen.*

DAY 60

WHEN IS JESUS COMING BACK?

*"For the Son of Man in his day will be like
the lightning, which flashes and lights up the sky
from one end to the other. But first he must suffer
many things and be rejected by this generation."*

LUKE 17:24, 25

What if I told you that Jesus is coming back in exactly 16 days, 10 hours, 4 minutes, and 34 seconds? What would you do? How would you live? If it was announced by God, *as a fact*, that He is returning to earth to finish what He said He was going to finish?…What would you change about your life if you knew the exact moment Jesus would be standing in front of you?…And why doesn't God just go ahead and tell us *when* He's coming back so we can be ready?

Now, to that last question, I actually have the answer: He wants you to *live* ready. He wants you to *choose* to love Him, not fake it just to get into heaven. Like a loving parent who is away on a trip, when He returns, He wants to see His house clean and in order—and only our faith in Jesus as our Savior can accomplish this feat.

I gotta be honest with you, when God put this subject on my heart this morning, I started to balk, I even argued a little, "Nobody wants to hear about such a difficult subject, give me something uplifting and encouraging for people." He replied through the Holy Spirit, "No, they need to be prepared for my return."

I used to just ignore God when it came to something like this—speaking about uncomfortable stuff—but now, I get over it real quick and become obedient. He's given me a gift of creative writing, so I *must* use it for Him. We all have gifts, YOU included. There is *something* God has placed in you that is very special and unique. He wants you to offer it up to Him daily by simply allowing Christ to live through you. Only then can your deepest level of purpose be fulfilled: *making heaven's population more dense.*

JESUS IS COMING BACK. We can try to live as if this is not true, or that it will never happen, but it *is* going to happen. This planet had a beginning, and it will have an end. Jesus said He will be like lightning across the sky. We can't compute this, just like an ant can't compute the Theory of Relativity. So we should *stay* ready by living out our lives how God approves.

Our ignorance about His return was talked about by Jesus Himself. He used the example of the time of Noah. As he built the ark while preparing for the flood, the people of the world made fun of him:

> *"Just as it was in the days of Noah, so also will it be*
> *in the days of the Son of Man. People were eating,*
> *drinking, marrying and being given in marriage*
> *up to the day Noah entered the ark. Then the flood*
> *came and destroyed them all." (Luke 17:24,25)*

"WELL MATT THAT SOUNDS LIKE A CRUEL GOD TO ME!" someone might say…Friend, this is all God's stuff, this is *His* creation and *His* rules. If He says something is evil and has to go, then that's that, no matter if we like it or not. He gives us plenty of warnings and opportunities to place our faith in Jesus, and He loves us. It is *us* who rejects *Him*, not the other way around.

You could also look at God flooding the earth like this: If He decides to sever off a foot that is infected with gangrene, it is to save the rest of the body from certain death. Noah kept warning these people that they needed to turn to God, yet they kept on *rejecting* God:

> *"The Lord saw how great the wickedness of the human race had become on the earth, and that every inclination of the thoughts of the human heart was only evil all the time." (Genesis 6:5)*

Just imagine a generation of people who *hated* God and everything about Him—a people who completely rejected Him and absolutely *refused* to acknowledge Him as God. Instead, they made themselves and "things" their *own* gods. "It's *my* way! So shut up! Don't tell *me* what to do! Mind your own business!"

To me, that sounds very familiar. I could pin those phrases on myself during the days of me ignoring God and saying, "NOPE! I'm handling this how I want!"

The million dollar question is, "Who knows when He's coming back?" I don't know, you don't know, nobody knows. Jesus said that He doesn't even know, nor do the angels—but *only* the Father knows (Mark 13:32). So when someone says they know, ignore that garbage, that's just plain stupid.

It could be today, it could be tomorrow, it could be in 1,000 years— all I know *for sure* is each day that passes by, we get closer. Right now, this moment, we *are* closer to Jesus' return than we were yesterday. What's it going to take for us to not just *accept* Jesus' spiritual perfection as our own, but also, allow Him to live *through* us?

What's it going to take for us to remove our self-righteous religious mindsets? A church-club, members only, conditional-grace mindset, that grows *rotten* spiritual fruit and repels the lost? When are we going to stop with the harsh judgments towards others, and making one sin worse than another? When are we going to STOP REFUSING to love everyone as Christ commands? And for the unbelievers, what will it take to remove your mindset of "There is no God."? What will it take for you to finally acknowledge a God who created *us*, instead of us creating Him?...More blessings? Less blessings? Or simply a return trip from Christ Himself?

It's a good thing God promised to never flood the earth again no matter our behavior. Each time you see a rainbow, that's a reminder of God's vow to Noah, which He gave after the flood (see Genesis 9:11-13).

We must begin to realize our Creator is reaching out to us through so many different outlets right now. His grace-filled, saving words are not just being preached in the church buildings for an hour on Sundays, but also throughout social media ministries, youtube videos, major motion pictures, books, podcasts, apps, tv shows, satellite radio—you name it—God is allowing technology to soar! And He's using *everything together* to do as Jesus said:

"Go into all the world and preach the
gospel to all creation." (Mark 16:15)

We have no more excuses! We aren't sitting in the woods any longer, trying to make fire just so we can have a hot meal! God's created beings, all of us, we have blossomed into something spectacular! We have quite possibly tapped into full potential of the capacity of our brains! It's only gonna get better from here! God will use ALL OF THIS to bring attention to Jesus' message, in order to amass more souls in heaven! Don't you want to be a part of that?!

God has blessed us and this planet on such a grand scale, that if we told Christians from 200 years ago what we can *now* do, to spread the gospel, they'd laugh! It would be unfathomable! The technology we have is amazing! As of the time of me writing this devotional, I can preach the gospel to over 300,000 people on my social media pages without even leaving the comfort of this big comfy chair—and if I pay for it, my message would go out to millions more.

GOD HAS MADE THINGS *SO* EASY FOR US! WHAT ARE WE DOING WITH IT?!

ARE WE HELPING PEOPLE GET READY FOR THE RETURN OF OUR CREATOR?!

WHAT. ARE. WE. DOING?!

I WAS DOING NOTHING. Instead, I was worried about the zeros in my bank account, the style of car I was driving, and how many likes I could get on Facebook. I was worried about making sure I had enough beer and shots to last the rest of the night, as well as how bad I could make my enemies pay. I wasn't allowing Jesus to live through me at all. Thankfully I *was* saved, I still would have gone to heaven because I asked Jesus into my heart at a very young age. However, there *are* people in this world who reject Jesus' free gift of forgiveness all the time. He had this to say about what will happen to them when He returns in the flesh:

> *"I tell you, on that night two people will be in one bed; one will be taken and the other left. Two women will be grinding grain together; one will be taken and the other left." (Luke 17:34,35)*

And no, we might not be "grinding grain"—although somewhere in the world someone will be—but we could be staring at our phones, or sitting at the bar, ignoring our kids, refusing to forgive a coworker or neighbor, putting on our clothes after having an affair, or gossiping about a relative…So why not *live* ready? Why not get in on the abundant life Jesus promised, right now? Why wait? Our lives aren't that great *without* letting Jesus live through us anyway. I thought *my* life was ideal, but until I got to know Christ deeply and began to allow Him to renew my mind, I didn't realize how miserable my life actually was.

So today, my friends, why not humble yourselves before God, repent of your unbelief in Jesus' forgiveness, and begin to allow Him to use you each day? If you will, when you finally meet Him in person He'll say:

> *"Well done, good and faithful servant! You have been faithful with a few things; I will put you in charge of many things. Come and share your master's happiness!" (Matthew 25:21)*

A prayer for you: *Good morning Lord! Thank you for another day! And thank you for helping me realize how wonderful you really are! Right now, I lift up all who are reading this, directly to you. For those who might have had fear overtake them while reading about Jesus' return, please help them understand you don't want them to be fearful, but instead, ready—just like Noah. You are not a God who uses fear to control us, but to warn us about coming danger. We NEED Jesus' forgiveness. We need it! You are sovereign, good, loving, and full of grace! Thank you for your graceful, free forgiveness, you've given us in Christ. If any of these readers want that forgiveness, all they must do is receive it today through belief in it as the truth for their sins! How simple you've made it! Help them develop a deep faith in what Jesus has done for them, beginning today! Because of His sacrifice at the Cross, we will enjoy your presence forever! Amen.*

ADDITIONAL BOOKS BY
MATT MCMILLEN

- 60 Days for Jesus, Volume 1

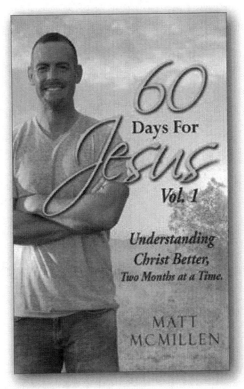

"I really like Matt's writing style. He makes understanding the gospel simple and real. I have found his daily devotions to be very helpful in guiding my walk with Christ. I highly recommend his book." Karen S. (Amazon customer review)

- True Purpose In Jesus Christ: *Finding The Relationship For Which You Were Made*

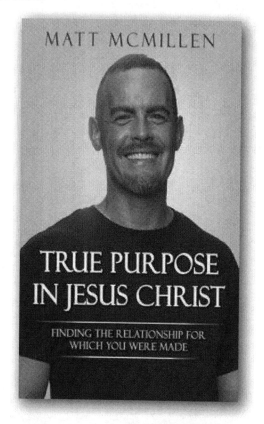

"One of the best books I've ever read! Matt's honesty about his life and what Jesus did to redeem him is amazing! He uses scripture throughout his book to back up everything he talks about. I bought 20 books so I could share with the lost. Absolutely life changing! Thank you, Matt for being obedient to Christ and writing this book!" -Terri L. (Amazon customer review)

- 60 Days For Jesus, Volume 3 (Coming Soon!)

45358926R00198

Made in the USA
Middletown, DE
02 July 2017